The State of Scots Law:
Law and Government after the Devolution Settlement

The State of Scots Law:
Law and Government after the Devolution Settlement

edited by

Lindsay Farmer, LLB, PhD
Professor of Law, University of Glasgow

and

Scott Veitch, LLB, PhD
Reader in Legal Theory, University of Glasgow

Butterworths
A Member of the LexisNexis Group

Members of the LexisNexis Group worldwide

United Kingdom	Butterworths, a Division of Reed Elsevier (UK) Ltd, 4 Hill Street, Edinburgh EH2 3JZ and Halsbury House, 35 Chancery Lane, London WC2A 1EL
Argentina	Abeledo Perrot, Jurisprudencia Argentina and Depalma, Buenos Aires
Australia	Butterworths, a Division of Reed International Books Australia Pty Ltd, Chatswood, New South Wales
Austria	ARD Betriebsdienst and Verlag Orac, Vienna
Canada	Butterworths Canada Ltd, Markham, Ontario
Chile	Publitecsa and Conosur Ltda, Santiago de Chile
Czech Republic	Orac sro, Prague
France	Editions du Juris-Classeur SA, Paris
Hong Kong	Butterworths Asia (Hong Kong), Hong Kong
Hungary	Hvg Orac, Budapest
India	Butterworths India, New Delhi
Ireland	Butterworths (Ireland) Ltd, Dublin
Italy	Giuffré, Milan
Malaysia	Malayan Law Journal Sdn Bhd, Kuala Lumpur
New Zealand	Butterworths of New Zealand, Wellington
Poland	Wydawnictwa Prawnicze PWN, Warsaw
Singapore	Butterworths Asia, Singapore
South Africa	Butterworths Publishers (Pty) Ltd, Durban
Switzerland	Stämpfli Verlag AG, Berne
USA	LexisNexis, Dayton, Ohio

© Reed Elsevier (UK) Ltd 2001

A CIP Catalogue record for this book is available from the British Library.

ISBN 0 406 94452 0

Typeset by Phoenix Photosetting, Chatham, Kent
Printed and bound in Great Britain by Thomson Litho Ltd, East Kilbride, Scotland

Visit Butterworths LexisNexis *direct* at : www.butterworthsscotland.com

Preface

The "state of Scots law" has been the subject of discussion, and not a little angst, for many years. Anyone who turns the pages of Lord Cooper's Selected Papers cannot help being struck by the elegiac tone of many of his speeches delivered in the late forties and early fifties: it is as if he felt that Scots law was passing away as nationalisation of many services and the emergence of tribunals dealing with public law disputes threatened the role of the courts and of the legal profession in Scotland. And, of course, much that had been familiar was indeed passing away. But institutions change all the time and what is surely most remarkable is the way in which, if sound, a legal system can and does adapt to these changes. The law is new every morning. Looking back, we can see that the very changes which seemed to be undermining the existence of the Scottish legal system were in fact to be the spur to new developments and new challenges. This book charts many of those developments and identifies the challenges confronting us today.

Perhaps the most striking feature of the essays is the variety of perspectives from which the authors contemplate the state of our law today. More particularly, many of the essays look at our system in the context of devolution and of the other political and constitutional developments of recent years. The result is a healthy corrective to the tendency to identify the state of Scots law with the state of Scottish private law. To legal nationalists such an identification may be attractive since many of the most distinctive parts of Scots law are to be found in the area of private law – though, significantly, those distinctive parts are rarely those where the main "action" is today. To those who prefer to take a more objective view public law is at least as important. Moreover, it is in the area of public law that the greatest developments have occurred in recent years under the influence of similar developments in English law and in Commonwealth systems. It is not hard to predict, either, that issues of constitutional and administrative law, and of human rights law, will be of great importance in the decades that lie ahead. As the writers in this collection recognise, when the history of these decades comes to be written, the real state of Scots law as a whole will have to be gauged just as much by the fate of, say, litigation about the *vires* of Acts of the Scottish Parliament as by any future twists and turns in the *Sharp v Thomson* saga.

Lindsay Farmer's fascinating account of the views of Andrew Dewar Gibb is a reminder that not all the roots of legal nationalism were healthy. But, in any event, it seems to me that, as in South Africa, the real dangers of a *bellum juridicum* are past. Rather, most people realise that Scots law is one among many systems of law wrestling with the problems thrown up sometimes by recent technological and social developments, but just as often by the kind of ingenuity that has been the hallmark of the good litigant since time immemorial. Whether we find the appropriate solutions to those problems in the classical Roman law of Julian, in the writings of Grotius, in the opinions of Lord Chancellor Brougham or in an article by some Australian academic seems to me to be, almost, a matter of indifference. We are, happily, citizens of a legal world which stretches not only backwards for more than two thousand years but outwards across the globe. Provided we abandon any notions of false superiority and go forward in that spirit, the future state of Scots law is likely to be happy. This book will do much to set us on the right course.

Rodger of Earlsferry
Lord President of the Court of Session
July 2001

Acknowledgments

We would like to thank a number of people and institutions for their assistance and support in the making of this collection: the Right Hon, Sir David Steel, MSP, and Judy Steel for permission to reproduce the painting "Scotland declares itself a nation"; the artist, Michael McVeigh, for allowing us to use it for this purpose; Lord Rodger, the Lord President, for his kind contribution of the Preface; the Law School at the University of Glasgow, for supporting the seminar series from which the essays have been drawn, and for financing research assistance in the later stages; and finally the staff at T & T Clark and Butterworths for their assistance and support.

Lindsay Farmer and Scott Veitch
University of Glasgow
July 2001

Contents

Preface   v
Acknowledgments   vii
Contents   ix
List of contributors   xi

Introduction   1

Chapter 1:   Constitutionalism, Judicial Review and "the Evident
               Utility of the Subjects within Scotland"   11

Chapter 2:   Lawyers in Contemporary Scottish Politics: a new
               "Dundas Despotism"?   27

Chapter 3:   Legislating for Diversity: Minorities in the New
               Scotland   37

Chapter 4:   Scots Law and European Private Law   59

Chapter 5:   Old and Foreign: History, Historiography and
               Comparative Law   75

Chapter 6:   Scottish Self-Government and the Unitary
               Constitution   97

Chapter 7:   Transitional Jurisprudence in the UK: A Very Scottish
               Coup?   121

Chapter 8:   Imagined Communities, Imaginary Conversations:
               Failure and the Construction of Legal Identities   135

Chapter 9:   Under the Shadow over Parliament House: The Strange
               Case of Legal Nationalism   151

Index   165

List of contributors

John Blackie is a Professor of Scots Law at the University of Strathclyde.

Rob Dunbar is a Lecturer in the Law School at the University of Glasgow.

Lindsay Farmer is a Professor of Law at the University of Glasgow.

James Kellas is a Professor of Political Science at the University of Glasgow.

Hector MacQueen is a Professor of Scots Law and Dean of the Faculty of Law at the University of Edinburgh.

Paul Maharg is a Senior Lecturer in Law at the University of Strathclyde.

Alan Page is a Professor of Law at the University of Dundee.

Scott Veitch is a Reader in Legal Theory at the University of Glasgow.

Neil Walker is a Professor of Law at the European University Institute, Florence and at the University of Aberdeen.

Introduction

Lindsay Farmer and Scott Veitch*

Many lawyers like to imagine that their work is purely technical, untouched by the wider currents of constitutional change and requiring little in the way of political choices. Others still firmly believe that the task, even the vocation, of the lawyer, lies precisely in the ability to insulate themselves from political, moral and ethical pressures, thus to represent more impartially the interests of their client and of the court. Justice is seen as best served through respecting the law and its institutions, and the continuity and stability that these provide. And in Scotland, where the authority and autonomy of the law stretches back into the distant past, a respect for the old, the traditional ways of doing things, has long been part of the professional world view. The lawyer can act, confident in the principled and just nature of the system – whatever temporary aberration has to be dealt with along the way.

The changes in the position of Scots law brought about by the Scotland Act 1998 and the Human Rights Act 1998 make this stance increasingly difficult to sustain. In combination these Acts have been, and will no doubt continue to be, the catalyst for an enormous upheaval in the world of the Scots lawyer, and as yet their full impact can scarcely be guessed at. In the period since the coming into force of these Acts, the public profile of lawyers and the legal system has been raised in ways that would not necessarily have been anticipated. The courts have had, as expected, to deal with difficult issues concerning the scope and application of human rights, but in doing so they have also been required to pass judgment on the legality and management of other institutions of government, such as the police and local authorities and even the Parliament itself. The enforcement of human rights has brought the judiciary directly into conflict with the new Scottish Executive, which in turn has thrown scrutiny back onto the judges' own background, politics and procedures for decision-making. All of this has happened in addition to the international scrutiny of Scottish criminal justice that has accompanied the staging of the Lockerbie trial, the so-called "trial of the century", at Camp Zeist in the Netherlands.

Such factors have given a critical public opinion an unprecedented opportunity to examine and challenge the procedures and substance of the

---

* We would like to thank Sarah Summers who assisted in the collection of material for the writing of this introduction and commented on the final version. Thanks also to Tom Mullen, Jim Murdoch and Tony Prosser for their help.

Scottish legal system. Just as the Scottish political nation has been brought to a crossroads by recent developments, so too has the Scottish legal system, and it is vital that at a time like this Scots lawyers begin to reflect on these developments and the choices that have to be made about the future of an independent and distinctive Scots law. Both lawyers and the lay public alike have increasingly been forced to address the question of what sort of legal system Scots law is, and what it ought to be in the future.

In order to encourage reflection on these issues a series of seminars was launched in the School of Law at the University of Glasgow under the title "The State of Scots law", and contributors to the seminar were invited to reflect on the past, present and future of the discipline of law in Scotland. The contributions are published here, and it is hoped that this book will stimulate further discussion of these important matters.

As a means of providing a backdrop and introduction to the following essays, and for the benefit of readers who are less familiar with the specifically legal developments of the past two years, what follows is a brief overview of some of the more significant challenges that the Scottish legal system has had to face in this period. Subsequently, we outline three significant themes that we see emerging around the role of law in Scotland today, and within which the contributions to this collection, and the legal and political developments more generally, may be set.

SCOTS LAW'S "YEAR OF LIVING DANGEROUSLY"

One measure of the way in which the landscape of Scots law has been transformed is the amount of litigation – or the threat of litigation – that has been generated. By this measure it is clear that a dramatic shift is occurring: as early as March 2000 there had been as many as 374 cases where issues involving the European Convention on Human Rights (ECHR) had been raised.[1] Although these claims were reported to have been successful in only ten cases, this does not seem likely to lead to any decrease in interest – and in fact the number of human rights challenges is only likely to increase following the full coming into force of the Human Rights Act 1998 in October 2000. In addition, it would appear that, possibly encouraged by the success of certain high-profile challenges, politicians, the media and the general public have all quickly adapted to the new discourse of human rights challenges and the questioning of the constitutional legality of the actions of government institutions. Of course, it might be argued that this merely reflects the novelty of the Acts rather than any lasting change in the law. It is, after all, always the case that new legislation will generate disputes over the meaning of key terms and concepts, and that this will tail off as a more settled meaning is established by the courts. However, an examination of some of the cases in which issues of human rights and devolution were considered by the courts would suggest that a more fundamental transformation of the legal system is underway.

---

1 Scottish Parliament Official Report, Vol 5, No 4, 2 March 2000, col 313.

Although the Human Rights Act 1998 did not come into force in the United Kingdom until 2 October 2000, a feature of the legislation establishing the Scottish Parliament was that certain provisions of the 1998 Act came into force in Scotland over a year earlier than in the rest of the UK. The Scotland Act 1998, which came into force on 20 May 1999, states in section 57(2) that no member of the Scottish Executive may act in any way that is incompatible with the ECHR. The same Act states in section 44(1) that the Lord Advocate, who has responsibility for, amongst other things, the prosecution of crime and the investigation of deaths in Scotland, is to be considered a member of the Scottish Executive. Thus the way was paved for the challenge of certain actions of the Lord Advocate, as a member of the Scottish Executive, under those provisions of the ECHR that relate to criminal procedure.

Article 6(1) of the ECHR states that "everyone is entitled to a fair and public hearing ... by an independent and impartial tribunal established by law", and it was the interpretation of this article that gave rise to most of the early challenges.

The first, and most celebrated, challenge came in the case of *Starrs v Ruxton*.[1] In this case, the complainers claimed that their prosecution on summary complaint before a temporary sheriff sitting in Linlithgow Sheriff Court contravened their right to a fair trial. The claim, while raising a number of technical legal issues, may be simply put: since the Lord Advocate took a crucial role in the Executive's appointment of temporary sheriffs, and since temporary sheriffs had no security of tenure but were reappointed annually, the impartiality and independence of those sheriffs could be called into question. It was not suggested that the sheriff had in fact acted in a partial or biased manner, but that the procedures surrounding the appointment of temporary sheriffs did not have the appearance of impartiality. The Appeal Court of the High Court of Justiciary upheld this claim in their decision, stressing that the important factor was less the fact that the Lord Advocate was involved in the appointment of the sheriffs, than that these appointments could be recalled at any time, and that the renewal or recall of their commissions was not subject to any regulation. The decision had an immediate impact on the criminal justice system, and led to widespread criticism of the Scottish Executive, and the Lord Advocate in particular, for their failure to anticipate this problem. It led to the suspension of temporary sheriffs, then 25% of the shrieval bench, causing delays in the hearing of cases through the loss of almost 6,000 court days, as well as causing difficulties in other courts as the Executive realised that other practices were open to challenge. It also became clear that further legislation would be required in order to establish appointment procedures that would not be open to challenge under the ECHR.[2]

This decision was followed by a number of cases which sought, with

---

1   *Starrs v Ruxton* 2000 SLT 42. For comment on the legal issues see A O'Neill, "The European Convention and the Independence of the Judiciary – the Scottish Experience" (2000) 63 Mod LR 429–41; S Tierney, "Human Rights and Temporary Sheriffs" (2000) 4 *European Law Review* 223–228.
2   See GW Anderson, "Using Human Rights Law in Scottish Courts" (2000) 25 *European Law Review Human Rights Survey* 3 at 11–12.

only a limited degree of success, to exploit this new understanding of the requirement for impartiality. In *Clancy v Caird*,[1] a civil case, it was held that a temporary judge in the Court of Session need not be in violation of Article 6(1) if there were sufficient security of tenure and the Crown were not involved in the case. In *Clark v Kelly*[2] it was held that the normal functions of the legal assessor in the District Court (who did not have security of tenure) would not breach the right to a fair trial. In *Millar v Dickson*[3] the Appeal Court rejected a claim that a conviction by a temporary sheriff prior to the decision in *Starrs v Ruxton* should be suspended. In a final case, *County Properties Ltd v The Scottish Ministers*,[4] counsel for the Scottish Ministers had to concede that procedures under Scots law for the operation of a planning inquiry fell foul of the requirement of Article 6(1).

If none of these cases generated the same level of media coverage or controversy as the earlier decision, it was not long before the courts were once again hitting the headlines in another case involving the interpretation of Article 6.[5] In *Brown v Stott*[6] a drunken woman was arrested outside an all-night supermarket under suspicion of having stolen a bottle of gin. The police then realised that she had a car in the car park. Suspecting that she might have driven the car, they required her to give the identity of the driver under section 172(2) of the Road Traffic Act 1988, bringing an admission that she had driven the car to the store. She was convicted of both theft and driving after consuming an excess of alcohol, but appealed against the conviction for the road traffic offence on the grounds that her right to remain silent and not incriminate herself had been violated. The Appeal Court held unanimously that the use of Brown's reply to the police in her prosecution violated the right to a fair trial guaranteed in Article 6. The case generated a considerable amount of negative publicity for human rights and the legal system. This was in part because the decision was depicted as having crippled police efforts to deal with road traffic crimes. Indeed, although the Crown had sought to argue that a potential consequence of the decision would be to prevent the use of roadside cameras in the detection of road traffic crime, the court had pointedly failed to regard this as a factor that was relevant to their decision.[7] In addition, this was a case where the accused was seen to have been "let off" on a technicality, leading to the portrayal of the ECHR as something that was not only foreign to the common sense of Scottish criminal procedure but also potentially dangerous.[8] It is perhaps ironic that it was the decision of a "foreign"

---

1   *Clancy v Caird* 2000 SLT 546.
2   *Clark v Kelly* 2000 SLT 1038.
3   *Millar v Dickson* 2000 SLT 1111.
4   *County Properties Ltd v The Scottish Ministers* 2000 SLT 965.
5   There have been a large number of other challenges under Article 6, on matters as diverse as the payment of fixed fees in criminal legal aid (see *Buchanan v McLean* 2000 SLT 928; *Gayne v Vannet* 2000 JC 51) and the delay in bringing an accused person to trial (see *McNab v HM Advocate* 2000 SLT 99; *HM Advocate v McGlinchey* 2000 SLT 995).
6   *Brown v Stott* 2000 SLT 379.
7   *Brown v Stott* 2000 SLT 379 at 396I–J.
8   This was similar to the views expressed following the decision in *McIntosh v HM Advocate* 2000 GWD 33-1284, 13 October 2000, in which the court upheld a petition challenging the legality of confiscation orders for the proceeds of drug trafficking.

court, the Judicial Committee of the Privy Council, that was to reverse the decision of the appeal court and restore the status quo.[1]

If these have been the most notable challenges to date, there is every likelihood that the number of challenges will continue to increase for the foreseeable future, placing a considerable burden on our legal system. There is, of course, always going to be a gap between those types of challenges under the ECHR which are deemed newsworthy and those which are likely to be successful. Pressure groups have been awakened to the effectiveness of domestic human rights litigation as a means of raising the public profile of an issue, notwithstanding that they may only rarely meet the technical requirements for bringing the issue before the courts. The litigation so far has demonstrated both the benefits and burdens of a human rights culture, in terms of the exposure of the potential abuse of powers and the costs of correcting these. Both should become even more apparent as future litigation moves into the yet more contentious areas, such as privacy (Article 8) and freedom of expression (Article 10). It is likely, then, that the courts will continue to hit the headlines as further failings in the ways that decisions are made by public bodies come to light.

It is clear that the increasing levels of scrutiny of the courts also mean that there are new responsibilities attaching to the role of the judge as a public figure. Few would dispute the need for a full and properly informed public debate on the incorporation of human rights into domestic law, nor deny the judiciary the possibility of participating in that debate. It is worthy of note then that one judge's very public contribution to this debate itself gave rise to further litigation on the meaning of the impartiality of the judiciary. Lord McCluskey, a senior member of the judiciary, suggested in a newspaper article that the incorporation of the ECHR would provide "a field day for crackpots, a pain in the neck for judges and legislators, and a goldmine for lawyers". These remarks then provided the basis for a successful appeal in the case of *Hoekstra v HM Advocate (No.2)*[2] where the appellants argued that this revealed a lack of impartiality on questions of human rights. In a second incident, the same judge's public criticisms of the Crown Office at the conclusion of the trial of one of the men accused of the murder of Surjit Singh Chhokar, and the public response of the then Lord Advocate, Andrew Hardie, were the basis for an appeal when it was claimed that the controversy had given rise to adverse publicity that would prejudice the possibility of a fair trial.[3] Although in this latter case the appeal was dismissed by both the Appeal Court and the Privy Council, this draws our attention to an important issue. It is absolutely essential to the development of legitimate and accountable legal institutions that judges should be able to engage in public debate.

---

1 *McIntosh v HM Advocate* 2001 SLT 304. This, in addition, has raised the spectre of an appeal to the House of Lords in criminal cases – something that has been steadfastly resisted by the Scottish legal system for the past 200 years.
2 *Hoekstra v HM Advocate (No 2)* 2000 SLT 605.
3 *Montgomery v HM Advocate* 2001 SLT 37. Hardie was later criticised for his resignation from the post of Lord Advocate to take a judicial post shortly before the commencement of the Lockerbie trial, partly for a lack of awareness of the political sensitivity of the situation, but also because of his institutional role in his own appointment as a judge.

There could be nothing worse than a return to the world where judges were remote and aloof figures, but it is clear that there are limits to the way that they can make a contribution to public debate, since judges must be aware of the immediate political dimensions of their words both in the context of judicial decisions and other public utterances.

It is surely right, however, that the judiciary should be subject to this extra degree of scrutiny, for the scope of their jurisdiction has been greatly enlarged. This growth in judicial powers has been recognised by the courts in cases such as *Whaley v Lord Watson*.[1] Here, confronted with the argument that the court's jurisdiction over the Parliament should be excluded, Lord Prosser stated:

> "If anything the need for such a jurisdiction is in my opinion all the greater where a body has very wide powers, as the Scottish Parliament has: the greater the powers, the greater the need to ensure that they are not exceeded."[2]

Thus, in addition to their powers under the Human Rights Act 1988, the courts might scrutinise actual or proposed legislation of the Scottish Parliament for its compatibility with the ECHR or its competence under the Scotland Act 1998.[3] And, since the Privy Council has taken a restrictive view of the definition of a "devolution issue" under the 1998 Act, they have, for the time being, passed the responsibility for the shaping of Scots law back to the domestic Scottish courts.[4] The legitimacy of the legal process in these areas – as also in cases where the legal system must respond to alleged miscarriages of justice – clearly depends on rather more than a technical understanding of the law. It will also depend on the continuing ability of the courts and the legal profession to attract public respect and support. Even if this does not necessarily entail that lawyers and judges should continue to "live dangerously", it certainly means that they must come to terms with their changing responsibilities towards the public.

THE STATE OF SCOTS LAW: THREE CENTRAL ISSUES

The surge of litigation and the need for speedy responses to often intractable questions with serious political and administrative consequences has meant that the period since the coming into force of the Scotland Act 1998 has been a trying time for Scots law. After centuries in which Scots law has often appeared to be cocooned from the modern world in the manner of a cosy gentleman's club, where its privileges have seemed to be part of the natural order, this transition has clearly not

---

1   *Whaley v Lord Watson* 2000 SC 340.
2   2000 SC 340 at 357.
3   The former was exercised in the case of *A v The Scottish Ministers* 2000 SLT 873, in relation to the Mental Health (Public Safety and Appeals) (Scotland) Act 1999.
4   See *Hoekstra v HM Advocate (No 3)* 2001 SLT 28 and *Brown v Stott* 2001 SLT 59. The Scottish courts, by contrast, have arguably widened the impact of the Scotland Act 1998, by treating questions about the competency of the judiciary as devolution issues.

always been an easy one for the legal system to make. It is crucial, then, in the face of these rapid changes, that we step back and reflect on the more general issues that have emerged. In order to aid such reflection, there are three central themes that may profitably be considered.

The first concerns the increasing legalisation of Scottish political culture – and, conversely, the politicisation of the legal culture. Several of the decisions noted in the previous section can be treated as reflecting this underlying, if nascent, trend. For present purposes, this has two aspects. On the one hand, the existence of a new constitutional framework provided by the two above-mentioned statutes has vastly increased the potential legal accountability of our political institutions and actors, and we can expect to see, for example, an increase in the number and range of challenges to the actions of politicians and the Executive. The democratic momentum initiated by the devolution settlement is, accordingly, being mediated through legal mechanisms and the immediate engagement of lawyers and the courts. However, we should also be aware that this may engender a defensiveness on the part of politicians and government agencies as they seek to render their procedures "judge-proof". This defensive mentality has the potential to outweigh any more positive gains that may be made. In either case this is new territory for both lawyers and politicians. Arguably what we are witnessing is the emergence of a type and style of legal politics for which there is little indigenous precedent. And whilst we are justified in expecting our political and legal institutions to come to terms with this, it nonetheless requires of lawyers and political actors a newly-oriented sensitivity to direct legal involvement in political procedures and strategies.

On the other hand, this necessarily puts the courts under an unaccustomed political pressure as they are forced to adjudicate on political disputes and to have these decisions held up to public scrutiny in the press and other media. The significance of the exposure of the judicial role to involvement in day-to-day issues of governance cannot be overestimated. Judges, individually and collectively, are becoming aware of their visible presence in structures of government, and the potential this may have for causing administrative chaos or the making of politically unpopular decisions. While some judges seem to relish the opportunity this provides for speaking out, others are less accustomed or able to deal with the fairly intense scrutiny that has been generated as the secret world of the legal profession has been exposed to the public. Moreover, the process of extending the democratic accountability of our political and administrative institutions leads inexorably to a demand for the accountability of our legal institutions. Specifically, the long-standing procedures and practices of bench and bar are now being forced into the public spotlight. This in turn calls for a re-configuration of expectations around the notion of what it means for Scotland to have an independent judiciary, involving dimensions as varied as accountability, employment opportunities and acceptable standards of impartiality. The way in which these concerns have been and will continue to be played out in front of the media will inevitably challenge a judicial practice and culture that has been largely shielded from such assessments – including self-assessments – of the serious political implications of its endeavours. The formal redefinition of the role of the courts, and their explicit insertion into the new machinery of government will have, in other words, important political consequences which we are only beginning to understand.

This leads into the second theme which concerns the impact of the public law revolution on Scots law. For many centuries Scots lawyers have been little concerned with public law and the British state, and have busied themselves with the cultivation of the principles of Scots private law – indeed in the absence of parliament or state there has been little public law for Scots lawyers to concern themselves with. Recent years have seen a dramatic reversal of this position with the increasing importance of "social legislation", the rise of regulative bodies fulfilling administrative decision-making functions, and the growth in judicial review in Scots law, due amongst other things to influence of European Community law. These trends look set to continue under the new constitutional arrangements and with the impact of the Human Rights Act 1998.[1] While one might remain agnostic as to the benefits of this revolution, it is nonetheless clear that this will have a great impact on the production and preservation of Scots law. As the practising Scots lawyer is increasingly concerned with issues both of public law and "foreign" influence, the question is how this will bear on legal practice and the self-image of Scots law.

The Scottish judiciary has signalled a clear willingness to face up to the new responsibilities that have been placed upon them in this regard. If, in terms of results, cases since 1998 suggest that the courts have adopted a cautious line in the recognition of the scope of human rights, many commentators have expressed surprise at the manner in which the courts have approached these questions. In contrast to the more conservative approach that has been taken to date in England and Wales, the Scottish courts have actively tried to graft human rights jurisprudence onto the existing law, and have demonstrated a clear willingness to draw on authorities from a wide range of jurisdictions.[2] This also gives an excellent illustration of the way in which, in practical terms, the Scotland Act 1998 and the Human Rights Act 1998 amount to a new constitutional "settlement". Legislation providing, for example, that in certain instances the judiciary will be required to assess the legality of actions of the executive and legislative branches of government provides a clear challenge to the traditional British doctrine of the sovereignty of parliament – at least insofar as this relates to Scottish affairs – although this admittedly is a transformation that was within the contemplation of the drafters of the legislation. With the concurrent rise in the use of regulatory bodies and procedures requiring administrative law supervision, we can expect such developments to play a key role in the future of Scots law as a whole.

Additionally, and specifically with regard to this public law revolution, we should also note its impact at a key level of the reproduction of legal ideas, namely, in legal education. The report last year of the Joint Standing Committee on Legal Education in Scotland noted unambiguously that,

---

1 For coverage and assessment of many of these developments see Clyde and Edwards, *Judicial Review* (W Green, Edinburgh, 2000).
2 See esp. G W Anderson, "Using Human Rights Law in Scottish Courts" (2000) *European Law Review Human Rights Survey* 3.

because "the content and practice of the law is markedly different from that in the 1960's when the present LL.B degree was conceived ... there would be considerable advantage in developing a new approach to the LL.B degree". Of the ten "substantive developments" the Report identified to justify such a shake-up, the majority were directly concerned with public, administrative and regulation law changes.[1] Undergraduate legal education is thus witnessing a shift in the balance between private and public law – occasionally to the despair of traditional private law teachers – as it readjusts curricular priorities in the light of perceived academic, student and employer requirements.

This leads finally to the third theme, which concerns the continuing status of the Scottish legal tradition.[2] Certain Scots lawyers have long had a fond belief in the existence of an organic connection between the simple and practical principles of the law and the character of the Scottish people. On this view the presence of a parliament in Edinburgh for the first time in almost 300 years would seem to represent the best means of protection against the incursion of foreign principles, and the best means also of the preservation of the distinctive identity of Scots law in its relation to the Scottish people. However, it is not at all clear that this will necessarily be the case. The presence of a parliament does mean that there is a greater potential for legislation than at any other point in our recent history. The early signs are that the Scottish Parliament has an appetite for law reform and this will put a great pressure on the capacity of bodies such as the Scottish Law Commission to produce and scrutinise the proposed legislation. However, the early signs are that the principal demand for legislation is in areas that go well beyond the traditional scope of Scots private law – and even if it were in this area there is no necessary reason why the Parliament should respect the traditional understandings and concepts of Scots law. It may be that the existence of a distinctive culture of Scots law is put under threat exactly at the moment at which it might have thought itself to be safe from foreign interference.

Indeed, even in the arena of private law we are increasingly forced to address the question of the extent to which there remains anything distinctive about the system of Scots law. Ironically perhaps, the status of Scots law as a "mixed system" – of Roman civil law and common law – may make it more amenable to influences that may ultimately be seen to detract from its claimed uniqueness. How should we understand, for example, the initiatives that seek to develop a new code of European private law? Are these the legal equivalent of the position that "there is no alternative" with regard to the increased economic forces and political harmonisation of the European Union? If so, should Scots lawyers be troubled by such developments? Or is this merely to practise the virtue of pragmatism which sees "the law develop as seem[s] best suited to the demands and fashions of the times"?[3]

---

1 "Scottish Legal Education in the Twenty-First Century": Report of Joint Standing Committee on Legal Education in Scotland (April, 2000). The Committee is made up of representatives from Universities, the Law Society, and the Faculty of Advocates.
2 For a classic treatment of this see M C Meston, W D H Sellar and Lord Cooper, *The Scottish Legal Tradition* (Saltire Society, Edinburgh 1991).
3 Alan Rodger, "Thinking about Scots Law" (1996) 1 ELR 3 at 24.

This may merely confirm that the mixed legal system of Scots law was never much more than the repository in a small jurisdiction of ideas and influences forged elsewhere and used in whatever way was most practically convenient.

In terms of influences tending towards a changing legal culture, we can already identify an expansion of the traditional idiom and grammar of Scottish jurisprudence as, for instance, the courts have shown greater willing to consider a range of cases and concepts from other jurisdictions. This suggests that, in an inversion of the conventional understanding of the Scottish tradition which stresses its cosmopolitan roots and homely resources, it is being revitalised by an infusion of "foreign" ideas. In terms of judicial influence, and in the words of Lord Reed, the magnetic north of legal influence may be shifting from London to Strasbourg.[1] This suggests that a reappraisal of the very notion of a Scottish legal tradition may be timely, and that – paradoxically – its very continuance may require scrutiny precisely at a point where democratic legitimacy seems to be edging slowly nearer to home.

Framed then by these three themes, and taking into account the particular and general nature of the changes to law in Scotland, such developments amount to a fundamental challenge to the ideas and institutions of Scots law. The following essays, arranged broadly according to the three themes which we have identified, are in different ways attempts to respond to these issues. The variety of the concerns and the different perspectives are an indication of an increasing breadth in Scottish legal scholarship, and will, we hope, represent the beginning, and not the end, of serious debate about the future of Scots law.

---

1 Lord Reed, "Human Rights: the Scottish Experience so far"—paper delivered at the Conference on Human Rights, University of Glasgow, 6 October 2000.

1 Constitutionalism, Judicial Review and "the Evident Utility of the Subjects Within Scotland"

Alan Page

"It is of little avail to ask whether the Parliament of Great Britain can do this or that without going on to inquire who can stop them if they do."[1]

"Writing a constitution that describes or implies judicial review is hardly the measure of the concept; how the pattern of judicial review evolves is more telling."[2]

INTRODUCTION

The constitutionalism to which the title of this chapter refers is the doctrine of the supremacy of the constitution, as opposed to the more familiar supremacy of statute; the ultimate source of norms is not parliament, or indeed the people, but the constitution. In *A Preface to Scots Law* Andrew Dewar Gibb wrote that it would be impossible to write a book or short essay on the constitution from a Scottish point of view "for today there is no Scottish Constitution. Whatever was written would of necessity be pure history ... To write at length on this subject in a book of Scots Law would be something of an absurdity".[3] Devolution, however, has once more made it meaningful to talk of a Scottish constitution. The new Scottish constitution is admittedly a very different creature from its pre-Acts of Union predecessor. It is the constitution not of a state but of a nation or region within a state. It is contained in an ordinary Act of the Westminster Parliament, as was the constitution of many of the countries that once formed part of the British Empire. It is also a constitution that, in theory at least, may be changed by the Westminster Parliament at any time; in Calvert's terms, it is a constitution that is completely rigid from a Scottish perspective, and completely flexible from a UK perspective.[4] It is a constitution nevertheless.

---

1 *MacCormick v Lord Advocate* 1953 SC 396 at 412, per Lord Cooper.
2 Volcansek, "Judicial Review in Italy: a Reflection of the United States?" (1990) 19 *Policy Studies Journal* 136.
3 Gibb, *A Preface to Scots Law* (W Green & Son, Edinburgh, 1964), p 2.
4 Calvert, *Constitutional Law in Northern Ireland* (Stevens & Sons, London, 1968), p 53.

"Judicial review" in the present context denotes the power of the courts to review the constitutionality of legislation as opposed to the more familiar power of the courts to review the legality of administrative action.[1] In the post-war period judicial review of legislation has become a "global phenomenon."[2] Originally confined to the United States, Canada and Australia, it was extended after the Second World War to Germany, Italy and Japan. More recently, it has been extended to France, Spain and Portugal and, in the last decade, to the "post-Leninist states" of Eastern Europe and the former Soviet Union.[3] It was where the traditions of parliamentary democracy were most firmly established, in the United Kingdom and France, that judicial review of legislation was most vigorously opposed; the doctrine of the sovereignty of Parliament and the analogous French doctrine of the sovereignty of the people "were the strongest barriers to the concept of the supremacy of the constitution, out of which constitutional jurisdiction evolved."[4] Now, however, with the incorporation of the ECHR and devolution to Scotland in particular, the United Kingdom has become part of this global phenomenon. Under the Human Rights Act 1998 the higher courts have power to declare Acts of Parliament incompatible with "Convention rights",[5] while under the Scotland Act 1998 the courts have the power to strike down Acts of the Scottish Parliament as outwith its legislative competence.[6]

The fact that the courts have no power under the Human Rights Act 1998 to strike down offending legislation has tended to obscure the fact that they will nevertheless be reviewing its constitutionality. The traditional orthodoxy was summed up by Lord Morris in *British Railways Board v Pickin:* "In the courts there may be an argument as to the correct interpretation of the enactment: there must be none as to whether it should be on the Statute Book at all."[7] Under the Human Rights Act 1998, however, there will be both.

The "evident utility of the subjects within Scotland" is the stipulation that, it will be recalled, Article XVIII of the Treaty of Union made in respect of changes to the separate system of Scots law affecting private rights. The law concerning public right could be changed freely, but the law concerning private right was not to be altered "except for the evident utility of the subjects of Scotland." However, the argument that the courts should take it upon themselves to rule on the conformity of Acts of Parliament with the fundamental law of the Union met with a distinctly cautious response

---

1 Russell, "The Diffusion of Judicial Review: The Commonwealth, the United States and the Canadian Case" (1990) 19 *Policy Studies Journal* 116.
2 Shapiro and Stone, "The New Constitutional Politics of Europe" (1994) 26 *Comparative Political Studies* 397.
3 Shapiro, "The Success of Judicial Review" in Kenney, Reisinger and Reitz (eds), *Constitutional Dialogues in Comparative Perspective* (Macmillan Press, London, 1999), p 199.
4 von Beyme, "The Genesis of Constitutional Review in Parliamentary Systems" in Landfried (ed), *Constitutional Review and Legislation: An International Comparison* (Nomos, Baden-Baden, 1988), pp 22–23; Cappelletti, *The Judicial Process in Comparative Perspective* (Clarendon, Oxford, 1989), p 190.
5 Human Rights Act 1998, s 4.
6 Scotland Act 1998, s 29.
7 *British Railways Board v Pickin* [1974] AC 765 at 789, per Lord Morris of Borth-y-Gest.

from the courts. T B Smith's forthright view was that: "Sixteen Scottish judges should certainly be better able to assess the 'evident utility' of Scotsmen than a legislature composed by an overwhelming majority of members who are not qualified to express a reasoned opinion on the matter."[1] But in *Gibson v Lord Advocate,* Lord Keith was of the view that:

> "the question whether a particular Act of the United Kingdom Parliament ... is or is not 'for the evident utility' of the subjects within Scotland is not a justiciable issue in this Court. The making of decisions upon what must essentially be a political matter is not a part of the function of the Court, and it is highly undesirable that it should be ... A general inquiry into the utility of specific legislative measures as regards the population generally is quite outside its competence."[2]

Under the Scotland Act 1998, however, it falls unequivocally to the courts to decide what is for the evident utility of the subjects within Scotland, as that notion is now defined in the 1998 Act.

Judicial review of legislation under the Scotland Act 1998 is likely to have a major impact on the devolved Scottish Parliament and Executive as well as on the courts. As if to underline the change that had taken place, no sooner had the Parliament's first bill been enacted, the Mental Health (Public Safety and Appeals) (Scotland) Act 1999, than a judicial ruling was sought on whether section 1 of that Act was within the Parliament's legislative competence.[3] It is also likely to be a considerable influence on relations between the devolved government of Scotland and Westminster. It is on those consequences that I want to concentrate in this chapter. But first I will say something about rationales for judicial review of legislation and the UK model of review.

RATIONALES FOR JUDICIAL REVIEW OF LEGISLATION UNDER THE SCOTLAND ACT 1998

Two explanations have been advanced for the post-war growth of judicial review. The first, a modified version of the traditional federalism hypothesis, is that it is designed to secure a division of powers—either vertically, between different levels of government, as in the United States, Germany or the European Union (membership of which has led the courts to review the compatibility of Acts of Parliament with the requirements of Community law),[4] or, less commonly, horizontally, between different branches of government, as in France where it was conceived as a means

---

1 T B Smith, *A Short Commentary on the Law of Scotland* (W Green, Edinburgh, 1962), p 58.
2 *Gibson v Lord Advocate* 1975 SC 136 at 144.
3 See *A v The Scottish Ministers* 2000 SLT 873. The Inner House of the Court of Session held that there was no conflict between s 1 of the Mental Health (Public Safety and Appeals) Scotland Act 1999 and the right to liberty guaranteed by Art 5 of the European Convention on Human Rights.
4 *R v Secretary of State for Transport, ex p Factortame (No 2)* [1991] AC 603; *R v Secretary of State for Employment, ex p EOC* [1995] 1 AC 1.

of ensuring that the legislature did not trespass on the preserve of the executive.[1] The second is that it is designed to secure the protection of individual rights and freedoms, in which connection it has been described as a necessary counterbalance to "the increasing significance of the principle of the democratic majority in a more and more politicised society."[2]

Applying these explanations to the Scotland Act 1998, judicial review is clearly rooted in division of powers concerns. However, the emphasis is on ensuring that the devolved institutions remain within the bounds of their constitutional competence, rather than guaranteeing a division of powers between London and Edinburgh on the federal model. In line with the devolutionary nature of the settlement, the Scotland Act 1998 expressly preserves the power of the Westminster Parliament to legislate for Scotland.[3] The UK Government has added to this the gloss that it "will proceed in accordance with the convention that the UK Parliament *would not normally* legislate with regard to devolved matters except with the agreement of the devolved legislature,"[4] but it has also emphasised that the Westminster Parliament retains authority to legislate on any issue, whether devolved or not,[5] and were it to do so there is no question that on current understandings the courts would be bound to give effect to its legislation. Whether in time the courts will come to treat the Westminster Parliament as having lost the power to legislate for Scotland on devolved matters is one of the many fascinating questions raised by the devolution settlement. Were that to happen it would indicate a fundamental change in the nature of the settlement. But for the moment the power undoubtedly exists, even if, as Bogdanor argues,[6] it is more theoretical than real.

Judicial review of legislation under the Scotland Act 1998 is also very much about the protection of individual rights and freedoms, much more so than has been openly acknowledged. A central unstated premise of the devolution project was that there should be some set of fundamental values by which the parliament and the executive would be bound; that the devolved legislature should not, in other words, inherit the unbounded legislative competence of the Westminster Parliament. This was to be achieved by making the Scottish Parliament subject to the European Convention on Human Rights. The decision to incorporate the ECHR for the United Kingdom as a whole has obscured this, but it appears that the decision to incorporate the Convention was taken subsequently and independently.

1 Shapiro, "The Success of Judicial Review", pp 194–199. (See note 3 on page 12 above.)
2 von Brunneck, "Constitutional Review and Legislation in Western Democracies", in Landfried (ed), *Constitutional Review and Legislation: An International Comparison* (Nomos, Baden-Baden, 1988), pp 221–222. See also Favoreu, "Constitutional Review in Europe" in Henkin and Rosenthal (eds), *Constitutionalism and Rights: The Influence of the United States Constitution Abroad* (Columbia University Press, New York, 1990), p 56.
3 Scotland Act 1998, s 28(7).
4 *Memorandum of Understanding and Supplementary Agreements between the United Kingdom Government, Scottish Ministers and the Cabinet of the National Assembly of Wales,* Cm 4444 (1999), para 13, emphasis added.
5 *Memorandum of Understanding,* para 13.
6 Bogdanor, "Devolution: Constitutional Aspects" in *Constitutional Reform in the United Kingdom: Practice and Principles* (Hart Publishing, Oxford, 1998), pp 12–13. In practice, it is being freely exercised—with the consent of the Scottish Parliament.

Scotland, in other words, was going to get the Convention regardless of what happened elsewhere in the United Kingdom. In contrast to its 1978 predecessor, therefore, the 1998 Act sets judicially enforceable limits on the potential of the Scottish Parliament for "arbitrary and oppressive action."[1]

Although judicial review has a role to play in ensuring that the devolved institutions remain within the bounds of their constitutional competence, it is important to note that both it and the allied powers of ministerial intervention conferred by sections 35 and 107 of the Scotland Act 1998 are conceived as remedies of last resort. The Memorandum of Understanding, which governs relations between the UK Government and the devolved administrations, establishes a Joint Ministerial Committee whose functions extend to the consideration of disputes between the administrations. Its purpose has been described by a senior civil servant as "to head off trouble before fires break out and end up in the rafters, or in constitutional terms, in the law courts. It will enable proper negotiations to take place before the UK Government has to use the 'nuclear option' of overriding a decision by a devolved Assembly."[2] It is only where efforts at intergovernmental mediation fail, therefore, that recourse to the courts is likely, although the possibility of such recourse, or of ministerial intervention in appropriate cases, will no doubt serve as a powerful incentive to agreement. Therefore, save where either side is keen to obtain a judicial ruling recourse to the courts is likely to be infrequent, in the case of executive bills at least. The same is much less likely to be true, however, of the courts' role in the protection of Convention rights.

THE UK MODEL OF REVIEW

A distinction is commonly drawn between United States and European models of review. The hallmark of US review is said to be that it is carried out by the ordinary courts in concrete cases; the hallmark of European review, which traces its origins to Hans Kelsen's Austrian constitutional court,[3] is that it is abstract as well as concrete but only carried out by a special constitutional court. "The difference between the two was that the former permitted determinations of constitutionality by ordinary courts in concrete cases and the latter permitted abstract as well as concrete review, but only by a special constitutional court."[4] The significance of judicial review on the European constitutional court model was that it was conceived as a way of keeping the ordinary courts within their traditional bounds. It had "the particular advantage of allowing for the *constitutional*

---

1 Daintith, "The Kilbrandon Report: Some Comments" in Calvert (ed) *Devolution* (Professional Books, London, 1975), p 31.
2 Osmond, *The National Assembly Agenda* (Institute of Welsh Affairs, Cardiff, 1998), p 355.
3 von Beyme, "The Genesis of Constitutional Review in Parliamentary Systems", pp 29–30. (See note 4 on page 12 above.)
4 Danelski, "The Origins of Judicial Review in the United States and Japan" (1990) 19 *Policy Studies Journal* 151; see also Favoreu, "Constitutional Review in Europe" in Henkin and Rosenthal (eds), *Constitutionalism and Rights: The Influence of the United States Constitution Abroad* (Columbia University Press, New York, 1990), pp 40–41.

review of legislation by special judges while preserving the main tenets of European separation of powers doctrines, tenets which had long enshrined an uncompromising hostility to *judicial review*."[1]

Judicial review under the Scotland Act 1998 follows the United States rather than the European model, but with important differences. First, the power of review is exercisable by the "ordinary" courts but this is combined with provision for the referral of "devolution issues", the definition of which includes the question whether an Act of the Scottish Parliament is within its legislative competence,[2] to the higher courts, with the possibility of an appeal to the Judicial Committee of the Privy Council. The Law Officers also have power to require a court or tribunal to refer to the Judicial Committee a devolution issue which has arisen in proceedings before it to which they are a party.[3] In theory, therefore, it should be possible to secure a rapid determination by a superior court of any serious questions as to the validity of legislation or executive action.[4]

Second, the Scotland Act 1998 makes provision for abstract as well as concrete review. Under section 33 of the Act, the Law Officers in both the UK and Scottish Executives may refer question of whether a bill is within the competence of the Scottish Parliament to the Judicial Committee for a decision.[5] A reference may be made within a month of the bill being passed (either for the first time or after being revised following a decision by the Privy Council that in its original form it was outwith the competence of the Scottish Parliament).[6] The effect of a reference under section 33 is to prevent a bill from being submitted for the royal assent, i.e. to prevent it from being enacted.[7] In addition, under Schedule 6 to the 1998 Act, the Advocate General and the Lord Advocate may institute proceedings for the determination of a devolution issue.[8] They may also refer to the Judicial Committee any devolution issue which is not the subject of proceedings.[9]

Why abstract as well as concrete review? Abstract review is typically justified as providing for a more complete, potentially systematic and therefore efficacious defence of the constitution within a hierarchy of judicial norms.[10] It permits clarification of the law before individuals are required to act, and

---

1 Stone, "The Birth and Development of Abstract Review: Constitutional Courts and Policymaking in Western Europe" (1990) 19 *Policy Studies Journal* 81, original emphasis. See more fully Cappelletti, *The Judicial Process in Comparative Perspective* (Clarendon, Oxford, 1989), pp 136–146.
2 Scotland Act 1998, Sch 6, para 1.
3 SA 1998, Sch 6, para 33.
4 Reed, "Devolution and the Judiciary" in *Constitutional Reform in the United Kingdom: Principles and Practice* (Hart Publishing, Oxford, 1998), p 26.
5 Scotland Act 1998, s 33(1).
6 SA 1998, s 33(2).
7 SA 1998, s 32(2).
8 SA 1998, Sch 6, para 4.
9 SA 1998, Sch 6, para 34.
10 Weber, "Le Controle juridictionnel de la constitutionalitie des lois dans les pays d'Europe occidentale" in (1987) *Annuaire International de Justice Constitutionnelle,* cited in Stone, "The Birth and Development of Abstract Review: Constitutional Courts and Policymaking in Western Europe" (1990) 19 *Policy Studies Journal* 88.

thus secures a beneficial certainty to the law.[1] Its disadvantage is that it is said to lead to less sound and less enduring judgments, despite the fact that, as Reitz points out, there is no reason to believe that abstract reviews involve any less genuine controversy or will be less diligently argued.[2] It is also said to weaken the court's claim to legitimacy and to lead to an undesirable expansion of judicial power.[3] From the point of view of the Scottish Parliament and Executive, however, the combination of abstract and concrete review means that they are subject to an exceptionally strong form of review. In France, Shapiro argues, "the exclusivity of abstract review was deliberately employed as a means of limiting judicial review"; in Germany, by contrast, "the combination of abstract and concrete review was deliberately employed to expand judicial review."[4] In Scotland, as in Germany, it is possible to seek review before legislation has been enacted, and before a concrete dispute has arisen, as well as once it is on the statute book.

Under the Scotland Act 1998, however, the right of referral is confined to the Law Officers to both the UK and Scottish governments. In contrast to other countries it does not extend to elected representatives. In Germany, the Federal Government, the governments of the Lander, or one third of the members of the Bundestag may initiate constitutional review. In France the right to seek review was initially confined to the President, the Prime Minister and the Presidents of the Senate and National Assembly, but a constitutional amendment in 1974 made it possible for 60 deputies or 60 senators to challenge the constitutionality of legislation before the Constitutional Council. Where the power is more widely conferred, as in France and Germany, abstract review has emerged as a powerful weapon of political opposition; "oppositions exploit abstract review procedures in order to win from constitutional courts what they can never win in parliament."[5] Since 1974, when the right of referral was extended in France oppositions have referred every budget and nearly every other important or controversial bill to the constitutional court.[6] The picture in Germany is no different: abstract judicial review is "a common weapon in Germany's political arsenal ... Governments and politicians continually threaten to drag their opponents "to Karlsruhe"— the location of the Court—when their interests are at stake."[7] "What

1 Reitz, "Political Economy and Abstract Review in Germany, France and the United States" in Kenney, Reisinger and Reitz (eds), *Constitutional Dialogues in Comparative Perspective* (Macmillan Press, London, 1999), pp 68–69.
2 Reitz, "Political Economy and Abstract Review in Germany, France and the United States", p 69. See also Bogdanor, *Devolution in the United Kingdom* (Oxford University Press, Oxford, 1999), p 206.
3 Reitz, "Political Economy and Abstract Review in Germany, France and the United States", pp 69–71.
4 Shapiro, "The Success of Judicial Review", p 199. (See note 3 on page 12 above.)
5 Stone, "Governing with Judges: The New Constitutionalism" in Hayward and Page (eds), *Governing the New Europe* (Polity Press, Cambridge, 1995), p 301.
6 Stone Sweet, "Constitutional Dialogues: Protecting Human Rights in France, Germany, Italy and Spain", in Kenney, Reisinger and Reitz (eds), *Constitutional Dialogues in Comparative Perspective*, p 24.
7 Kommers, "The Federal Constitutional Court in the German Political System" (1994) 26 *Comparative Political Studies* 470 at 475.

makes abstract review so politically sensitive", Kommers argues, "is the capacity of any of the three parties to transpose a political conflict directly into a constitutional one."[1]

It may be surmised that the restriction of the power of referral to the Law Officers was with the intention of preventing its use as a weapon of political opposition. This is not to suggest that it may not be used by the Law Officers as a means of opposition, putting opponents in baulk, only to underline that the power is confined to the Scottish and UK governments. Notwithstanding all that has been said about a more inclusive form of politics, abstract review under the Scotland Act 1998 is not conceived as a means of opposing executive dominance at the regional or national level. It is a weapon of executive control not a weapon of opposition. Given its potential as a means of opposition, however, it would be surprising if attempts were not made to widen the circle of those who can initiate reviews, for example, by way of a challenge to a Law Officer's refusal to refer. I come back to this possibility below.

The third and final difference is that the final court of appeal in devolution matters is not the House of Lords but the Judicial Committee of the Privy Council. The reasons why the Judicial Committee was preferred to the House of Lords have been thoroughly rehearsed. The Lord Chancellor has indicated that the main reason was that because there is no appeal in criminal matters to the House of Lords there was thought to be less risk of offending nationalist sensitivities if the final appeal on devolution issues were to lie to the Privy Council.[2] Additional considerations adduced by Lord Reed include the fact that the Privy Council's constitutional role as adviser to Her Majesty makes it an appropriate means of resolving disputes over whether the royal assent should be given to Scottish bills; and the fact that since, unlike the House of Lords, it does not form part of the Westminster Parliament there is no question of one parliament being subject to review by another.[3] The Judicial Committee can also sit during the parliamentary recess, again unlike the House of Lords which can sit only if Parliament is recalled.[4]

The Judicial Committee's emergence as an ad hoc constitutional court is in line with the post-war trend away from the multi-purpose, multi-jurisdictional supreme court towards specialist constitutional tribunals.[5] One factor that this trend reflects is the growth of court-based control of executive and legislative action on "higher law" constitutional grounds.[6]

---

1 Kommers, "The Federal Constitutional Court in the German Political System" (1994) 26 *Comparative Political Studies* 470 at 474.
2 Irvine of Lairg, "Keynote Address" in *Constitutional Reform in the United Kingdom: Principles and Practice* (Hart Publishing, Oxford, 1998), p 3; see also Hope, "Edinburgh v Westminster and Others" (1997) 42 *JLSS* 142.
3 Reed, "Devolution and the Judiciary" in *Constitutional Reform in the United Kingdom: Principles and Practice* (Hart Publishing, Oxford, 1998) p 25.
4 Reed, "Devolution and the Judiciary", p 25.
5 McWhinney, *Supreme Courts and Judicial Law-Making: Constitutional Tribunals and Constitutional Review* (Nighoff, Dordrecht, 1986), p 272 and earlier at p xiv.
6 McWhinney, *Supreme Courts and Judicial Law-Making: Constitutional Tribunals and Constitutional Review*, p 1.

Whether in time it will give way to a fully-fledged constitutional court, as has been proposed, remains to be seen.

THE CONSEQUENCES OF JUDICIAL REVIEW

General

The German jurist Carl Schmitt is said to have opposed the establishment of an organ with the power of constitutional review on the grounds that it would lead either to "judicialisation of politics" or to the "politicisation of justice".[1] By the "judicialisation" or "juridification" of politics is meant that judicial decisions become a factor in political decision-making; political outcomes are determined by judicial decisions.[2] By the politicisation of justice is meant that judges make the law instead of interpreting and applying it; they find themselves deciding between competing rights claims instead of disinterestedly applying the law. "Of course", Stone comments in relation to France, "from the perspective of policy-makers, it led to both."[3]

A danger with the language of judicialisation and politicisation is that it may lead us to treat as wholly new already existing features of our constitutional arrangements. If we take the judicialisation of politics, for example, the response of the courts has long been a crucial factor in executive and parliamentary approaches to legislation: considerations of legal effectiveness require legislation to be drafted with a view to how that legislation is likely to be interpreted by the courts.[4] The question to be asked in my view, therefore, is whether and to what extent judicial review of legislation will intensify these already existing features of our arrangements, rather than whether it will lead to their emergence for the first time. With this caveat in mind, we may turn to the consequences of judicial review of legislation for the executive, parliament and the courts.

Judicial review and the executive

Devolution in combination with the incorporation of the ECHR represents a massive increase in uncertainty for the executive, at the UK, as well as devolved levels. The growth of judicial review of administrative action in recent years has accustomed the executive to the idea that such action might fall foul of the courts. Outside the sphere of Community law, however, it has not yet had to seriously contend with the possibility that the same fate might befall legislative action, at least when that action has taken the form of primary legislation.

---

1 Carl Schmitt, quoted in Stone, *The Birth of Judicial Politics in France: The Constitutional Council in Comparative Perspective* (Oxford University Press, New York, 1992), p 253.
2 "The legislative process is juridicised to the extent that court decisions and the threat of future censure alter legislative outcomes": Carl Schmitt, quoted in Stone, p 9.
3 Carl Schmitt, quoted in Stone, p 253.
4 Daintith and Page, *The Executive in the Constitution: Structure, Autonomy and Internal Control* (Oxford University Press, Oxford, 1999), pp 241–242.

The number of successful challenges to executive legislation will depend in part on how successful the executive is in "judge proofing" its own legislation. Faced with the possibility of judicial censure, we would expect the executive to respond by strengthening the internal machinery for the scrutiny of legislative proposals in an effort to avoid the possibility of legislation being struck down. The White Paper *Scotland's Parliament* anticipated that in drafting legislation for consideration by the Scottish Parliament, the Scottish Executive would take legal advice to ensure that the provisions brought forward were within the Scottish Parliament's powers. In any cases of uncertainty, there would be consultation with the Scottish Executive Law Officers and, as necessary, more widely. These and equivalent pre-legislative checks by the Presiding Officer would ensure that any potential difficulties were identified at the earliest possible point.[1]

The Scotland Act 1998 itself acknowledges the importance of pre-legislative scrutiny in reducing the risk of judicial censure. Under the 1998 Act a member of the Scottish Executive in charge of a Bill must, on or before its introduction in the Scottish Parliament, state that in his view the provisions of the Bill would be within the Parliament's legislative competence.[2] Like section 19 of the Human Rights Act 1998, the purpose of this provision is to ensure that the issue is properly addressed before legislation is introduced.[3]

As well as being subject to scrutiny by the Scottish Executive, Scottish legislative proposals will also be subject to scrutiny by the UK government, with the possibility of recourse to the Joint Ministerial Committee and thereafter to the courts, or ministerial intervention, should questions as to *vires* not be satisfactorily resolved. The Scottish Executive is required to send copies of legislative proposals when they are first published to the office of the Advocate General, to the office of the Secretary of State for Scotland and to Whitehall departments which have a policy interest in the subject-matter of the legislation.[4] The focus of such scrutiny is likely to be on ensuring that the devolved institutions do not trespass on reserved matters rather than Convention rights. It is unlikely to offer any assurance therefore as to the compatibility of legislative proposals with Convention rights.

The effectiveness of the Scottish Executive's arrangements for the pre-legislative scrutiny of legislative proposals from the point of view of their compatibility with Convention rights attracted a certain amount of critical comment in the first year of devolution. These criticisms would have been fuelled had the Inner House found the Mental Health (Public Safety and Appeals) (Scotland) Act 1999 to be in breach of the Convention. What should not be overlooked, however, is the inherent difficulty of the task. In response to criticisms of the effectiveness of the largely informal system of "Strasbourg proofing" of Acts of the Westminster Parliament, which was

---

1   *Scotland's Parliament* Cm 3658 (1997), para 4.16.
2   Scotland Act 1998, s 31(1).
3   Daintith and Page, *The Executive in the Constitution: Structure, Autonomy and Internal Control* (Oxford University Press, Oxford, 1999), p 270.
4   *Guidance Note on Common Working Arrangements* (Scottish Executive, Edinburgh, 1999), para 5.7.

in operation until its overhaul in anticipation of the incorporation of the ECHR, departmental lawyers argued that the width of the Convention combined with the generality of many of its provisions and the confusion of its jurisprudence made it very difficult to predict whether a particular provision of domestic law was likely to lead to a breach of the Convention. They also pointed with pride to the many unrecorded occasions when they had persuaded ministers (with difficulty) away from policies "which sailed too close to the Strasbourg wind".[1] Nor is "Strasbourg proofing" of legislation an activity of which the government legal service in Scotland has necessarily had a great deal of experience, given the relative infrequency of Scottish legislation at Westminster.

Judicial review also has major implications for the Law Officers—UK as well as Scottish—who occupy a crucial position in the machinery of legislative co-ordination and control. In addition to being responsible for legal advice, the Lord Advocate is also responsible, as we have seen, for decisions on referrals, as well as for the criminal prosecution system. The effect of recent controversy on the Lord Advocate's position remains to be seen. At the very least, it may be thought, it is likely to make it much more difficult to pass off decisions on referrals as decisions taken without an eye to political advantage,[2] while adding still further to the pressure for a redefinition of the Lord Advocate's role. The Law Officers are also likely to find themselves subject to a much closer degree of parliamentary scrutiny than has traditionally been the case.

Judicial review and Parliament

The uncertainty generated by judicial review is no less a problem for the Scottish Parliament than for the Executive; in fact it is a greater problem in that it will be dealing with legislative proposals from parliamentary committees as well as from the Executive. As in relation to the Executive, judicial review is likely to lead to increased parliamentary scrutiny in an effort to avoid the risk of legislation being found incompatible. The White Paper anticipated that it would be for the Presiding Officer of the Scottish Parliament to satisfy himself or herself that legislation, whether brought forward by the Executive or by others, was *intra vires* before giving approval to introduction,[3] but the Scotland Act 1998 merely requires the Presiding Officer to decide whether or not in his view the provisions of a bill would be within the Parliament's legislative competence and "state his decision."[4] An adverse decision will not block a Bill's progress, but it will highlight the conflict of views that exists between the Bill's sponsors and the Presiding Officer. As Bogdanor points out, this provision could easily prove controversial.[5]

Judicial review of legislation also opens up the prospect already mentioned of the "judicialisation" of politics. As has been suggested, judicialisation is a matter of degree. An extreme version of the

---

1 Daintith and Page, *The Executive in the Constitution*, p 269.
2 Cf. *Gouriet v Union of Post Office Workers* [1978] AC 435.
3 *Scotland's Parliament* Cm 3658 (1997), para 4.16.
4 Scotland Act 1998, s 31(2).
5 Bogdanor, *Devolution in the United Kingdom* (Oxford University Press, Oxford, 1999), p 205.

judicialisation thesis may be derived from Landfried's account of the development of judicial review in the Federal Republic of Germany. That version, which finds strong echoes in Stone's account of the development of the jurisdiction of the French Constitutional Council, is one in which, as a result of a combination of an overactive judiciary and a less confident legislature, the executive and parliament find themselves enmeshed in an increasingly dense network of constitutional interpretations, with less and less scope for the exercise of effective political choice.[1] For Landfried judicialisation to this degree is replete with danger for democracy. "As constitutional courts have only a limited democratic legitimacy," she argues, "it is detrimental to a democracy when courts frequently decide political problems and, with a dense network of constitutional interpretations, reduce the political alternatives for future generations."[2]

Landfried, it should be stressed, is not opposed to judicial review. The starting point for her analysis is "the conviction that constitutional courts are suitable instruments for an effective control of the legislature and for the protection of the rights of individuals and minorities."[3] What she is opposed to is an excess of judicial review and an overloading of the political process with legal arguments, to which politicians as much as judges may contribute. If judges do not practice self-restraint and parliamentarians lack political self-confidence and continually defer to the courts, she argues, there is a risk of judicial review becoming a danger to democracy.[4] The solution she sees as lying in working out an appropriate division of labour between courts and parliaments, and she offers some criteria by which an appropriate division might be sought.

Whether judicial review will lead to the extreme version of the judicialisation thesis propounded by Landfried remains to be seen. We have already seen some evidence of the judicialisation of politics in the Westminster Parliament following the incorporation of the ECHR, e.g. in relation to the Financial Services and Markets Bill, and there have been early indications of it in relation to the legislative programme of the Scottish Executive. But with only six bills enacted by the Scottish Parliament at the time of writing, it is too early to say whether debates will become overloaded with legal argument. The determined efforts which were made to prevent the introduction of a Bill to ban fox-hunting may, however, offer a glimpse of things to come.[5]

Judicial review and the courts

Judicial review also opens up the possibility of the "politicisation" of constitutional justice, with judges deciding between competing rights

1 Landfried (ed), *Constitutional Review and Legislation: An International Comparison* (Nomos, Baden-Baden, 1988), p 12. See also Stone, *The Birth of Judicial Politics in France: The Constitutional Council in Comparative Perspective* (Oxford University Press, New York, 1992), p 242. Landfried's view by no means commands unqualified assent; for a dissenting view, see Mahrenholz, in Landfried, pp 175–176.
2 Landfried (ed), *Constitutional Review and Legislation: An International Comparison* (Nomos, Baden-Baden, 1988), p 16.
3 *Constitutional Review and Legislation: An International Comparison,* p 8.
4 *Constitutional Review and Legislation: An International Comparison,* p 16.
5 *Whaley v Watson* 2000 SLT 475.

claims instead of disinterestedly applying the law. Built into the Scotland Act 1998 are devices designed to minimise conflicts between the legislature and judiciary: the duty to choose the interpretation, assuming more than one is possible, which is compatible with the Scotland Act 1998,[1] for example, is designed to minimise such conflicts.[2] In addition, if the court decides that an Act of the Scottish Parliament is outwith its competence, or that subordinate legislation is *ultra vires*, it has power under section 102 of the 1998 Act to make an order removing or limiting any retrospective effect of the decision for any period and on any conditions to allow the defect to be corrected. There is also the possibility of executive intervention to mitigate the effects of judicial decisions.[3] But the possibility of conflict cannot be discounted. The spectre of a "gouvernement de juges" has already been raised,[4] and judicial concern expressed that "the inescapable fact" that the Scottish Parliament is not a sovereign Parliament has not been appreciated by the electorate.[5]

How, against this background, the courts will approach the exercise of their constitutional review jurisdiction is one of the most fascinating questions raised by the devolution settlement. Will they adopt an "activist" or "passive" approach to the exercise of this jurisdiction?[6] Will they in particular adopt a cautious approach to their abstract review jurisdiction, which theory suggests is inherently more "political" and "legislative" than other modes of review?[7] "The invalidation of legislation pursuant to concrete review" Stone argues, "is generally viewed as more benign, and far less politically provocative, than rulings of unconstitutionality pursuant to referrals by parliamentary minorities."[8] Or will they, like the Canadian Supreme Court, adopt an "ultra-permissive" approach which offers "a field day to politically sectarian action groups that have lost out by the ordinary democratic political processes"?[9]

The early signs indicate caution. Lord Hope has noted the reduced likelihood of conflict between parliament and the courts where, to employ the language used in *R v Panel on Takeovers and Mergers, ex p Datafin*,[10] review proceeds on a "historic" rather than "contemporaneous" basis. The longer legislation remains on the statute book "the less obvious, and thus the less

---

1 Scotland Act 1998, s 101.
2 Kommers, "The Federal Constitutional Court in the German Political System" (1994) 26 *Comparative Political Studies* 470 at 477.
3 Scotland Act 1998, s 107.
4 O'Neill, "The Scotland Act and the Government of Judges" (1999) SLT (News) 61 66.
5 Hope, "Opinion: Devolution and Human Rights" (1998) 4 *European Human Rights Law Review* 373.
6 Kommers, "The Federal Constitutional Court in the German Political System" (1994) 26 *Comparative Political Studies* 470 at 478.
7 Stone Sweet, "Constitutional Dialogues: Protecting Human Rights in France, Germany, Italy and Spain" in Kenney, Reisinger and Reitz (eds) *Constitutional Dialogues in Comparative Perspective* (Macmillan Press, London, 1999), p 30.
8 Stone, "Governing with Judges: The New Constitutionalism" in Hayward and Page (eds), *Governing the New Europe* (Polity Press, Cambridge, 1995), p 295.
9 McWhinney, *Supreme Courts and Judicial Law-Making: Constitutional Tribunals and Constitutional Review* (Nighoff, Dordrecht, 1986), pp 99–102.
10 *R v Panel on Takeovers and Mergers, ex p Datafin* [1987] 1 All ER 564.

offensive, will be the potential for collision between the processes of judicial review and that of legislation by the democratically elected Parliament."[1] He has also floated the idea of a "discretionary area of judgement" within which "the judiciary will defer, on democratic grounds, to the considered opinion of the elected body or person whose act or decision is said to be incompatible with the Convention."[2]

On the question of who has standing to refer bills, Lord Reed does not rule out the possibility that the circle of those who might have standing might be widened, e.g. by way of judicial review of a refusal to refer, but comments that the difficulties would appear substantial:

> "One might have thought ... that a person seeking to challenge a Bill, as distinct from an Act, might have difficulty in establishing title and interest to sue, and in overcoming the related problem of prematurity (after all the Bill might not be enacted). Any person wishing to challenge a Bill on the basis of the Convention would in addition have to be a 'victim' for the purposes of Article 34 of the Convention, in terms of section 100(1) of the Act. I would be sceptical whether the victim test could be satisfied in respect of merely potential legislation".[3]

The courts can also afford to take a strict approach to abstract review in the knowledge that concrete review is not precluded.[4]

CONCLUSION

Central to the debate about judicial review of legislation is the question of its legitimacy. In *Supreme Courts and Judicial Law-Making*, McWhinney argues that the question that confronts legal scholars is no longer whether judges make law, but on what basis they do it and according to what values. There has been a shift, he argues, towards issues of political and constitutional legitimacy, and whether it is right and proper in democratic terms for non-elected judges to exercise wide and constitutionally uninhibited discretionary powers:

> "Judicial values ... become a legitimate subject of public-political examination and enquiry, and if need be of public-political debate and criticism, of a sort that would hardly have been thought admissible or tolerated by the judges in that earlier era of postulated judicial neutrality on great societal issues and conceived absolute separation of the Courts from politics ..."[5]

Looked at in the context of devolution, it seems to me that there are two possible answers to the criticism that the courts are meddling in matters

---

1 Hope, "Judicial Review of Acts of the Scottish Parliament", 1989 SCOLAG 107 at 110.
2 See *R v DPP, ex p Kebilene* [1999] 3 WLR 972 at 994.
3 Reed, "Devolution and the Judiciary" in *Constitutional Reform in the United Kingdom: Principles and Practice* (Hart Publishing, Oxford, 1998), p 5.
4 See Shapiro "The Success of Judicial Review" in Kenney, Reisinger and Reitz (eds), *Constitutional Dialogues in Comparative Perspective* (Macmillan Press, London, 1999), p 199.
5 McWhinney, *Supreme Courts and Judicial Law-Making: Constitutional Tribunals and Constitutional Review* (Nighoff, Dordrecht, 1986), p 270.

that are no part of their concern. The first, which does not take us much further forward, is that in contrast to judicial review under the Treaty of Union the process is statutorily ordained: "the functions which the judges will have to perform have come to them, not as a result of any judge-made law, but because they have been given these functions by the Act."[1] The second, on which the Scotland Act 1998 is predicated, is that individual rights and freedoms are more effectively protected by judicial than by parliamentary means; the courts are better defenders of the rights of the individual than parliaments. The Human Rights Act 1998 is more reticent but the underlying premise is the same.[2] For Stone the key question is whether constitutional courts, "in fact protect rights—and therefore legislate—better than governments and parliaments do, or would do in the absence of constitutional review."[3] How effective a protector of individual rights a Scottish parliament would have been in the absence of judicial review we shall never know. How effective the courts will be we shall have the opportunity to judge for ourselves in the years to come.

---

1   Hope, "Judicial Review of Acts of the Scottish Parliament" 1989 SCOLAG 107 at 107.
2   *Legislation on Human Rights With Particular Reference to the European Convention: A Discussion Document* (Home Office, London, 1977).
3   Stone, "Constitutional Politics: The Reciprocal Impact of Lawmaking and Constitutional Adjudication" in Craig and Harlow (eds), *Lawmaking in the European Union* (Kluwer Law International, London, 1998), p 132.

2 Lawyers in Contemporary Scottish Politics: a new "Dundas Despotism"?

James G Kellas

Devolution has brought in a new Scottish political system, and it has also inaugurated a new Scottish legal system. It has opened a Pandora's Box for Scots lawyers, who have new jobs to do in the Scottish Parliament and Scottish Executive, as well as those attached to the Scotland Office in London, in judicial scrutiny and review of Scottish legislation and Executive actions and in drafting Bills for the Scottish Parliament, either Executive Bills, Committee Bills or Members' Bills. Law firms may even prepare draft Bills on their own account, to sell them to MSPs who are looking for Bills to present in a properly drafted form. Some firms like McGrigor Donald in Glasgow have special devolution sections. McGrigor Donald has its Scottish Parliament Group with Alan Boyd as Director. These enrol subscribers for a Briefing Service, and offer legal services to clients relating to devolution. Law Schools in Scotland are of course active in teaching the law of devolution, and at least three law textbooks were published on the Scotland Act 1998 in 1999.

My interest in this from a political science point of view is to explain the changing role of Scotland in the Constitution, and here to consider the position of lawyers in the government of Scotland. My subtitle is "A new Dundas Despotism?", which of course refers to Henry Dundas, 1st Viscount Melville (1742–1811), and his son Robert Dundas, 2nd Viscount Melville (1771–1851). The elder Dundas was Lord Advocate after 1775, and effectively operated as "Scotland's Manager" for the UK Government. His son continued in this role after his father died in 1811, although the Government position he held was First Lord of the Admiralty. This was the era of the unreformed House of Commons, in which the few Scottish voters could be persuaded to vote for Government candidates in return for securing favours and positions for their family and friends. In 1827 the unofficial post of Scotland's Manager disappeared and the Home Secretary took over responsibility for Scotland in the Government. But the Lord Advocate was the official adviser on Scotland, and was responsible for drafting and introducing Scottish Bills in Parliament. While the electoral system was greatly changed by the Reform Act of 1832, it was not until 1885 that the Lord Advocate was replaced as Scotland's chief minister in the British Government by the Secretary for Scotland, and even then the relationship between the Scottish Secretary and the Lord Advocate remained an uneasy one in matters of law and order, administration of the courts and so on.

Today we can see how the Lord Advocate's roles are confused as between his prosecuting role and his judicial appointments role.[1] Historically, more attention was paid to the confusion between his political and legal roles. As the Government minister responsible for introducing Scottish Bills on education, local government, crofting and so on, his partisan and prosecuting roles were even more mixed up than they are today. This led to the demand for a non-legal post in the Government to speak for Scotland, which was to be the Scottish Secretary, established in 1885.

If we jump to 1999 and the advent of devolution, we find that the Scottish Secretary has been replaced for most purposes by a First Minister, and the Scottish Office by a Scottish Executive in Edinburgh. But is there a return to a kind of "Dundas Despotism"?: a rule of lawyers, who in the words of Donald Dewar at his 1999 John Mackintosh Memorial lecture, might "bind Scotland to the UK" even under devolution.[2]

The Dundas Depotism was intended to bind Scotland to the UK, especially in the wake of the Jacobite Rebellions, and it gave a peculiar political role to practising lawyers. We can see this binding process again today, even with devolution, and lawyers are once again prominent Scottish politicians. What binds the United Kingdom together now is what in the United States federal system is called a "government of laws, not of men". This means that the British system of government is more legalised and less purely political, with a crucial role for courts and lawyers to adjudicate between the rival claimants to democratic legitimacy in London and Edinburgh. While lawyers on both sides of the border respect the letter of the law (here especially the Scotland Act 1998), there is room for interpretation, as there is in the United States. There, the "living constitution" is what matters to the Justices of the Supreme Court, and so it will be in a devolved Britain. What gives a constitution life is the political context, and with two Parliaments and Governments political and legal loyalties are divided between Edinburgh and London in a new way.

My use of the phrase "Dundas Despotism" is to draw attention to this enhanced role of lawyers and judicial review in the devolution system. This is something new in British politics, since it subjects the legislative branch to scrutiny and control by the judicial branch. I deal first with lawyers in Scottish politics, and then with the wider constitutional changes brought about by devolution.

LAWYERS IN SCOTTISH POLITICS

Lawyers have always straddled Scottish "civil society" and the formal apparatus of the British state in its London and Scottish forms. The Act of Union guaranteed the Scottish courts' position, and thus the continued existence of the Scottish legal profession. To be a practising lawyer in Scotland meant having a Scots Law qualification, and this effectively

---

1 See *Starrs v Ruxton* 2000 SLT 42.
2 He was referring to an odd idea that a reformed House of Lords could be a revising chamber for Scottish legislation emanating from the Scottish Parliament.

excluded English lawyers from practising in Scotland. Scots going south (such as Derry Irvine and his predecessor as Lord Chancellor, Lord Mackay of Clashfern) were able to practise in London if they qualified there, or had become Lord Chancellor through political patronage and had no English legal training. Lord Mackay was in the latter category, but was made an Honorary Member of the Bench at the Inner Temple from 1979. The Scottish legal "closed shop" matches that of Scottish teachers who also need a Scottish qualification or equivalent to register with the General Teaching Council. These rules are an important bulwark of Scottish civil society against a take-over by the English.

How does devolution affect this? First, the legal section of Scottish civil society is peculiarly fitted to occupy positions of importance in Scottish devolved politics, because practising lawyers can combine their practices with being MSPs, especially as the Scottish Parliament does not sit as long as the House of Commons. Of course this does not apply so well to members of the Scottish Executive, who are full-timers.

Looking at the personnel of the Scottish Parliament and Executive we find a goodly representation of lawyers. The Presiding Officer, The Rt Hon Sir David Steel (otherwise Lord Steel of Aikwood) is an LLB of Edinburgh, but did not practise as a solicitor (but he may be glad of his legal training, as we shall see later). The first First Minister, Donald Dewar, was a Glasgow LLB and former practising solicitor (latterly in the prominent Conservative Ross Harper's firm!). The Deputy First Minister, Jim Wallace, is an Edinburgh-trained QC. The Leader of the Conservatives, David McLetchie, is a Writer to the Signet, and his Deputy, Annabel Goldie, is a solicitor with a Strathclyde LLB. The Conservative Chief Whip, Lord James Douglas-Hamilton, is an Advocate. The SNP can boast several lawyers among its prominent MSPs. "Madame Ecosse" herself (Winnie Ewing) is of course a Glasgow LLB, as is her son, Fergus. Nicola Sturgeon is another Glasgow LLB, and is a prominent spokesperson. Roseanna Cunningham has an Edinburgh LLB and practised as a solicitor, as did Kenny MacAskill. And one should not forget Professor Neil MacCormick, holder of the Regius Chair of Public Law in Edinburgh, now an MEP, or Elspeth Attwooll, the Liberal Democrat MEP, formerly of the School of Law, Glasgow University.

Add to these Colin Boyd (who replaced Lord Hardie as Lord Advocate after his elevation to the Bench), a Scottish Law Officer in the devolved Edinburgh Executive, and Lynda Clark QC, in the newly-established post of Advocate General for Scotland in the British Government. With her are 30 Scots lawyers attached to the Scotland Office in Dover House, Whitehall. Perhaps not a "Dundas Despotism" exactly, but maybe a "government of lawyers, not men".

In the new devolved system, law has an enhanced role. The Scotland Act 1998 is the Scottish Constitution as far as the legislative and executive branches are concerned. The judicial branch still harks back to the Act of Union, wherein are to be found its guarantees.[1] While Scotland soon lost its control over civil cases to the House of Lords after 1707, the devolved

---

1 Act of Union, s XIX.

government now comes under the scrutiny of the Judicial Committee of the Privy Council.[1] This adjudicates in cases arising under the Scotland Act 1998, but not so as to deny the sovereignty of the UK Parliament, which continues to have "the power ... to make laws for Scotland".[2] Thus, the Judicial Committee may strike down an Act of the Scottish Parliament, but not one of the UK Parliament.

The Judicial Committee does not appear to be involved with the powers of the Scottish Executive, as it is not mentioned in the corresponding sections of the Scotland Act 1998.[3] But even if they are not justiciable, the powers of the British Government over the Scottish Executive are greater than those of the UK Parliament over the Scottish Parliament. The Secretary of State for Scotland (or other UK Secretary of State) can by order direct that a proposed action by the Scottish Executive shall not be taken if he has reasonable grounds to believe that such an action would be incompatible with any international obligations.[4] He can also require that action be taken by the Scottish Executive if he believes such action is required to give effect to international obligations. Presumably, such UK interventions are not justiciable, as the Judicial Committee of the Privy Council is not mentioned here.

In general, questions of legislative jurisdiction as between devolved and reserved matters can be referred by the Advocate General (UK Law Officer for Scotland), or the Lord Advocate, or the Attorney General (UK Law Officer) to the Judicial Committee of the Privy Council for decision.[5] Moreover, the Secretary of State may make an order prohibiting the Presiding Officer from submitting a Bill for Royal Assent if that Bill would "make modifications of the law as it applies to reserved matters" and he has "reasonable grounds to believe [it] would have an adverse effect on the law as it applies to reserved matters."[6] However, this tortuous language is not clear about what is involved (are these clearly trespasses into reserved matters, or just some indirect effect on reserved matters?) and whether such a decision would be justiciable (e.g. on appeal by the Lord Advocate).

The Presiding Officer of the Scottish Parliament (at present Sir David Steel, LLB) also has a quasi-judicial role in declaring whether a Bill in the Scottish Parliament is *ultra vires*. In section 31(2) of the Scotland Act 1998, it is stated that he "shall ... decide whether or not in his view the provisions of the Bill would be within the legislative competence of the Parliament and state his decision." It is unclear if that decision is justiciable, though in practice the decision is not final as to legality and Parliament can proceed to discuss the Bill and normal legal channels can subsequently be followed.

Another novelty arising under devolution, switching powers to the courts and helping to produce a kind of "Dundas Despotism", is the

---

1 Scotland Act 1998, Sch 6.
2 SA 1998, s 28(7).
3 The effect of the legislation is unclear, although the Scottish Executive is limited by Human Rights and EU legislation, as well as being subject to conventional judicial review mechanisms.
4 Scotland Act 1998, s 58.
5 SA 1998, s 33.
6 SA 1998, s 35(b).

power to review and challenge the procedures of the Scottish Parliament. While the procedures of the UK Parliament cannot be reviewed in a court, those of the Scottish parliament can. Thus, we have already had two cases in the Court of Session. First, the "Lobbygate Case" in which *The Scotsman* newspaper challenged the right of the Standards Committee to sit in private. The Committee went public right away, and *The Scotsman* withdrew its case on 18 November 1999. However, there was no question that the Standing Orders of the Parliament were not a matter for the Parliament alone but could be challenged in court on various grounds.

The second case also surfaced at this time. The fox-hunting lobby challenged (Lord) Mike Watson's right to introduce a Bill banning hunting, since he had been funded in this by an anti-hunting organisation. This went to the Court of Session whose very consideration of the matter suggested an augmented role for the courts.[1] Where previously such issues would have been considered a matter for the Parliament alone, it is clear that the new range of justiciable matters under the Scotland Act 1998 increases the Court's powers in the parliamentary realm.

There is, of course, another aspect of Scottish Devolution which is new to Britain. This is the application of the European Convention on Human Rights in Scotland since May 1999 (unlike England which had to wait until October 2000 before it came into force). Devolution has brought the UK Human Rights Act 1998 into play in Scotland with the European Convention now part of domestic Scottish law. The Scotland Act 1998 did this in section 29(d) concerning the Parliament, and section 57(2) concerning the Executive. The Scottish legal system has thus been placed under scrutiny and found wanting. There was the Court of Session's condemnation of the Lord Advocate's power to appoint and dismiss temporary sheriffs.[2] The sheriffs have gone, and perhaps Justices of the Peace and other judges will follow. Thus, devolution has opened up the question of the relationship between the different parts of the judicial branch and between the executive and judicial branches. No doubt the English legal system is quaking as the roles of the Lord Chancellor and the Attorney General could now be condemned. Another human rights issue has surfaced in Scotland. It has been suggested that the offence of breach of the peace is too vague in terms of human rights in the Convention. That may be challenged in court.[3] Clearly, devolution has brought in two new dimensions to Scottish public law: judicial review of legislation and the European Convention of Human Rights—all this since May 1999.

POLITICS AND THE DEVOLUTION SETTLEMENT

I should like to move more clearly to the politics side of the subject. Looking first at the British Constitution, it seems that it has changed, but

---

1 See *Whaley v Lord Watson* 2000 SLT 475.
2 See *Starrs v Ruxton* 2000 SLT 42.
3 See *The Scotsman*, 24 November 1999.

that this was not the intention of the British Government and Parliament. The legislation that was passed, the Scotland Act 1998, the Government of Wales Act 1998, and the Northern Ireland Act 1998 were all different forms of devolution, and nothing was legislated for England as such. It was hoped that the British Constitution would remain untouched in essentials. Parliament remained sovereign, the Queen was still head of state and exercised her various Prerogatives as before. It was not exactly "Her Majesty's Government" in Edinburgh, for the only "Ministers of the Crown" in the Scotland Act 1998 were UK Ministers. But Her Majesty appoints the First Minister and he or she holds office at Her Majesty's pleasure.[1] There is a difference with London here. Holyrood had to vote the First Minister into office, while the House of Commons does not vote for a Prime Minister. Moreover, while Her Majesty appoints and dismisses all Scottish Ministers, "The First Minister shall not seek Her Majesty's approval for any appointment . . . without the agreement of the Parliament".[2] So there is a "vote of confidence" right at the start of the appointing process for Scottish ministers, a different procedure than in Westminster.

I should like to think that John Swinney, the Convener of the SNP, heads "Her Majesty's Loyal Opposition", but I am not so sure. No such post is mentioned in the Scotland Act 1998, and there is no special salary for his position as main Opposition leader.

Looking at the politics of "devolved" and "reserved" matters (rather than the strictly legal aspects), we find a deal of confusion. Gordon Brown's budget speech in 1999 announced policies which could be seen to straddle devolved and reserved matters. He said that the fuel duty escalator would go and that any fuel duty increase would be ring-fenced to be spent on roads and public transport. What he did not clarify was how a UK Minister could ring-fence spending in a devolved function such as roads, for such spending was within the devolved powers, and so is most of public road transport. He also said that increases in tobacco duties would be ring-fenced for spending in the National Health Service, also devolved. No one queried this at the time, and the assumption must be that using the funds coming down to Scotland via the Scottish Consolidated Fund based on the Barnett Formula, Scotland would be using the cash for the purposes mentioned by the Chancellor. But there is nothing in the Scotland Act 1998 to ensure that that would happen. Only party solidarity would lead the Scottish Labour Party to follow the British Labour Party, coupled with the expectations of the Scottish people that their UK taxes would come back to them in the form of the benefits which Brown enunciated.

Somewhat different was the Queen's Speech on 17 November 1999. An analysis of the proposed measures revealed that at least 11 of the total number of bills (34) would be in matters which were apparently devolved (mostly relating to local government, social work, and so on), and in some of the so-called UK Bills there seemed to be devolved matters involved. After devolution, the Westminster Parliament is acting in part as the English Parliament when it legislates only for England, and holds ministers to account whose remit is England alone. Previously it really was the

---

1 Scotland Act 1998, s 45(1).
2 SA 1998, s 47(2).

UK Parliament, for it legislated for all parts of the UK even when some laws applied only in Scotland, England, Wales or Northern Ireland. Devolution *has* made a difference here, for now the Scottish Parliament is alone in legislating in devolved matters. Thus, Scottish education, health, roads, local government, social work, etc, cannot be in the Queen's Speech at Westminster, and any reference to such topics must be considered not to apply in Scotland. So this is an English Parliament in devolved-equivalent (but not reserved) matters.

Now the "West Lothian Question" is heard once again and the Conservative Party and some English Labour MPs, such as Frank Field, have called for the exclusion of Scottish MPs from voting on matters relating to England which have been devolved to Scotland. The revival of an English Grand Committee in the House of Commons is likely, but more unlikely is the setting up of an English Parliament. Given the unwillingness of the English to carry through a solution to this demand for English Home Rule, Westminster is likely to remain the English Parliament in the present circumstances.

Meanwhile, another anomaly in the UK system of government has emerged in the new status of the office of Secretary of State for Scotland. The empire that was once the Scottish Office has been dismembered even more effectively than the break-up of the Soviet Union. The "Evil Empire" has gone but the Governor-General, who is the Scottish Secretary, is still there. The name of the department was changed in 1999 from the Scottish Office to the Scotland Office, but Dover House is still its headquarters in London. Where there were seven ministers in the Scottish Office before May 1999, there are now only two. In the House of Lords there is only an Official Spokesperson, in 1999 Baroness Ramsay, who is not a minister. The holder of the new post of Advocate General for Scotland is Lynda Clark QC, and she has 30 lawyers on her staff, almost half of the total Scotland Office staff at present (it is expected to rise to 100). What they do I am not sure; in 1999, for example, there were no Scottish Bills in the Queen's Speech. The executive functions of the Scotland Office are few, and about 30 were taken away recently. One of the few remaining competences is the conduct of elections in Scotland. That will bring in the new proposals for funding parties. In 1999–2000, the Budget of the Scotland Office dropped from £15,000 m per annum to £5 m.

Scottish Question Time in the House of Commons still goes on, once in four weeks, but reduced from 45 minutes to 30 minutes. It is a strange spectacle. The Scottish Secretary and the Minister of State take it in turn to answer, and the Advocate General sits quietly nearby. But there are no questions of substance relating to ministerial responsibilities, just general queries about what the Scottish Secretary does. He tries to defend his position, but it is not easy, and most of the time is spent in countering the SNP, on the one hand, and the Tories on the other, both of which parties would like to see the Office abolished. Even former Secretary of State, John Reid, was not clear if he saw the Scotland Office as permanent. The Secretary attends the Cabinet, and the Home Page on the internet says that the Secretary acts as an "honest broker as appropriate in disputes or otherwise intervening as required by the Scotland Act". But can a minister in one Government be an honest broker in disputes between that government and another government?

It is part of the old political culture that devolution does not represent a break with the past but a continuation of the past by other means. What happens in Westminster and what happens in Holyrood are wholly harmonious, according to this philosophy, and the whole is based on co-operation. This is also the language of the Concordats negotiated between the UK Government, the Scottish Executive and the Welsh Executive in October 1999, and the Memorandum of Understanding issued at the same time between the three Governments (Northern Ireland would have been included if it had existed at that time). This is all fine in the context of a unified Labour Party running every part of the UK, but what if these parts have minds of their own? Perhaps then the old "Westminster Sovereignty" would show its fangs, and co-operation would be replaced with conflict.

An adversarial approach is not unknown in legal circles, and there seems to be no reason why it should not be found in devolution as in the House of Commons. A bland culture of co-operation between London and Edinburgh would kill the whole point of devolution. Tony Blair at first assumed that he could control the Scottish, Welsh and London devolved bodies, but he learned the hard way that he could not. In fact, the British state is now broken into its national components, and it is no longer possible to put it together again as "control freaks" or party loyalists would like. Henry McLeish (the new First Secretary) may be Labour but he is now Scottish Labour too. His "Queen's Speech" is different from Tony Blair's and he is not bound by Blair's Cabinet.

CONCLUSION: A DUNDAS DESPOTISM?

It is more true today that at any time in the last 300 years that Scots law is made in Scotland for Scots. The position has changed from 1858 when Lord Cranworth, in the House of Lords appeal *Bartonshill Coal Co v Reid* (another Reid!), stated: "In England the doctrine must be regarded as well settled; but if such be the law of England, on what ground can it be argued not to be the law of Scotland? The law as established in England is founded on principles of universal application ... I think that it would be most inexpedient to sanction a different rule to the north of the Tweed."[1] Many lawyers, like the celebrated T B Smith, have long been devolutionist and even nationalist for Scots law. It is now the turn of the politicians and the academics to show that there can be a different parliament, government, and policies north of the Tweed and that what is English is not necessarily appropriate for Scotland.

After the first two years of Scottish devolution it is possible to see how far a new "Dundas Despotism" is under way. Politics has become more legalised, for the Scotland Act 1998 has opened up a new role for the

---

1 Quoted in T B Smith, *British Justice: The Scottish Contribution* (Stevens, London 1961), p 85. There are echoes of Lord Cranworth in the statement in January 2000 by the Quality Assurance Agency for Higher Education in the UK that the Scottish MA should be replaced by the BA because it is too confusing to have Scottish degrees called something different from English degrees. This despite the fact that higher education is devolved!

courts, and subjected the Scottish Parliament and Executive to tests of *ultra vires* not found at the level of British Government. The main challenges so far have come from private citizens and civic bodies rather than from governmental institutions. Thus, the Court of Session has entertained cases from citizens, the media and the fox-hunting lobby challenging temporary sheriffs, parliamentary arrangements, and an MSP's private member's Bill respectively. And only the first case has been successful, and it involved the European Convention on Human Rights rather than devolution as such. Nevertheless, this is a growth area and the Scottish Parliament must obey the courts in a way that the sovereign British Parliament does not.

Devolution disputes between Scotland and London have not yet emerged, with the Judicial Committee of the Privy Council so far inactive. Nevertheless, the potential is there, and in the cases against the Scottish Parliament and against an MSP, the Court of Session, while exercising restraint, did not disclaim its right to decide. The law has been politicised by devolution, and in the future we are likely to see the rise of judicial activism.

3   Legislating for Diversity: Minorities in the New Scotland

Robert Dunbar

In 1998 there appeared a remarkable anthology of Scottish poetry or, perhaps more accurately, poetry composed by people who once lived in Scotland. Indeed, to refer to the poetry in this anthology as "Scottish" poetry would be problematic, because the poetry was composed by people who likely did not conceive of themselves as Scottish, at least in a way that is meaningful to us, nor would they likely have perceived of many of their neighbours living in this part of the British Isles as fellow Scots. This anthology, entitled *The Triumph Tree*,[1] is the first collection of Scotland's earliest poetry, and spans the years 550 to 1350 AD, a period, in the words of the editor, Thomas Owen Clancy, not himself a Scot, of course, but an American, "neglected by modern scholars and anthologists, and virtually unknown to the general public".[2] Clancy argues that this remarkable omission is "because the approach to our literary history has for long been Anglocentric, concentrating on the English-language tradition of Scotland, and that of its northern cousin, lowland Scots". In the fourteenth century, Scots begins to be used as a major literary language in Scotland and, coincidentally, "something like a national consciousness about the kingdom of the Scots" is firmly established.[3] So, 1350, or thereabouts, is a sort of "cultural year zero", to steal James MacMillan's wonderfully provocative turn of phrase.

The Triumph Tree is a remarkable piece of work, not least because it required the efforts of five skilled translators; this is because Scotland's earliest poetry was written in five different languages—Latin, Welsh, Old Irish or Gaelic, Old English and Norse. In fact, one of the poems in the anthology, *Fergus of Galloway*, was almost certainly composed in Scotland, but in a northern dialect of Old French. Yet another language, Pictish, was widely spoken in Scotland for at least the first part of this period, but little evidence of it remains except in a large number of placenames.[4] It is remarkable to consider that the oldest surviving "Scottish" poem was not composed in English, Scots or even Gaelic, but in Welsh: *Y Gododdin*, about

---

1   T O Clancy (ed), *The Triumph Tree* (Canongate, Edinburgh, 1998).
2   *The Triumph Tree*, p 5.
3   *The Triumph Tree*, p 5.
4   W J Watson, *The Celtic Placenames of Scotland* (Birlinn, Edinburgh, 1993), esp. Ch 2.

a warrior tribe of the same name, who occupied the territory of the Lothians and had as their main fortress Din Eidyn, or Edinburgh as we know it. The poem chronicles the unsuccessful struggle of this Welsh-speaking Celtic tribe to resist the incursion of the English tribes who were to bring to Scotland its two most widely spoken modern languages, Scots and English.

The Triumph Tree is important not least because it reminds us of two fundamental points: Scotland has always enjoyed a remarkable mixture of peoples, languages and cultures; and the Scotland we know today is a comparatively recent construct. Scotland remains a diverse mix, a diversity which has been stoked by considerable immigration over recent generations. It is not likely that we shall ever return to the cacophony of the period 550–1350: the powerfully integrative, even assimilationist mechanisms of the modern state, the economy, and perhaps most important of all, the modern communications media will see to that. But we will have to continue to confront diversity, perhaps a more kaleidoscopic diversity than ever before. As we enter the twenty-first century, are we prepared to do so? What policies will guide our choices? Will we value and nurture this diversity, or will future generations of Scots be as isolated from our diversity as we are from that of our early medieval forebears?

THE POLICY CONTOURS OF A LEGAL REGIME FOR MINORITIES

In the early 1990s, Tamara Hervey commented on British minority policy in these terms:

> "[T]here is in Britain no forum, language or even belief in the necessity for the recognition of minorities and their rights. There are legal measures prohibiting discrimination; there are measures which preserve the nature of the British Constitution as one of four 'Kingdoms' united. But completely lacking in political thought in Britain is a coherent approach to the question of what to do with minority groups: how best to nurture those groups, how best to protect the rights of minorities as groups against the 'tyranny of the majority'".[1]

Sebastian Poulter has come to a broadly similar conclusion, although in perhaps a more nuanced way. He has argued that Britain has moved away from a policy of assimilation to what he describes as a policy of cultural pluralism. Broadly speaking, assimilation entails the "absorption" of minorities into the mainstream culture of the majority community, the surrendering of their separate identities in order to blend into the wider society.[2] Cultural pluralism, on the other hand, which has also been described as "integration", seeks to affirm the positive value of greater

---

1 T K Hervey, "Which Rights, Whose Rights? The Identification and Protection of Minorities in British Law" in J Packer, K Myntti (eds) *The Protection of Ethnic and Linguistic Minorities in Europe* (Abo/Turku, Abo Akademi Univ., 1993) p 123.

2 S Poulter, *Ethnicity, Law and Human Rights: The English Experience* (Clarendon, Oxford, 1998) pp 12–13.

diversity in enriching national life, and rejects the idea that minorities should be encouraged to surrender their identities.[1] This ideal was expressed as early as 1966 by the then Labour Home Secretary, Roy Jenkins:

> "Integration is perhaps a rather loose word. I do not regard it as meaning the loss, by immigrants, of their own national characteristics and culture. I do not think we need in this country a melting pot, which will turn everybody out in a common mould, as one of a series of carbon copies of someone's misplaced vision of the stereotypical Englishman ... I define integration, therefore, not as a flattening process of assimilation but as an equal opportunity, coupled with cultural diversity, in an atmosphere of mutual tolerance".[2]

Poulter argues that this approach has been more or less the dominant one in British politics for a generation. Indeed, the UK's commitment to this policy has recently been restated in the UK's first State report to the Council of Europe under the Council's "Framework Convention for the Protection of National Minorities" (the "Framework Convention"):[3]

> "UK policy on integration is based upon the principle that cultural diversity should be valued and promoted. Our aim is to enable members of ethnic minorities to play a full part in national life, with all the rights and responsibilities which that entails, whilst still being able to maintain their own culture, traditions, language and values."[4]

Yet in spite of this steady and long-standing commitment—indeed, perhaps because of the malleability of the concept of cultural pluralism or integration—no coherent approach to minority issues has emerged in Britain. According to Rowena Arshad, director of the Centre for Education for Racial Equality in Scotland, this general state of confusion is certainly evident in Scotland:

> "Why does Scotland continue to marginalise issues of multiculturalism and racism? We need to ask what it is that generates complacency on racial issues in Scotland. When will we stop playing the numbers game? When will we stop questioning whether Scotland is multicultural or not? Multiculturalism is now a reality, it is not something in which we might believe or with which we might agree: it exists. For New Scotland, the question is how we might choose to respond to this reality and to devise strategies to redress the imbalances".[5]

---

1 *Ethnicity, Law and Human Rights: The English Experience*, p 16.
2 Roy Jenkins as quoted by Poulter in *Ethnicity, Law and Human Rights: The English Experience*, p 17.
3 The Council of Europe's "Framework Convention for the Protection of National Minorities" opened for signature on 1 February 1995, came into force on 1 February 1998, and has been signed by 40 European States and ratified or acceded to by 32.
4 *Report Submitted by the United Kingdom pursuant to Article 25, paragraph 1 of the Framework Convention for the Protection of National Minorities* (Received 26 July 1999, Council of Europe ACFC/SR (99) 13), para 92.
5 R Arshad, "Racial Inclusion and the Struggle for Justice" in G Hassan and C Warhurst, (eds) *A Different Future: A Moderniser's Guide to Scotland* (The Centre for Scottish Public Policy, Edinburgh, 1999), p 225.

SPECIFIC RESPONSES: SUPPRESSION, PROTECTION AND PRESERVATION AND PROMOTION

But what should this response be? There are broadly three sorts of legal regime which may be applied in respect of minorities. One could be described as comprising measures of "prohibition" or "suppression"; that is to say, statutory or other measures which seek to prohibit or suppress certain practices of minority groups. Such measures are directed against minority practices which fall "so far outside the minimum standards of acceptable behaviour [in the community] that they must be suppressed".[1] Examples in our law would be restrictions on polygamous practices,[2] a ban on female circumcision,[3] invalidation of certain forms of marriage (child marriages),[4] and so on.[5] While all such measures are "assimilationist" in the sense that they prohibit minority practices which deviate from community norms, they are not necessarily the exclusive property of those pursuing a broadly assimilationist agenda; even many cultural pluralists accept that there may have to be some limits on the diversity of cultural practices where such practices offend deeply held principles, particularly the fundamental human rights of others. The question of where one draws the line between "acceptable" and "unacceptable" cultural diversity has become a more pressing and difficult issue, particularly with increased numbers of immigrants from non-Christian backgrounds.

A second legal regime could broadly be described as one which expresses what could be called the "protective" principle. One element of such a regime is the protection of members of minority groups from acts of discrimination. The other element is their protection from acts of violence and abuse, both physical and verbal.

The principle of non-discrimination is strong in our law. Under the Race Relations Act 1976, for example, discrimination, both direct and indirect, on "racial grounds" is made unlawful in employment, in education, training and related matters, in the provision of goods, facilities, services and premises, and in the disposal of premises.[6] For these purposes, "racial grounds" is defined to mean colour, race, nationality or ethnic or national origins.[7] In addition to giving affected individuals access to the courts and employment tribunals in order to obtain remedies, this Act established the Commission for Racial Equality (CRE) to work towards the elimination of discrimination, to promote equality of opportunity and good relations

---

1 Poulter, *Ethnicity, Law and Human Rights: The English Experience* (Clarendon, Oxford, 1998), p 59.
2 *The Laws of Scotland: Stair Memorial Encyclopaedia* (Butterworths, Edinburgh, 1995), Vol 8, para 846.
3 Prohibition of Female Circumcision Act 1985.
4 Marriage (Scotland) Act 1977, s 1(1); *The Laws of Scotland: Stair Memorial Encyclopaedia*, (Butterworths, Edinburgh, 1995), Vol 8, para 816.
5 See, generally, E Sutherland, *Child and Family Law* (T & T Clark, Edinburgh, 1999) para 1.30 at pp 15–16.
6 See A W Bradley and K D Ewing, *Constitutional and Administrative Law*, 12th edn (Longman London, 1997).
7 Race Relations Act 1976, s 3(1).

between persons of different racial groups generally, and to review the operation of the 1976 Act.[1] The Human Rights Act 1998 has made various provisions of the European Convention on Human Rights (ECHR) part of British law, including Article 14, which provides that the enjoyment of the various rights and freedoms provided under the ECHR shall be secured "without discrimination on any ground such as sex, race, colour, language, religion, political or other opinion, national or social origin, association with a national minority, property, birth or other status". It has been remarked that the incorporation of Article 14 into British law is not, in itself, likely to add much to existing anti-discrimination legislation such as the Race Relations Act 1976 in fields where such legislation already applies, but that Article 14 may have a significant impact in other areas, in particular public law and immigration law, where the Race Relations Act 1976 does not apply.[2]

The second aspect of the "protective" principle, the protection of minorities from acts of violence and abuse, also finds expression in our law. The Public Order Act 1986, for example, creates the offence of inciting racial hatred. This offence occurs where a person uses or displays, publishes, distributes recordings of or broadcasts programmes which contain material which is threatening, abusive or insulting and where either the person intends to stir up racial hatred with such material or such material is simply likely to stir up racial hatred, having regard to all the circumstances.[3] "Racial hatred" is defined in section 17 of the 1986 Act to mean hatred against a group of persons in Great Britain by reference to colour, race, nationality (including citizenship) or ethnic or national origins (this is essentially the definition of "racial group" in the Race Relations Act 1976). The Broadcasting Act 1990 requires that the Independent Television Commission ensures that "nothing is included in [programming in the independent sector] which offends against good taste or decency or is likely to incite crime or to lead to disorder or to be offensive to public feeling".[4] The BBC's Producers' Guidelines and Charter and Agreement contain similar provisions, while for the non-broadcast media, the Press Complaints Commission's Code of Practice states that "the press should avoid prejudicial or pejorative reference to a person's race, colour, religion … and should avoid publishing details of a person's race, colour, religion … unless these are directly relevant to the story".[5] These sorts of measures also engage fundamental freedoms such as the freedom of expression and opinion, now protected under the Human Rights Act 1998, and it is not

---

1 RRA 1976, s 43.
2 J Wadham and H Mountfield, *Blackstone's Guide to the Human Rights Act 1998* (Blackstone, London, 1999).
3 See the Public Order Act 1986, ss 18–23.
4 Broadcasting Act 1990, s 6(1)(a).
5 The effectiveness of non-statutory guidelines is open to question, and the PCC may not apply in respect of print pieces which contain non-specific pejorative material directed at an ethnic group as a whole, as opposed to material directed at an identifiable individual or group of individuals who could be directly affected thereby. See, generally, UK State Report, *Report Submitted by the United Kingdom pursuant to Article 25, paragraph 1 of the Framework Convention for the Protection of National Minorities* (received 26 July 1999, Council of Europe ACFC/SR (99) 13), at paras 129 and 130.

altogether clear which principles Scottish and the wider British courts will use to resolve potential conflicts between the protective principle and these fundamental freedoms.

Before leaving the protective principle, brief reference should also be made to the Crime and Disorder Act 1998, section 33 which, through an amendment to the Criminal Law (Consolidation) (Scotland) Act 1995, creates a new offence of racially-aggravated harassment. A course of conduct is racially-aggravated if either at the time of the conduct the offender evinces malice or ill-will based on the victim's membership or presumed membership of a racial group, or the conduct was in fact motivated by such malice or ill-will. The definition of racial group once again follows the Race Relations Act 1976 definition, namely a group of persons defined by reference to race, colour, nationality (including citizenship) or ethnic or national origins. In the wake of the Imran Khan and Surjit Singh Chhokar incidents, the importance of the "protective" principle for minorities in Scotland cannot be overstated.[1] Indeed, the recent report by the Rowntree Trust, *We Can't All Be White*,[2] found that racist bullying and harassment is endemic in Britain but is unrecognised by officialdom and unchallenged by wider society. The latest CRE figures showed that Scotland's black/minority ethnic groups were at least three times as likely to suffer racist incidents as black/ethnic minority people in England and Wales.[3] Significantly, the Scotland Act 1998 provides that matters relating to the Race Relations Act 1976 and broadcasting are reserved matters,[4] with the result that these pillars of the protective principle are outwith the legislative scope of the Scottish Parliament. This is not to say, however, that the Scottish Parliament cannot continue to develop and extend the protective principle, particularly in the criminal law, subject to the limits placed on it by the Human Rights Act 1998.

The protective principle is clearly one which is consistent with, and supportive of, an integrationist approach. It could be argued that the principle is not necessarily inconsistent with an assimilationist approach; after all, it is possible to hope for the elimination of differences based on ethnicity, if not colour and race, while opposing incidents of discrimination, abuse and violence. On the other hand, as Poulter notes, an assimilationist approach often takes for granted that the dominant culture of the majority is superior to that of minorities and that it is desirable to ensure an homogeneous society through "acculturation" on the part of

---

1 On 29 November 2000, the Lord Advocate, Colin Boyd, QC, commissioned an independent judicial inquiry into the decision-making process in the prosecution of three men who had been accused of the murder of Surjit Singh Chhokar: Scottish Executive Press Release, SE3074/2000. The murder was itself thought to have been racially motivated, and the failed prosecution led to allegations of institutional racism being levelled against the Crown prosecution office.

2 *We Can't All Be White* (Rowntree Trust, London, 1999).

3 Arshad, "Racial Inclusion and the Struggle for Justice" in G Hassan and C Warhurst, *A Different Future: A Moderniser's Guide to Scotland* (The Centre for Scottish Public Policy, Edinburgh, 1999), pp 221–222.

4 See the Scotland Act 1998, s 29(2)(b) and s 30(1), and Sch 5, Section L2 (c), and Section K1.

minorities.[1] Such assumptions may, at the very least, create a climate in which exclusion and marginalisation of minorities is acceptable.

The third sort of legal regime which may be applied in respect of minorities involves positive measures of State support aimed at preserving, and perhaps even promoting, the distinctive identity of minority groups. Such a regime is clearly integrationist, although opponents of such policies often characterise them as promoting a "separatist" agenda which itself ultimately deepens divisions in society. Opponents of separate state-funded Roman Catholic schools in Scotland, for example, have over many decades accused such schools of being a source of division in Scottish society, an accusation which, as Gerry Finn notes, is often a "prejudicial confounding of cause and effect".[2] Recently, an Edinburgh Councillor, in a Council debate on the establishment of a Gaelic-medium school in the city, reportedly referred to Gaelic-medium education as educational "apartheid", a gross misunderstanding of the reasons for, and nature of, such education. Even cultural pluralists are not agreed, however, on the degree to which a promotional regime is desirable. For some it is enough to respect difference through a regime of protection, which allows minorities to maintain their distinctiveness if they should so desire, within the private realms of family, church/mosque/synagogue, and local community, without adopting measures in the public domain that seek to foster distinctiveness. At the start of a new century, however, such a limited approach to minority groups is under considerable pressure.

THE BROADER CONTEXT: INTERNATIONAL OBLIGATIONS, INTELLECTUAL TRENDS

With respect to legal norms, developments in the European context, in particular, are likely to impinge increasingly on British and, of necessity, Scottish minority law and policy. A good example of the new approach to minorities is provided by the Framework Convention, by the terms of which the United Kingdom is bound.[3] The Framework Convention is the first legally binding multilateral instrument specifically devoted to minorities issues. The preamble to the Framework Convention recognises the need to protect the existence of national minorities within the territories of signatory States. It also asserts that a pluralist and genuinely democratic society should not only respect the ethnic, cultural, linguistic and religious identity of each person belonging to a national minority but also create appropriate conditions enabling them to express, preserve and develop this identity. The preamble also notes that the creation of a climate of toler-

---

1 Poulter, *Ethnicity, Law and Human Rights: The English Experience* (Clarendon, Oxford, 1998), p 13.

2 G P T Finn, "'Sectarianism' and Scottish Education" in T G K Bryce and W M Humes, *Scottish Education* (Edinburgh University Press, Edinburgh, 1999), p 877.

3 See also, for example, the 1990 *Document of the Copenhagen Meeting of the Conference on the Human Dimension of the CSCE*, and the United Nations General Assembly *Declaration on the Rights of Persons Belonging to National or Ethnic, Religious and Linguistic Minorities*, UN Doc A/RES/47/135 of 18 December 1992.

ance and dialogue is necessary to enable cultural diversity to be a source and a factor, not of division, but of enrichment for each society.

As is noted in its explanatory report, the Framework Convention contains mostly programme-type provisions setting out the broad objectives which States undertake to pursue; the implementation of these principles is left up to the States themselves.[1] The Framework Convention contains strong expressions of both aspects of the protective principle; it guarantees members of national minorities a right to be free of discrimination, and enjoins States to take measures to protect persons who may be subject to threats or acts of discrimination, hostility or violence as a result of their ethnic, cultural, linguistic or religious identity.[2] Article 5 provides that States shall refrain from policies or practices aimed at the assimilation of persons belonging to national minorities against their will. But the Framework Convention also recognises that the protective principle is not sufficient to ensure diversity. Thus, Article 4, for example, provides that States "undertake to adopt, where necessary, adequate measures in order to *promote*, in all areas of economic, social, political and cultural life, *full and effective equality* between persons belonging to national minorities and those belonging to the majority" (emphasis added). This, in turn, implies certain positive measures of support for such minorities.[3] Article 5 states this obligation even more clearly: "The Parties undertake to promote the conditions necessary for persons belonging to national minorities to maintain and develop their culture, and to preserve the essential elements of their identity, namely their religion, language, traditions and cultural heritage".[4] Subsequent Articles make reference to a number of specific rights, many of which have particular relevance to linguistic minorities, such as a right to minority language education,[5] a right to minority language services in administrative contexts,[6] a right to access to the media[7] and so forth.

This concept of "cultural rights" as embodying positive measures of support to members of cultural minorities, a concept which has gained expression in instruments such as the Framework Convention, has also found support from a number of legal and political theorists. Their arguments are premised on the idea that individuals are, to a significant degree, embedded within their own cultural identities, with the result that these identities affect how individuals perceive the available choices and possibilities of life.[8] A supportive cultural environment is, it is argued, essential for both the well-being and personal autonomy of every individual; members of cultural minorities, however, are less likely to enjoy that

---

1 Explanatory report, para 11.
2 Framework Convention, Art 4, para 1, Art 6, paras 1 and 2.
3 This is recognised in the other international instruments referred to in note 3 on page 43 above.
4 See F Benoit-Rohmer, *The Minority Question in Europe: Texts and commentary* (Strasbourg; Council of Europe, 1996) pp 38–51, and references therein, for an analysis.
5 Framework Convention, Arts 13 and 14.
6 Framework Convention, Art 10, para 2 and Art 15.
7 Framework Convention, Art 9.
8 See, for example, P Keller, "Rethinking Ethnic and Cultural Rights in Europe" (1998) 18 *Oxford Journal of Legal Studies* 29 at 39.

secure and supportive cultural environment. In order to redress this, the traditional "difference blind" model of equality, which attempts to ensure freedom from discrimination or unwarranted interference, must be supplemented by a "difference aware" equality, which involves an equality of respect and recognition, under which "the public culture and institutions of a society also need to reflect and accommodate the languages, religions and cultural practices of minority groups".[1] Since this right to maintain and develop a cultural identity is in principle a universal right, it has been argued that there is therefore no reason to make formal distinctions between types of ethnic minorities—particularly between the rights of long-established "traditional" minorities and more recently arrived immigrant groups.[2]

While measures of positive support for certain minorities are already evident in Scotland, the present legal regime with respect to minorities can be described as event-driven, unprincipled and incomplete. For a number of reasons, this state of affairs will be increasingly difficult to manage. First, there are the UK's existing commitments under international instruments such as the Framework Convention. Second, on 2 March 2000, the United Kingdom signed up to another Council of Europe treaty, the European Charter for Regional or Minority Languages, and from 2 July 2001, the date on which this treaty came into force for Britain, the United Kingdom will assume special obligations in respect of both the Gaelic and Scots languages (as well as Irish and Welsh). Third, there are increasingly strong demands from ethnic minority communities themselves. Finally, the interaction of existing and developing measures with the Human Rights Act 1998 and the Race Relations Act 1976, particularly with the non-discrimination provisions therein, may complicate the picture even further, and will certainly require some serious thinking.

OBSTACLES TO A LEGAL REGIME FOR MINORITIES: DEFINING OUR MINORITIES

A fundamental problem in Scottish and, indeed, British minority law and policy is our understanding of the concept of minorities itself. There exists, for example, much confusion about such basic concepts as ethnicity, as opposed to race, colour or religion, even amongst minority activists, the CRE, government officials and the courts, to say nothing of the general public. The result is a tendency to overlook certain types of minorities, perhaps because they do not fit within predominant assumptions and stereotypes about such matters.

The first periodic British State report under the Framework Convention provides a good illustration. As noted above, the Framework Convention creates a range of standards with respect to "national minorities";

---

1 Keller, "Rethinking Ethnic and Cultural Rights in Europe" at 40–41.
2 Keller, "Rethinking Ethnic and Cultural Rights in Europe", at 43; in a British context, "traditional" minorities would include Welsh- or Gaelic-speakers; Urdu- or Cantonese-speakers would fall into the second category.

however, it does not define the term "national minority", leaving it up to States themselves to interpret and apply this term. The UK has decided to define the term by using the definition of "racial group" within the Race Relations Act 1976.[1] This has both strengths and weaknesses. A strength is that it is generally an inclusive definition; it does not restrict the concept of "national minorities" to longstanding indigenous, or "autochthonous" groups, but includes newer immigrant communities. There is a tendency in the minority rights discourse at the European and international level to focus on the former, due in part no doubt to the serious problems being experienced by such autochthonous minorities in central and eastern Europe, in particular. But if, as cultural rights theorists have argued, a right to culture is, in principle, a universal right, distinctions between "traditional" and newer immigrant minority communities are often unjustified. On the other hand, our understanding of which groups are entitled to protection of the Race Relations Act 1976 is itself somewhat confused, with the result that Britain's own indigenous or "autochthonous" minorities such as the Gaels are too often overlooked.

Both of these tendencies can be seen in the UK State Report under the Framework Convention itself, in which it is noted that Britain's minority population, within the meaning of the Framework Convention and therefore within the meaning of "racial group" as defined by the Race Relations Act 1976, is mainly made up of "'ethnic minorities' or 'visible minorities'",[2] thereby implying that these are essentially the same category.

The State Report goes on to note that case law has determined that the Scots, Irish and Welsh, who originate from what were formerly independent nations, are defined as a racial group by virtue of their national origins.[3] Significantly, the State Report does not distinguish between Gaelic-speaking and non-Gaelic speaking Scots, Welsh-speaking and non-Welsh speaking Welsh, and Irish-speaking and non-Irish speaking Irish, although in reporting on State commitments with respect to the educational rights of national minorities, for example, the State Report does recognise this distinction by making reference to Gaelic-, Welsh- and Irish-medium education.[4] This is presumably based on the assumption, made explicit at paragraph 47, that these are the languages and cultures of the Scots, Welsh and Irish. This is a most peculiar assumption, however, in that it implies a linguistic and cultural unity which does not exist. As a practical matter, something less than 20 per cent of the Welsh population speaks Welsh, less than 10 per cent of the Northern Irish population claims a knowledge of Irish (the percentage which speaks Irish with some fluency is likely less than 1 per cent), and about 1.5 per cent of the Scottish population speaks Gaelic.[5] While a significant proportion of the nationalist community in Northern

1 See the UK State Report, *Report Submitted by the United Kingdom pursuant to Article 25, paragraph 1 of the Framework Convention for the Protection of National Minorities* (received 26 July 1999, Council of Europe ACFC/SR (99) 13), para 46.
2 UK State Report, para 45.
3 UK State Report, para 47.
4 UK State Report, paras 198–203.
5 Based on figures from the 1991 census, and other sources. See, generally, R Dunbar, "Implications of the European Charter for Regional or Minority Languages for British Linguistic Minorities" (2000) 25 *European Law Review Human Rights Survey* 44.

Ireland feel an affinity with the Irish language and culture, this is generally not the case amongst the Unionist population, a majority of which tend to view Irish with suspicion, if not hostility[1]; if they were to identify with a language and culture other than English, many Unionists would look to the Ulster variant of the Lowland Scots tongue. While attitudes in Scotland are not nearly as hardened, there is, as I will argue, still an important divide between Gaels and non-Gaels.

Part of the reason for this confusion is due to the approach which has emerged in British courts with respect to the meaning of "racial group" under the Race Relations Act 1976. "Racial group" is defined under section 3(1) to mean a group of persons defined by reference to colour, race, nationality or ethnic or national origins. The manner in which British courts have interpreted the term "ethnic origins" betrays a deep-seated misunderstanding of the concept of ethnicity, as opposed to race, nationality and so forth. Things started out well enough. In the leading case of *Mandla v Dowell Lee*,[2] the House of Lords set out a number of factors to be considered in determining whether an "ethnic group" within the meaning of section 3(1) exists. Lord Fraser stated that there were two "essential" characteristics, and several other " relevant" characteristics. The two "essential" characteristics were: (1) a long shared history, of which the group is conscious as distinguishing it from other groups, and the memory of which it keeps alive; and (2) a cultural tradition of its own, including family and social customs and manners, often but not necessarily associated with religious observance. The five "relevant" characteristics of an ethnic group were: (1) either a common geographical origin, or descent from a number of common ancestors; (2) a common language, not necessarily peculiar to the group; (3) a common literature peculiar to the group; (4) a common religion different from that of neighbouring groups or from the general community surrounding it; and (5) being a minority or being an oppressed or dominant group within a larger community.[3]

While the tests of ethnicity as set out in *Mandla* sensibly come to terms with the concept of ethnicity, they have on occasion been mishandled. Take, for example, the decision of the Employment Appeal Tribunal in *Northern Joint Police Board v Power*.[4] This case involved a claim by an applicant for the post of Chief Constable for the Northern Constabulary that he was not shortlisted for the position because he was English rather than Scottish, and had therefore been discriminated against on racial grounds, within the meaning of section 3(1) of the Race Relations Act 1976. The tribunal was of the view that the English and Scots may be distinct racial groups based on their "national origins" but not based on their "ethnic origins". Quoting with approval from another tribunal case, *Boyce v British Airways plc*,[5] the Tribunal in *Power* argued that the category "ethnic origins" "must ... have a racial flavour to it". The Tribunal continued:

---

1   See, for example, A MacPoilin, "Taig Talk" in G McCoy and M Scott (eds), *Aithne nan Gael/ Gaelic Identities* (The Institute for Irish Studies, Queen's University Belfast, Belfast, 2000), pp 88–95.
2   *Mandla v Dowell Lee* [1983] ICR 385, [1983] 2 AC 548.
3   *Mandla v Dowell Lee* [1983] ICR 385 at 390, [1983] 2 AC 548 at 562.
4   *Northern Joint Police Board v Power* [1997] IRLR 610.
5   *Boyce v British Airways plc* EAT/385/97.

"Whether it is correct to categorise that factor [i.e. a racial flavour] as an essential precondition to determining whether the definition is satisfied seems to us to beg the essential question, which relates to whether or not the group being identified *has* common characteristics within all its members of a racial nature, and not, by contrast, members drawn from various ethnic backgrounds".[1]

Scots could not be a group identified by ethnic origins, the Tribunal concluded, because:

"given the wide variations in origin, background and, indeed, race, within Scotland, all of whom can be categorised as 'Scots', we cannot find the common racial element within the group being addressed as Scots which meets the test plainly laid down by the House of Lords *before* the individual tests enunciated by Lord Fraser are considered".[2]

In other words, the Tribunal was able to arrive at its conclusion by, in effect, ignoring the test of ethnicity set out by Lord Fraser in *Mandla*, to reintroduce a racial basis for ethnicity.[3] This decision shows a remarkable attachment to a concept of ethnicity which is discredited sociologically and, after *Mandla*, legally.

Fortunately, this confusion was redressed to some extent in the recent decision of the Inner House of the Court of Session in *BBC Scotland v Souster*,[4] which involved a claim by a presenter that he did not have his contract renewed owing to his membership in a racial group (he was an Englishman working on a Scottish rugby show). The Inner House recognised that the English could be a "racial group" under the Race Relations Act 1976 by virtue of national origins, but rejected the claim that the English were an "ethnic group".

However, Lord Cameron of Lochbroom noted that to the extent that the Tribunal in the *Power* case[5] required some racial element or racial flavour to be found before applying the *Mandla* tests,[6] the Tribunal was wrong. The only tests of the existence of an ethnic group were those of *Mandla*.[7] Lord Cameron of Lochbroom concluded that neither the Scots nor the English fit within the *Mandla* tests, because they partook in a "much wider and broader based cultural tradition than that which would constitute one of the two essential conditions or characteristics for an ethnic group".[8]

Significantly, Lord Cameron of Lochbroom thought that there may be groups in Scotland which could claim to be "ethnic groups", and referred specifically to the Gaels.[9]

---

1 *Northern Joint Police Board v Power* [1997] IRLR 610 at 613.
2 [1997] IRLR 610 at 613.
3 In *Mandla*, Lord Fraser recognised that "ethnic" conveys a flavour of race "but it cannot, in my opinion, have been used in the Act of 1976 in a strictly racial or biological sense": *Mandla v Dowell Lee* [1983] ICR 385 at 389.
4 *BBC Scotland v Souster* 2001 SLT 265.
5 See *Northern Joint Police Board v Power* [1997] IRLR 610.
6 See *Mandla v Dowell Lee* [1983] ICR 385.
7 *BBC Scotland v Souster* 2001 SLT 265 at 272.
8 *BBC Scotland v Souster* 2001 SLT 265 at 273.
9 *BBC Scotland v Souster* 2001 SLT 265 at 273.

However, even when the courts have remained true to the *Mandla* tests, they have still run into some difficulties. Take, for example, the case of *Gwynedd County Council v Jones*,[1] also heard by the Employment Appeal Tribunal. This case involved applicants for jobs as assistants at a local authority residential home who were refused employment because they did not speak Welsh. They alleged unlawful discrimination under the Race Relations Act 1976 on the basis that they were members of a protected racial group, namely an English-speaking Welsh ethnic group. The industrial tribunal whose decision was being appealed against had ruled that the Welsh as a whole were both a separate nation and an ethnic group—a point which the Appeal Tribunal agreed was "obvious", which is surprising given the decision in *Power* as to the meaning of "ethnic group"—but went on to conclude that the Welsh ethnic group could and should be subdivided into two distinct ethnic groups, namely English-speaking Welsh and Welsh-speaking Welsh. The Appeal Tribunal rejected this subdivision, and therefore dismissed the claim that the applicants had been discriminated against on racial grounds.[2] It did so because it considered that it was wrong in law to use language differences alone to create a separate racial group. Based on the tests in *Mandla*, this is no doubt correct, because although language is mentioned as a factor which can constitute a separate ethnicity, it is only one of Lord Fraser's five "relevant" factors, and is not one of the two "essential" factors. Where, however, there is a separate language, many of the other factors, both essential and relevant, will also exist, and it is disappointing that the Tribunal chose not to consider the presence of any of these other factors, and instead focused on irrelevancies:

> "We cannot believe that, for example, a Mrs Jones from Holyhead who speaks Welsh as well as English is to be regarded as belonging to a different racial group from her dear friend, a Mrs Thomas from Colwyn Bay who speaks only English. This concept seems to us to be as artificial as the proposition that 5,000 or so spectators at Cardiff Arms Park who are fluent in Welsh are a different racial group from the 45,000 or so whose command of the Welsh tongue is limited to the rendering of the Welsh national anthem, or 'Sospan fach.'"[3]

No doubt the Sikh plaintiffs in *Mandla* had non-Sikh friends living near them in Birmingham, and they may even have at some point supported England at Wembley; such considerations are rightly irrelevant to a determination of separate ethnic identity. Indeed, the whole point of legislation such as the Race Relations Act 1976 is to promote such cross-cultural

---

1 *Gwynedd County Council v Jones* [1986] ICR 833.
2 In fact, the conclusion that Welsh-speaking Welsh were not a separate ethnic group was likely not necessary for the Tribunal to find that no act of discrimination had occurred, because it is not clear that the restriction in this case would have amounted to "discrimination" contrary to the Race Relations Act 1976, and in any case there is a provision in the 1976 Act which creates a defence in circumstances such as these where a particular requirement such as the ability to speak Welsh is required for the proper performance of a task. See W McLeod "Autochthonous language communities and the Race Relations Act" [1998] 1 WebJCLI, www.webjcli.ncl.ac.uk/1998/issue1/mcleod1.html.
3 *Gwynedd County Council v Jones* [1986] ICR 833 at 836–837.

harmony within a non-ethnic nationhood. Had the Appeal Tribunal actually asked a Mrs Jones or the 5,000 Welsh speakers at Cardiff Arms Park as to their perceptions of their ethnicity, and the basis on which Welsh-speaking and non-Welsh-speaking Welsh people differ, they may have come to a more nuanced and, in my view, appropriate conclusion.

As the foregoing case law suggests, it is not surprising that the ethnic identity of Britain's autochthonous communities tends to be overlooked. In a Scottish context, the Gaelic community tends to be completely ignored in any discussion of ethnicity, and therefore in any consideration of an appropriate minorities law and policy. This is surprising because, based on the *Mandla* tests[1] properly applied, there is a strong—perhaps irrefutable— argument that Gaels are a distinct racial group based on their "ethnic origins", even though these Gaelic-speaking Scots would consider that they and non-Gaelic-speaking Scots are all part of a Scottish nation and would, no doubt, cheer together for Scotland at Hampden or Murrayfield, while generally accepting a common British nationality. As noted, Lord Cameron of Lochbroom seemed to recognise this very point in *BBC Scotland v Souster*.[2]

Anyone with a passing familiarity with the Gaelic community and, in particular, with the large corpus of Gaelic poetry and literature, much of it retained and transmitted orally, will have no doubt that the Gaelic community satisfies both of the "essential" factors and four of the five "relevant" factors which Lord Fraser used to determine the existence of a separate "ethnic group" in *Mandla*.[3] Indeed, the only factor which this community would not satisfy is that of a "common religion different from that of ... the general community surrounding [them]": in spite of the association of Gaeldom with strict Sabbatarian Calvinism, Catholicism remains strong in many Gaelic communities.[4] It is not, of course, necessary that Gaels satisfy all five of these characteristics to be considered an "ethnic group". Most important, perhaps, is that the distinct ethnic identity of Gaelic-speaking and non-Gaelic-speaking Scots has been recognised by both groups for centuries. Evidence of this awareness amongst non-Gaels dates from John of Fordun's famous comment of the 1380s:

> "The manners and customs of the Scots vary with the diversity of their speech ... The people of the coast are of domestic and civilised habits, trusty, patient, and urbane, decent in their attire, affable and peaceful, devout in Divine worship ... The Highlanders and people of the Islands, on the other hand, are a savage and untamed nation, rude and independent, given to rapine, ease-loving, of a docile and warm disposition, comely in person, but unsightly in dress, hostile to English people and language, and owing to diversity of speech, even to their own nation, and exceedingly cruel."[5]

1 See *Mandla v Dowell Lee* [1983] ICR 385.
2 *BBC Scotland v Souster* 2001 SLT 265.
3 See, for example, M Newton, *A Handbook of the Scottish Gaelic World* (Four Courts Press, Dublin, 2000).
4 See, for example, D E Meek, *The Scottish Highlands: The Churches and Gaelic Culture* (World Council of Churches, Geneva, 1996).
5 As quoted in Newton, *A Handbook of the Scottish Gaelic World*, on p 55.

From a Gaelic perspective, non-Gaelic speakers are fellow Scots, but are viewed as culturally distinct. Dr John MacInnes, perhaps the most perceptive interpreter of this divide, characterises the situation in these terms:

> "To sum up, the Gaelic perception of the Lowlands is in essential agreement with that of the medieval Scots writers who regard the Gaels of their time as 'contemporary ancestors', people who preserve the language and culture which were once shared by all. But from the Gaelic point of view, we the Gaels are the disinherited, the dispossessed."[1]

Perhaps because Gaels are an unrecognised minority, it is still acceptable to subject them to an abuse, often in the pages of the so-called "quality" broadsheets such as *The Scotsman* and *The Sunday Times*, which is quite exceptional in a modern, tolerant society. In 1995, for example, Peter Clarke wrote in the pages of *The Scotsman* that "[t]here is nothing in Gaelic that is worth passing on to the rest of mankind", and that the language was "a low level peasantish sort of debris".[2] In 1997, Allan Brown wrote in the pages of *The Sunday Times* that "everything about Gaelic and those who promulgate it is fairly loathsome", justifying an ill-tempered and ill-informed attack on Gaelic-medium television with this observation: "The inevitable interface with the modern world that television occasions points up all that is twee and antediluvian about this wretched idiolect".[3] Recently, Michael Kelly launched a scathing attack on Gaelic, and in particular, the tiny numbers of hours of Gaelic-medium programming aired each week, all because a Gaelic children's program interrupted viewing of a golf match; "[w]hat a farce to pump out programmes in a meaningless language to a hostile audience".[4] Such hostile outbursts have deep historical antecedents in Scotland, as Krisztina Fenyo has illustrated in a recently-published survey of attitudes towards the Gaels as expressed in Scottish newspapers in the mid-nineteenth century.[5]

In spite of the overwhelming evidence of this Gaelic ethnic distinctiveness, and an often sullen antipathy towards them, Gaels continue to be Scotland's forgotten minority, even amongst those elites who are appointed—or self-appointed—to consider such issues. The CRE itself offers an interesting illustration. *The Herald* reported on 26 May 1999 that the CRE was to sponsor a "Threads in the Tartan Festival", to be held in the year 2000 in order to "explore the importance and meaning of being Scottish at the start of a new century". *The Herald* story reported that the CRE, as main patron of the festival, would identify "the 10 main black and

---

1 J MacInnes, "The Gaelic Perception of the Lowlands", in W Gillies (ed), *Gaelic and Scotland/Alba agus a' Ghaidhlig* (Edinburgh University Press, Edinburgh, 1989) p 99.
2 "Who needs the Gaelic?", *The Scotsman*, 11 March 1995, "Weekend" magazine, p 24.
3 "Restless Native", *The Sunday Times*, 19 October 1997, Section 12, "Ecosse", p 2.
4 "Enough of this Gaelic television farce", *The Scotsman*, 17 October 2000, p 12.
5 *Contempt, Sympathy and Romance: Lowland Perceptions of the Highlands and the Clearances during the Famine Years, 1845–1855* (Tuckwell, East Linton, 2000). Fenyo concluded that in "the mid-nineteenth century, the Highland Gaels were viewed in many ways—from inferior race to picturesque and poetic heroes—but, with a few exceptions, they were never seen as equal, fellow human beings": pp 183–184.

minority ethnic communities in Scotland". Among the 10 communities chosen were those which one would expect to find, including the Pakistani, Italian, Jewish, Chinese and Irish communities. Some of these have been fairly long-established in Scotland, others are relatively newly-arrived; some have become completed integrated, even assimilated, while others have only begun this process. Interestingly, Scotland's Gaelic-speaking minority had been completely overlooked as one of the 10 main minority ethnic communities. This exclusion is all the more remarkable when one considers the aims of the festival, among which were to deal with issues such as emigration and immigration, exclusion, persecution, and simplistic stereotyping. Gaels have been affected by all of these processes, even right up to the present.

Another example of this blind spot came from Bashir Maan, a leading minority rights activist. In *The Herald*'s analysis of the first elections to the new Scottish Parliament, Maan lamented the fact that no members of Scotland's "black and minority ethnic communities" had been elected to the 129–member Parliament, a fact he found surprising given that "there are now between 70,000 and 80,000 people from black and minority ethnic communities" in Scotland.[1] Indeed, the 1991 census showed that some 62,600 people in Scotland reported themselves members of "ethnic minorities", which number included 21,200 Pakistanis, 10,476 Chinese and 10,050 Indians. However, such figures are misleading. First, the groups included in the category "ethnic minorities" in the census were all non-white minorities; white ethnic minorities were simply lumped in with the general population. The same census figures also showed, moreover, that there were some 69,510 people who reported themselves as Gaelic-speakers, the overwhelming majority of whom would be native speakers of the language. If Gaels were included, the size of Maan's ethnic minority community would double; it would also have some representation in the Scottish Parliament, because two native Gaelic speakers were among those elected. Maan's main point is completely appropriate: the under-representation of non-whites in Scotland's institutions, political and otherwise, is a shame, and the problems suffered by these Scots are most serious and in need of urgent attention. The example is merely meant to show the over-whelming tendency to conflate the categories "ethnic group" and "visible minorities", to the exclusion of certain groups which also deserve our attention, including our autochthonous communities such as the Gaels.

This problem may also in part be one of metropolitan, as opposed to local, perceptions. National institutions such as the CRE—and, for that matter, the Westminster Parliament—cannot help but have a national perspective and, perhaps, a perspective that is sharpened by the reality of life in modern London. Nationally, for example, 3,015,000 people were reported in the 1991 Census as belonging to non-white ethnic minorities, representing about 5.5 per cent of the national population of 55 million. About 45 per cent of the UK's non-white population, or some 1,346,800 people, lived in greater London, where they made up roughly 20 per cent

---

1 "How the ethnic minorities have been excluded", in "Scotland's Decision", *The Herald*, Saturday, 8 May 1999, p 9.

of the population. Nationally, the Gaelic population is by comparison miniscule, as is that of the UK's autochthonous populations such as the Welsh-speaking community (some 500,000 speakers in Wales), and the Irish-speaking community (some 142,000 people in Northern Ireland with some knowledge of Irish). Such linguistic minority communities are, practically speaking, invisible in London. It remains to be seen whether the creation of a Scottish Parliament will allow us to begin to develop a broader and more inclusive notion of the minority concept which is reflective of a local reality which includes both "traditional" autochthonous and more recent immigrant minority communities. It certainly gives us the opportunity to do so, at least in areas, such as education, which are within the legislative remit of the Parliament.

CONCLUSION: STRUGGLING TOWARDS A LEGAL REGIME FOR MINORITIES

If there is still considerable confusion in Scotland as to which groups are ethnic minorities, there is perhaps even more confusion as to whether, and how, minorities should receive positive measures of State support. At present, such measures generally fall into two main categories. First, there is strong statutory support, through successive Education (Scotland) Acts since the Education (Scotland) Act 1918, for State-supported Roman Catholic primary and secondary education. Second, there is, ironically enough given the preceding discussion, a patchwork of mostly ad hoc provisions of relatively limited effect for Gaelic, almost all of which have been put in place over the last 15 or so years, following decades, if not centuries, of neglect.[1] Since 1918, there has also been an obligation under various Education (Scotland) Acts to provide for "the teaching of Gaelic in Gaelic-speaking areas",[2] although the precise nature and extent of this obligation has never been tested, and it is certain that the expansion in State-funded Gaelic-medium education which has taken place since it was created in 1985 has not been based on this provision but on decisions by local education authorities, financially supported by a system of Scottish Office grants for Gaelic-medium education which was put in place in 1986, pursuant to Grants for Gaelic Language Education (Scotland) Regulations 1986.[3] As noted earlier, the European Charter for Regional or Minority Languages, which commits States to taking a range of measures for certain "regional or minority languages", has recently come into force in the United Kingdom. These languages include minority languages of long

---

1 For a discussion, see R Dunbar, "Legal and Institutional Aspects of Gaelic Development" in G McCoy and M Scott, (eds), *Aithne nan Gael/Gaelic Identities* (The Institute for Irish Studies, Queen's University Belfast, Belfast, 2000), p 67.
2 See, for example, the Education (Scotland) Act 1981, s 1(5).
3 Although Gaelic-medium education received passing mention in the Standards in Scotland's Schools etc Act, passed by the Scottish Parliament in June 2000, and reference has also been made to Gaelic in the "national priorities" scheme under that statute, the Scottish Executive is not as yet prepared to accede to the demands of Gaelic groups for a specific statutory right to Gaelic-medium education.

standing, but not the languages of more recent immigrant communities. In the Scottish context, only Gaelic and Scots are covered. Above and beyond the Charter, Gaelic organisations have been campaigning for a Language Act, similar to the Welsh Language Act 1993, which would have the effect of creating an integrated statute-based mechanism for the preservation and promotion of the language.

I shall conclude by considering one aspect of minority law and policy a little more closely: minority educational rights. While the provision of State-supported Roman Catholic and Gaelic-medium education is commendable and in keeping with the sort of cultural pluralist approach described above, it must be remembered that there are other claims to minority education which are not yet being heard. There is, for example, a sizeable East Indian population in Scotland, centred primarily on Glasgow and Edinburgh. While not yet as numerous as Scotland's Catholic community or its Gaelic-speaking community, there are significant concentrations of Muslims and Urdu-speakers—generally an overlapping constituency—in Scotland's main cities. Although there is one State-supported Jewish school, there are not yet any State-supported Islamic schools in Scotland.[1] Likewise, there are no Urdu-medium schools, and the provision of even community language teaching—that is, instruction in the language as a subject in an English-language curriculum—is sparse, despite the well-documented research evidence on the cognitive benefits of bilingualism and the maintenance of the mother-tongue.[2] If requests for such education come, as they almost certainly will, how shall we deal with them? Gerry Finn has framed the argument in this way:

> "Catholic schools, as the supposed source of so-called sectarianism, are used to substantiate the argument that racism and prejudice would be increased by providing Islamic schools. In turn, Islamophobia is used to delegitimise the rights of Catholics to attend Catholic schools. Funding for Catholic, Episcopalian and Jewish schools within a national system has set a precedent for the provision of Islamic schools within the same national system, on exactly the same basis and conditions. Only Islamophobes and racists need fear that eventuality. Worries that this development must lead to more anti-Asian racism are ill-founded."[3]

A positive response to the eventuality of a wider range of religious and ethnic minority schools would not only be in keeping with broader European and international trends and standards, described above, but may, indeed, be necessary within the context of the non-discrimination provisions of the ECHR, brought into domestic law under the Human Rights Act 1998. While the principle of non-discrimination attempts to ensure that speakers of minority languages are not subject to discrimination at the hands of the

---

1 G P T Finn, "'Sectarianism' and Scottish Education" in T G K Bryce and W M Humes, *Scottish Education* (Edinburgh University Press, Edinburgh, 1999), p 878.
2 R Arshad, "Racial Inclusion and the Struggle for Justice" in G Hassan and C Warhurst, *A Different Future: A Moderniser's Guide to Scotland* (The Centre for Scottish Public Policy, Edinburgh, 1999), p 882.
3 Finn, "'Sectarianism' and Scottish Education", p 878.

State, it does not ensure that such persons obtain governmental services through the medium of their language, or full "difference aware" equality, as proponents of cultural rights would describe it. In the *Belgian Linguistic Case (No 2)*,[1] for example, the European Court of Human Rights rejected the notion that the principle of non-discrimination set out in Article 14, read together with the right to education set out in Article 2 of the First Protocol to the ECHR, conferred a general right to minority language education.

The principle of non-discrimination may, however, give rise to difficult questions where promotional measures are offered to one group only. The recent decision of the United Nations Human Rights Committee in *Waldman v Canada*[2] provides an illustration. A communication was made by the father of two children enrolled in a private Jewish day school. Under the law of the Province of Ontario, Roman Catholic schools are the only non-secular schools that receive full and direct public funding; indeed, such funding is guaranteed by the Canadian constitution of 1867. Waldman argued that the public funding for Roman Catholic schools alone violated Article 26 of the UN International Covenant on Civil and Political Rights, like Article 14 of the ECHR, a non-discrimination provision, albeit of broader effect, on the basis that it created a distinction or preference which was based on religion and which had the effect of impairing the enjoyment or exercise by all persons, on an equal footing, of their religious rights and freedoms. He argued that the conferral of a benefit on a single religious group could not be sustained.[3]

The Human Rights Committee determined that there had been a violation of Article 26. The Committee stated that

> "... the Covenant does not oblige States parties to fund schools which are established on a religious basis. However, if a State party chooses to provide public funding to religious schools, it should make this funding available without discrimination. This means that providing funding for the schools of one religious group and not for another must be based on reasonable and objective criteria."[4]

The Committee found that the differential treatment here was not based on such "reasonable and objective" criteria. Significantly, the Committee noted that the fact that a distinction is enshrined in a constitution does not render it reasonable and objective. While there may have been some basis for the special protection of Roman Catholics in Ontario when the constitution was enacted in 1867, the Committee found no evidence that Roman Catholics were presently in a disadvantaged position compared to members of the Jewish community. The Committee did not comment on the State party's argument that the extension of funding to other groups could result in the fragmentation of Ontario's public school system, a

---

1 *Belgian Linguistic Case (No 2)* (1968) 1 EHRR 252.
2 *Waldman v Canada* (Communication No. 694/1996, CCPR/C/67/D/694/1996, of 5 November 1999).
3 Waldman also made claims under Arts 18(1) and 27, taken in conjunction with Art 2; in light of its conclusions with respect to Art 26, the Committee did not feel it necessary to comment on these other claims.
4 *Waldman v Canada* at para 10.6.

system reputedly designed to foster tolerance and cross-cultural under-standing, or on the State party's arguments concerning the potentially serious cost implications of extending public funding to other schools.

In his individual opinion, in which he concurred with the Committee's conclusion, Martin Scheinin speculated on the implications that this deci-sion may have for minority language education. With respect to minority language education, Scheinin wrote that:

"[P]roviding for education in minority languages for those who wish to receive such education is not, as such, discrimination, although care must of course be taken that possible distinctions between different minority languages are based on objective and reasonable grounds."[1]

He did not provide guidance as to what those grounds should be, although he suggested that "constant demand" for minority language education may be a relevant factor. He later reiterated the numerical criterion, suggesting that "whether there is a sufficient number of children to attend [the minority school] so that it could operate as a viable part in the overall system of education" was relevant.[2]

The use of demand as a basis for determining which minority groups will benefit from positive measures of support is problematic. But the use of other criteria in determining how entitlement to positive measures is to be determined is also fraught with difficulties. In practice, states do make provision for publicly-funded minority language education which is restricted to only certain linguistic groups.[3] In Scotland, for example, does the provision of Gaelic-medium education to Gaelic speakers without similar provision of Urdu-medium education to the Urdu-speaking community constitute a violation of Article 14, read in combination with Article 2 of the First Protocol? If not, what "objective and reasonable grounds" distinguish the two communities?

On the one hand, it could be argued that Scotland's Gaelic-speaking minority is entitled to special treatment. It is a "traditional" minority which, given its small numbers, is in a precarious state.[4] Given that Gaelic is not spoken as a community language anywhere else, it could be argued that the United Kingdom has a special duty to this community.[5] Furthermore, as noted, the United Kingdom has signed the European Charter for Regional or Minority Languages which provides for special measures of support to such "traditional" linguistic communities,[6] and

---

1 *Waldman v Canada*, Appendix, para 5.
2 *Waldman v Canada*, Appendix, para 5.
3 In Britain, for example, Welsh- and Gaelic-medium education is provided by the state in Wales and Scotland, respectively, while in Canada, French- and English-medium public education is guaranteed in provinces in which French or English, as the case may be, is a minority language; however, other linguistic minorities are not provided with similar measures of support.
4 The 1991 UK census revealed that there were only 69,510 Gaelic speakers in Scotland.
5 In the only other such community outside of Scotland, in Cape Breton, Nova Scotia, Canada, the language is almost extinct.
6 The explanatory report to the Charter refers to such "traditional" linguistic minorities as "autochthonous" groups.

excludes so-called "immigrant" languages. Finally, it could be argued that the United Kingdom facilitated the decline of this linguistic group through its state policies, and therefore owes the community a special duty.[1]

If, on the other hand, language rights are based on a universal right to maintain and develop a cultural identity, there is, as Keller has noted, no intrinsic reason for favouring "traditional" minorities over more recently-arrived immigrant groups.[2] Significantly, the Human Rights Committee did not make reference to the relative length of historical linkage that the two religious minority communities had with Canada. Indeed, to the extent that the provisions in the Canadian constitution of 1867 relative to education of religious minorities could be considered to be an historical compromise in respect of a "traditional" minority, *Waldman* could be interpreted as giving expression to the approach which is consistent with a broader entitlement to maintain and develop cultural identity. And if considerations such as numbers and concentrations of speakers and vitality of the linguistic community are relevant criteria for making distinctions between minorities, Urdu-speakers, who tend to be concentrated in closely-knit urban communities, may have a stronger claim for certain positive measures of support than Gaels, a significant number of whom live in scattered and isolated rural and island communities.

In formulating minority education law and policy in the new Scotland, and minority law and policy in general, we should not allow ourselves to be drawn into this cul-de-sac, and instead take a more open and even-handed approach to all our minority groups. As Gerry Finn argues:

> "Scotland needs to learn to take pride in its continued provision of different educational experiences within a common national framework for specific ethno-religious communities; that recognition of, and support for, social diversity ought to be seen as a healthy sign of a mature, pluralist democracy."[3]

Indeed, I suggest that this would be a sensible starting place for the development of a broader Scottish minority policy.

---

1 See, for example, V E Durkacz, *The Decline of the Celtic Languages* (John Donald, Edinburgh, 1996), C W J Withers, *Gaelic in Scotland, 1698–1981: The Geographical History of a Language* (John Donald, Edinburgh, 1984), C W J Withers, *Gaelic Scotland – The Transformation of a Culture Region* (Routledge, London, 1988), or K J MacKinnon, *Gaelic: A Past and Future Prospect* (Saltire Society, Edinburgh, 1991).
2 P Keller, "Rethinking Ethnic and Cultural Rights in Europe" (1998) 18 *Oxford Journal of Legal Studies* 29 at 43.
3 G P T Finn, "'Sectarianism' and Scottish Education", in T G K Bryce and W M Humes, *Scottish Education* (Edinburgh University Press, Edinburgh, 1999), p 879.

4   Scots Law and European Private Law[1]

Hector L MacQueen

It is a crucial aspect of the history of Scots private law that in its history influences from the Common Law of England have been unavoidable from the beginning and waxed particularly strong after the Union of the Parliaments of the two kingdoms, with a common legislature, final court of appeal (the House of Lords), and the familiarity which comes from proximity, accessibility and a common language. But unlike English law, Scots law was also open from the very beginning to what was to become the Continental European *ius commune* (common law). The substance of the law was much affected by the universal law of the church (the canon law) and the Roman or Civil law taught in the Continental universities at which, until the eighteenth century, many Scots lawyers underwent their initial legal education. A further effect was that when Scots lawyers wrote treatises on their law, they used the systematics and concepts of the learned laws of Europe, further reinforcing its *ius commune* characteristics. If this Civilian dimension weakened after the 1707 Union, and in particular from the Victorian era on, Scots private law nonetheless remains significantly distinct from that of England, and in comparative law terms it is correctly classified as a "mixed" system.[2]

In 1924 the distinguished French comparatist Professor Lévy-Ullmann observed that "Scots law gives us a picture of what will be some day the law of the civilised nations, namely a combination between the Anglo-Saxon and the Continental system".[3] Fifty years later two equally distinguished German comparatists, Professors Zweigert and Kötz, wrote: "... it is clear that Scots law deserves particular attention from comparative lawyers as a special instance of the symbiosis of the English and Continental legal traditions; this may be of some assistance to those who

---

1   An earlier version of this paper appeared as *Scots Law and the Road to the New Ius Commune* (Ius Commune Lectures in European Private Law No 1, Universities of Maastricht, Utrecht, Leuven and Amsterdam, February 2000).

2   For a more detailed survey with literature references see H L MacQueen, "Mixture or muddle? Teaching and research in Scottish legal history" (1997) 5 *Zeitschrift für Europäisches Privatrecht* 369, responding to N R Whitty, "The Civilian tradition and debates on Scots law" (1996) *Tydskrif vir die Suid-Afrikaanse Reg* 227 and 442; see further W D H Sellar, "Scots law: mixed from the very beginning? A tale of two receptions" (2000) 4 *ELR* 3.

3   H Lévy-Ullmann (trans F P Walton), "The law of Scotland" (1925) 37 *Juridical Review* 370 at 390.

embark on the great project of the future, namely to procure a gradual approximation of Civil Law and Common Law."[1] Such thinking can be extended to mixed legal systems more generally: "mixed systems can be regarded as points of reconciliation and as models of the symbiosis of legal systems. They may even be depicted as the 'ideal systems' of the future."[2] As Jacques du Plessis of Stellenbosch has noted, "it can be argued that mixed systems have the potential of being legal 'battlefields' where rules from different systems have to fight for their survival so that only the fittest or best rules survive".[3]

But "they [mixed systems] have not yet become the ideal systems of the future as was hoped, however."[4] It is fair to say that, at least until recently, and despite the very flattering remarks of great comparative lawyers, Scots law and other mixed legal systems have not in fact received much attention outside Scotland and the other mixed systems themselves.[5] Thus, it is not altogether surprising to find that, in the recent renaissance of interest in the idea of harmonising and unifying the private law of Europe, perhaps even in the form of a European Civil Code, relatively little attention has been given to Scots law as a potential model for (in the words of Zweigert and Kötz) "a gradual approximation of the Civil Law and Common Law"; if anything, the reverse has been the case, with Scots lawyers being concerned to see what can be learned from this new *ius commune*.[6] Indeed, Scots lawyers themselves have at times seemed to lack faith in the merits of being a mixed system and to see only a future of gradual assimilation within the Common Law.[7]

---

1   K Zweigert and H Kötz, *Introduction to Comparative Law* (trans T Weir) 3rd edn (Clarendon Press, Oxford, 1998) p 204. The statement also appeared in the first and second editions.
2   E Örücü, E Attwooll and S Coyle (eds), *Studies in Legal Systems: Mixed and Mixing* (Kluwer, The Hague, London and Boston, 1996), p 350. For another recent analysis of mixed systems, see W Tetley, "Mixed jurisdictions: Common Law vs Civil Law (codified and uncodified)" (1999) 4(ns) *Uniform Law Review* 591.
3   J du Plessis, "The promises and pitfalls of mixed legal systems: the South African and Scottish experiences" (1998) 3 *Stellenbosch Law Review* 338 at 343.
4   *Studies in Legal Systems: Mixed and Mixing*, p 351. (See note 2 above).
5   But see H David, *Introduction a l'étude du droit écossais* (Pichon, Paris, 1972) and H Weber, *Einführung in das schottische Recht* (Wissenschaftliche Buchgesellschaft, Darmstadt, 1978). Other non-Scots to write extensively about Scots law include Klaus Luig (Cologne) and Peter Birks (Oxford). Christian von Bar's *The Common European Law of Torts* (Clarendon Press, Oxford, 1998) makes frequent reference to Scots law. Recently Reinhard Zimmermann (Regensburg) and a number of South African scholars have begun to take a comparative interest in Scots law: see the two-volume *History of Private Law in Scotland*, ed K G C Reid and R Zimmermann, (Oxford University Press, Oxford, 2000).
6   J W G Blackie and N R Whitty, "Scots law and the new *ius commune*" in H L MacQueen (ed), *Scots Law into the 21st Century* (W Green, Edinburgh, 1996); H L MacQueen, "Remedies for breach of contract: the future development of Scots law in its European and international context" (1997) 1 *ELR* 200.
7   See most recently R Evans-Jones, "Receptions of law, mixed legal systems and the myth of the genius of Scots private law" (1998) 114 LQR 228. Compare, however, T Weir, "Divergent legal systems in a single Member State" (1998) 6 *Zeitschrift für Europäisches Privatrecht* 564, emphasising "how very different, after nearly three centuries of political unification in an unquestionably single market, the laws of Scotland and England continue to be" (at 565).

The reasons why this might be so have been well expressed by du Plessis:

> "[T]he mere fact that a system has the promise of being able to select from a broader variety of rules obviously does not imply that the best rule necessarily is going to be selected. The pitfall is that it could be the worst rule for that matter, in which case one would not have a particularly exciting 'mixed' legal system, but a rather, as some would say, depressing 'mixed up' legal system ... Ultimately, there is nothing inherently admirable or exciting about a rule derived from a mixed legal system. It entirely depends on what is mixed."[1]

On the other hand, Jan Smits has written, in a lecture of 19 May 2000 inaugurating his tenure of the chair of European Private Law at Maastricht in the Netherlands:

> "It is my profound belief that the experience mixed legal systems already have with the mixing of the civil law and the common law can be of great significance for the venture of establishing a European Private Law. Many times, the *Rechthonoratien* of these systems were able to pick from both the civil law and the common law what they considered to be the best solution for a specific problem."[2]

In his lecture, Smits illustrates this thesis by drawing critically upon the experiences of Scotland, South Africa, Quebec and Louisiana in considering the "duty to rescue" and the rewarding of the Good Samaritan, treating it as part of the new *ius commune*. It seems to me that it is only by analyses of this kind that we can find out whether or not mixed systems do embody the best—or at least good or defensible—choices between the contrasting rules of the Common and the Civil Law, and thus have a role to play in the convergence of legal systems in Europe.

With Smits, therefore, I take the view that more heed should be given to the words of Lévy-Ullmann, Zweigert and Kötz by those following the road to what is sometimes described as the new *ius commune* of Europe. Indeed, I would go further and suggest that it is not only Scots law, but also the world's other mixed legal systems which should receive attention in this regard.[3] The argument is based upon an analysis of the outcome so far of the new *ius commune* project in which I have myself been involved, namely the Commission on European Contract Law chaired by Professor Ole Lando. The Commission is a private initiative, with a membership drawn from all the legal systems in the European Union. I have been the

---

1 J du Plessis, "The promises and pitfalls of mixed legal systems: the South African and Scottish experiences" (1998) 3 *Stellenbosch Law Review* 338 at 343.
2 J M Smits, *The Good Samaritan in European Private Law: on the perils of principles without a programme and a programme for the future* (Kluwer, Deventer, 2000) p 35. See also ibid, p 49; idem, "European private law as a mixed legal system" (1998) 5 *Maastricht Journal* 328, and *Europees privaatrecht in wording* (Instentia, Antwerp, 1999).
3 For a recent analysis of mixed systems, see W Tetley, "Mixed jurisdictions: Common Law vs Civil Law (codified and uncodified)" (1999) 4(ns) *Uniform Law Review* 591. A perceptive older study is J McKnight, "Some historical observations on mixed systems of law" (1977) 22(ns) *Juridical Review* 177.

Scottish representative since 1995, when I succeeded the late Professor W A Wilson. The aim of the Commission is the production of a set of rules—the Principles of European Contract Law—which will represent an ideal system of contract law.[1]

The intellectual origin of the Principles lies in the successful conclusion in 1980 of the Vienna Convention on the International Sale of Goods (CISG), which includes a number of rules on general contract law reconciling the conflicting traditions of the Common and the Civil Law.[2] But CISG applies only to sale contracts, and one aim of the Lando Commission is to create a system for all contracts in the context of the European Union. A similar objective with regard to the global marketplace has been successfully pursued by Unidroit, the International Institute for the Unification of Law, which published its Principles of International Commercial Contracts in 1994.[3]

Although the very similar Unidroit and Lando Principles may one day be the basis for the contract law of a unified Europe, that is not their immediate goal. They are also designed to be capable of adoption by contracting parties engaging in cross-border transactions but anxious not to tie them to particular systems for purposes of either the applicable law or dispute settlement. The Principles may thus take effect in international commercial arbitrations. They are also expected to influence law reform in the Member States and by the European Community itself, and to be a basis for teaching in the law schools.[4]

The work of the Lando Commission is now drawing to a conclusion, with the publication of Parts I and II of the Principles at the end of 1999, and work on the third and final Part expected to finish early in 2001. The time is therefore ripe to examine its results and to consider how far they reflect the position in the Scots law of contract. My approach will be to draw attention to some major rules in the Principles which can be said to approximate to those of the modern Scots law of contract but on which there are significant divisions between the approaches of the Civil Law and the Common Law. I will divide the discussion according to whether the rules are of Civilian or Common Law origin.

---

1 The Principles of European Contract Law (henceforth PECL) are only partly published. Part I (Performance, Non-performance and Remedies) appeared in 1995: see O Lando and H Beale (eds), *Principles of European Contract Law* (Kluwer, Dordrecht, London, Boston, 1995). This Part has now been revised and another added, dealing with formation, agency, validity, interpretation, contents and effects: see O Lando and H Beale (eds), *Principles of European Contract Law Parts I and II* (Kluwer, Dordrecht, London, Boston, 1999). A final Part is in preparation.
2 For the text of the Convention on the International Sale of Goods (Vienna, 1980), see F D Rose (ed), *Blackstone's Statutes on Commercial and Consumer Law 1997–8* (Blackstone Press, London, 1997, pp 468–485.
3 UNIDROIT, *Principles of International Commercial Contracts* (Rome, 1994). See M J Bonell, *An International Restatement of Contract Law: the UNIDROIT Principles of International Commercial Contracts*, 2nd revised edn (Transnational Juris Publications, Irvington, NY, 1997).
4 See H Beale, "Towards a law of contract for Europe: the work of the Commission on European Contract Law" in G Weick (ed), *National and European Law on the Threshold to the Single Market* (Peter Lang, Frankfurt am Main, 1993); H Beale, "The 'Europeanisation' of contract law" in R Halson (ed), *Exploring the Boundaries of Contract* (Dartmouth, Aldershot, 1996).

RULES OF CIVILIAN ORIGIN

No consideration—the unilateral promise

The Principles state that a contract is concluded if (a) the parties intend to be legally bound and (b) they reach a sufficient agreement. There is no further requirement (Article 2:101). Thus, the English requirement of consideration (to say nothing of the French *cause*) plays no part in the Principles, any more than it does in Scots or German law.[1] One consequence in Scots law is the enforceability of the unilateral or gratuitous promise;[2] and likewise the Principles hold that "a promise which is intended to be legally binding without acceptance is binding"(Article 2:107).

Irrevocable offers and postal acceptances

The Principles, while stating a general proposition that offers are revocable, allow them to be made irrevocable by an indication to that effect (Article 2:202). The Scots law concept of promise allows a party to make offers irrevocable or "firm" by an appropriate statement in the offer.[3] In French law, offers are revocable but nonetheless an offeree may have a claim in damages if the offeror abuses his right, while in Germany offers are irrevocable unless otherwise stated. Offers are always revocable in English law, however, unless the offeree provides consideration. The problems which this limitation creates are overcome to some extent by the distinctive rule of English law, under which a postal acceptance concludes a contract at the time and place of posting rather than when and where it is communicated to the offeror.[4] This rule has also been received into Scots law, although in a report published in 1993 the Scottish Law Commission has recommended its abolition.[5] Given that the Principles start on the basis that offers are revocable, it has to do something to protect offerees where the parties are not dealing face to face; the solution is to provide that offers can no longer be revoked once the offeree has dispatched an acceptance (Article 2:202(1)), but the contract is not concluded until the acceptance reaches the offeror (Article 2.205(1)).

---

1 For the comparative position see Zweigert and Kötz, *Introduction to Comparative Law* pp 389–399.
2 See most recently W W McBryde, "Promises in Scots law" (1993) 42 *International and Comparative Law Quarterly* 48; W D H Sellar, "Promise" in Reid and Zimmermann (eds), *History of Private Law in Scotland*, vol 2, pp 252–282; H L MacQueen and J M Thomson, *Contract Law in Scotland* (Butterworths, Edinburgh, 2000) pp 63–69.
3 W W McBryde, *The Law of Contract in Scotland* (W Green, Edinburgh, 1987) pp 65, 68–70; *The Laws of Scotland: Stair Memorial Encyclopaedia* (Butterworths, Edinburgh, 1987–1996, henceforth SME), vol 15, para 617; MacQueen and Thomson, *Contract Law in Scotland*, pp 45–46.
4 For all the foregoing see Zweigert and Kötz, *Introduction to Comparative Law*, pp 356–364.
5 Report on Formation of Contract: Scottish Law and the United Nations Convention on Contracts for the International Sale of Goods (Scot Law Com No 144, 1993).

Contracts for the benefit of third parties

The Principles follow the Continental and Scots legal systems in recognising that contracting parties may create enforceable rights for third parties by appropriate terms in their contract (Article 6:110).[1] English law by contrast has traditionally started from the doctrine of privity, under which only the contracting parties can acquire rights under a contract, even if they intend to confer a benefit upon a third party. The Law Commission of England and Wales produced a report on this subject in 1996, recommending the abandonment of privity and the introduction of a system of third party rights.[2] Significantly, one of the reasons for this change given by the Commission was the need for English law to be brought into harmony with the approach elsewhere in Europe. Even more significantly, on the highly symbolic date of 11 November 1999 (the anniversary of Armistice Day) the report was given effect as law when the Contracts (Rights of Third Parties) Act received Royal Assent.

Performance as the primary right of a creditor

The Principles provide a range of remedies for breach of contract, or non-performance, as the Lando Commission has preferred to term the matter. First among them is the aggrieved party's entitlement, or right, to specific performance of the other party's obligation (Article 9:102(1)). Here again the model being followed is that of the Continental systems,[3] and under Scots law too the creditor's primary remedy is an order for specific implement.[4] In English law, by contrast, the aggrieved party is not entitled to specific performance, which is an equitable remedy subject to the discretion of the court and which will not be granted in a number of circumstances. Scots law has been influenced by English law in this area, to the extent that the courts exercise an equitable control over the grant of the remedy and have borrowed many of the rules which limit specific performance in England. Moreover, in practice on the Continent specific performance is granted only relatively rarely. This means that the outcome in particular cases is often much the same in England, Scotland and the Continent. The Principles reflect this, and indeed the development of Scots law, when they qualify the right to specific enforcement with a number of exceptions mainly drawn from the English rules on the subject (Article

---

1 For third party rights in Scotland See SME, vol 15, paras 824–852, and H L MacQueen, "Third party rights in contract: *jus quaesitum tertio*" in Reid and Zimmermann (eds), *History of Private Law in Scotland*, vol 2, pp 220–251. For the Continent see Zweigert and Kötz, *Introduction to Comparative Law*, pp 456–469.
2 Report on Privity of Contract: Contracts for the Benefit of Third Parties (Law Com No 242, 1996).
3 Zweigert and Kötz, *Introduction to Comparative Law*, pp 472–479; G H Treitel, *Remedies for Breach of Contract: a comparative account* (Clarendon Press, Oxford, 1988) pp 43–63 (note also pp 71–74 on mixed systems).
4 MacQueen and Thomson, *Contract Law in Scotland*, pp 221–224. See also A D Smith, "Some comparative aspects of specific implement in Scots law" (Edinburgh University PhD, 1989).

9.102(2)). Nevertheless, that a difference exists between a system where specific performance is a right rather than a remedy within the discretion of the court is suggested by the contrasting outcomes of recent cases in Scotland and England on so-called "keep open" clauses in commercial leases. In both countries commercial leases are typically of several years' duration. In the cases, changing commercial circumstances led the tenants to withdraw prematurely from the leases. In England, the House of Lords refused to grant specific performance to the landlords, on the grounds that the order could not be used to compel someone to trade at a loss,[1] whereas the Scottish courts upheld the landlords' claim and ordered the tenants to continue to implement the contract.[2] While there may seem to be economic inefficiency in compelling a party to trade at a loss and against its will, the Scottish approach seems preferable to me in upholding the sanctity of contract and the overall risk allocation in long-term bargains; it also means that the onus of finding a new tenant falls on the existing tenant rather than the landlord, that is to say, the contract-breaker pays the costs of breach up-front, rather than later in a claim for damages.

The exceptio non adimpleti contractus—retention

Another remedy in the Principles (Article 9:201) which is found in Scots and Continental contract laws is the right to withhold performance until the other party performs—the *exceptio non adimpleti contractus* (defence of the unperformed contract).[3] The remedy is in the nature of a suspension of performance, and there is no precise equivalent in the English law of remedies,[4] which emphasises termination and damages, although its rules on conditions precedent and subsequent and on order of performance provide some analogues.[5]

RULES OF COMMON LAW ORIGIN

Unified concept of breach

In general, the Principles and Scots law adopt a unified approach to breach or non-performance of contract; that is to say, the remedies apply to any failure to perform in accordance with the contract, whether by total or

---

1 *Cooperative Insurance Society Ltd v Argyll Stores (Holdings) Ltd* [1998] AC 1.
2 *Retail Parks Investments Ltd v The Royal Bank of Scotland Ltd (No 2)* 1996 SC 227; *Highland Universal Properties Ltd v Safeway Properties plc* 2000 SC 297. See further H L MacQueen and L J Macgregor, "Specific implement, interdict and contractual performance" (1999) 3 ELR 239, and A D Smith, "Keep on keeping open" (2000) 4 *ELR* 336.
3 The comparative position receives detailed treatment in Treitel, *Remedies for Breach of Contract: a comparative account*, pp 245–317. For the Scots law of retention and mutuality see MacQueen and Thomson, *Contract Law in Scotland*, pp 195–205, and for comment on the latest cases (*Bank of East Asia v Scottish Enterprise* 1997 SLT 1213, and *Macari v Celtic Football Club* 1999 SC 658), see W W McBryde, "Mutuality retained" (1996) 1 *ELR* 135, and J M Thomson, "An unsuitable case for suspension" (1999) 3 ELR 394.
4 Treitel, *Remedies for Breach of Contract: a comparative account*, pp 299–317.
5 Treitel, *Remedies for Breach of Contract: a comparative account*, pp 255–299.

partial non-performance, delayed or late performance, or defective performance. This is essentially the approach of English law and, indeed, of modern French and Dutch law; however, it contrasts with German law, where remedies for non-performance depend upon whether it results from delay or impossibility. This limitation has given rise to great difficulties in Germany, only partially alleviated by the development in the courts of the further idea of "positive breach of contract".[1] Before the nineteenth century, Scots law showed some signs of developing a similar idea of non-performance as either delay or impossibility, but this was given up largely under English influence.[2] Impossibility came to be treated quite separately from breach, under the heading of frustration (another concept borrowed from English law). The Principles do not go quite this far: a concept of non-performance excused by an impediment beyond a party's control is deployed instead (Article 8:108), and under this head, the remedies of specific performance and damages are precluded but those of withholding performance and termination (see below) are allowed. Apart from this, however, the Principles do not impose any requirement of fault before remedies for non-performance become available, and again this is akin to the position in Scots and English law. A final point under this heading is that the Principles follow Scots and English law in allowing the cumulation of remedies so long as they are not incompatible with each other (Article 8:102). Again there is a contrast with the German position under which, for example, an aggrieved party must choose between termination and restitution, on the one hand, and damages protecting its expectation or performance interest on the other.[3]

Repudiation as breach

Breach of contract by repudiation—that is, refusal to perform including anticipatory refusal before performance has fallen due—is an invention of English law which is not exactly paralleled in the Continental systems.[4] A party may consequently be released from its contract by the refusal without having to wait to see whether or not it is fulfilled when performance is due. It is a doctrine of immense value in commercial situations which Scots law received in the later nineteenth century, and it is recognised in several Articles of the Principles (e.g. Articles 8:105, 9:101(2), 9:201(2), 9:304).

"Self-help" remedies for non-performance

Another distinctive characteristic of the English law of remedies for breach which has only limited parallels on the Continent is the informal and "self-help" nature of some, such as termination, meaning that it is not necessary

---

1   For all the foregoing see Zweigert and Kötz, *Introduction to Comparative Law*, pp 487–515.
2   See H L MacQueen, "Remedies for breach of contract: the future development of Scots law in its European and international context" (1997) 1 *ELR* 200 at 203.
3   BGB §§ 325, 326.
4   Treitel, *Remedies for Breach of Contract: a comparative account*, pp 379–81.

in law to go to court or to give the other party special notice to invoke them.[1] This means that the remedies can be exercised speedily and without immediate cost, again features attractive to commerce. Once more Scots law borrowed the English approach here in the nineteenth century, and the Principles follow suit with regard to its remedies of withholding performance and termination of the contract.

Undisclosed principal in agency/representation

Moving away from remedies, a final example of an English doctrine based upon commercial utility rather than strict conceptual purity which has found its way into Scots law and the Principles, but not into Continental systems, is that of the undisclosed principal in cases of agency.[2] The gist of this doctrine is that an agent who has not revealed to his co-contractant that he is an agent may nonetheless bind together in a contract his principal and the other party.

These examples suffice to make my basic point, which is the simple one that in a number of important respects the mixed Scots law of contract has anticipated the position arrived at by the Lando Commission in considering what is the best rule of contract law to deal with particular situations. The same might be said of other mixed systems, such as that of South Africa, which likewise rejects consideration, gives immediate effect within limits to postal acceptances, allows third party rights, favours specific performance, adheres broadly to a unified concept of breach, and has adopted the doctrines of repudiation, self-help remedies and the undisclosed principal.[3] Of course it is not suggested that all the Lando Commission had to do when it began work in 1982 was visit the law libraries of Edinburgh and Glasgow Universities, consult Professor Walker's then new book on contract,[4] and codify the Scots law of contract—in fact, the law's deficiencies and gaps are highlighted by much of the Commission's work[5]—but it might have provided a useful point of departure, perhaps alongside some of the other mixed systems.

Another interesting dimension is that Scots law reached its position largely through the decisions of the courts, i.e. it reflected problems that actually arose in practice. There was no worthwhile systematisation of

---

1 Treitel, *Remedies for Breach of Contract: a comparative account*, pp 323–340.
2 Zweigert and Kötz, *Introduction to Comparative Law* pp 433–444, 436–441. For Scots law see SME, vol 1, paras 616–623, 625–627, 637, 657.
3 For discussion of these points see R Zimmermann and D Visser (eds), *Southern Cross: Civil Law and Common Law in South Africa* (Juta, Cape Town, 1996), pp 165–180, 303–334, 342–344. Note that offers are generally revocable in South Africa.
4 D M Walker, *Law of Contracts and Related Obligations in Scotland*, (now 3rd edn T&T Clark, Edinburgh, 1995) first appeared in 1979.
5 The Lando and the Unidroit Principles are drawn upon for comparative purposes throughout MacQueen and Thomson, *Contract Law in Scotland*. For an example of how the Principles may be used to clarify and develop Scots law, see the discussion of the applicability of the principles of good faith and pre-contractual liability to be found in PECL, arts 1:201 and 2:301, in my "Good faith in the Scots law of contract: an undisclosed principle?", in A D M Forte (ed), *Good Faith in Contract and Property* (Hart Publishing, Oxford, 1999).

contract law by a text writer until 1914,[1] by when many of the modern features had been laid down by the judges. Some of the nineteenth-century developments show the flexibility of approach which may not be possible with a code. The law of breach provides a particularly good example: the move to adopt some major characteristics of the English system took place quite suddenly in the middle of the century, and provides a striking contrast to the difficulties of German law, hampered by its ossification in the concepts of the BGB of 1900. There are other examples in areas of contract law which I have not so far mentioned. For instance, it was judicially noted in 1868 that Scots law knew only five grounds for the reduction of a contract—incapacity, force and fear, facility and circumvention, fraud and error.[2] Eleven years later, the same judge presided in the court which borrowed a sixth ground from English law, namely undue influence.[3] Similarly, challenges to contracts based on the originally English doctrine of misrepresentation gained ground in Scotland in the latter part of the nineteenth century, overlapping confusingly with the established rules of error,[4] while fraud was significantly narrowed down by acceptance of the English doctrine laid down by the House of Lords in 1889 in *Derry v Peek*.[5]

The factors underlying this reception of English law in the nineteenth century, which can be paralleled in areas of the law other than contract, have often been discussed, and were most likely multiple: as already mentioned, they probably included a common language, ready access to sources and texts of English law contrasting with a relative paucity of indigenous material, and the existence of a common appeal court in the House of Lords. In addition, there may well have been a judicial perception that the unified commerce and increasingly unified culture of a great imperial nation required at the least a harmonised or common approach to legal issues.[6] A further possibility which has not yet received the attention it probably deserves is the influence, or even reception, of Civilian concepts and thinking in nineteenth-century English law,[7] which may have made it seem more intelligible to lawyers brought up in another tradition altogether.

Legislation, from Westminster since the 1707 Union and from Brussels since 1973, has also been a factor in the convergence of Scots and English

---

1 W M Gloag, *The Law of Contract: a Treatise on the Principles of Contract in the Law of Scotland* (W Green, Edinburgh, 1914). The second edition of 1929 remained the only book-length treatment of the subject until the late 1970s. Before 1914 there were only treatments within more general works on private law.

2 *Tennent v Tennent's Trs* (1868) 6 M 840 at 876 per Lord President Inglis. Facility and circumvention is really a sub-category of fraud. Compare with the Inglis list the classical Civilian grounds of invalidity: incapacity, violence, fraud and error. Note also PECL, Arts 4.103–4.108.

3 *Gray v Binny* (1879) 7 R 332.

4 McBryde, *The Law of Contract in Scotland*, pp 187–203; see further MacQueen and Thomson, *Contract Law in Scotland*, pp 155–171, especially at pp 165 ff.

5 (1889) 14 App Cas 337; McBryde, *The Law of Contract in Scotland*, pp 207–209.

6 A recent discussion is A F Rodger, "Thinking about Scots law" (1996) 1 *ELR* 1.

7 See e.g. A W B Simpson, "Innovation in nineteenth-century contract law" (1975) 91 *LQR* 247, and, more generally, M Reimann (ed), *The Reception of Continental Ideas in the Common Law World 1820–1920* (Duncker & Humblot, Berlin, 1993).

contract laws, although mainly at the level of particular contracts such as sale of goods. In many areas of legislation, in particular those associated with commerce, employment, welfare and taxation, it is increasingly difficult to see any specifically Scottish dimension, and it is possible to talk properly of UK law, or indeed EC law. But in the traditional areas of private law, legislation has, in recent times, often contributed to the continuation of a distinct Scottish dimension. This can be attributed largely to the existence since 1965 of the Scottish Law Commission, which has greatly improved Scottish legislation in private law. The Commission works by detailed research on Scots law and the comparative position, wide consultation and the presentation of generally well-argued reports and draft Bills. In contract law, the Commission has been responsible for the modernisation of the rules on requirements of writing;[1] the undoing of the parole evidence rule, another piece of nineteenth-century borrowing from England;[2] and the de-Anglicisation of the sale of goods legislation to some extent by the removal of ambiguous references to the condition/warranty dichotomy in the rules on implied terms and buyer's remedies.[3] In addition, the Commission has proposed adoption of a number of the general contract formation rules in the Vienna Convention,[4] and has been examining the rules on the interpretation of contracts, penalty clauses and breach of contract with the Unidroit and Lando Principles very much in mind.[5]

At least in the domain of contract law, therefore, it is already possible to query the pessimism of Zweigert and Kötz when they write:[6]

> "It is an open question whether Scots law will be able in the long run to resist the influence of Common Law and whether in the future the area within which it can develop its own solutions may not become more and more restricted. One must realise that Scots law is not reinforced by codification, as the law of Louisiana is, nor by using a separate language, like the law of Quebec; nor is Scotland in the position of South Africa of being its own legislator, for Scotland must often trim its legal sails to the winds blowing from Westminster."

Moreover, there is a further new factor in the Scottish legal scene to qualify the last observation in this quotation—the devolved Parliament which from July 1999 has sat in Edinburgh with power to legislate in the field of

---

1 Requirements of Writing (Scotland) Act 1995. For the background see Report on Requirements of Writing (Scot Law Com No 112, 1988).
2 Contract (Scotland) Act 1997, s 1. For the background see Report on Three Bad Rules in Contract Law (Scot Law Com No 152, 1996).
3 Sale and Supply of Goods Act 1994. For the background see Report on Sale and Supply of Goods (Scot Law Com No 104, 1987).
4 Report on Formation of Contract: Scottish Law and the United Nations Convention on Contracts for the International Sale of Goods (Scot Law Com No 144, 1993).
5 Report on Interpretation in Private Law (Scot Law Com No 160, 1997); Report on Penalty Clauses (Scot Law Com No 171, 1999); Report on Remedies for Breach of Contract (Scot Law Com No 174, 1999).
6 Zweigert and Kötz, *Introduction to Comparative Law*, p 204. The same statement appears in the first and second editions.

Scots private law. Pleasingly, this is defined in terms reflecting the traditional divisions of the law into persons, things and actions, as:

> "the following areas of the civil law of Scotland—
>
> (a) the general principles of private law (including private international law),
> (b) the law of persons (including natural persons, legal persons and unincorporated bodies),
> (c) the law of obligations (including obligations arising from contract, unilateral promise, delict, unjustified enrichment and negotiorum gestio),
> (d) the law of property (including heritable and moveable property, trusts and succession), and
> (e) the law of actions (including jurisdiction, remedies, evidence, procedure, diligence, recognition and enforcement of court orders, limitation of actions and arbitration) . . ."[1]

What can the Parliament do with this power? The attentive reader will have noted the time-lag which often exists between the making of Scottish Law Commission reform proposals and implementing legislation, and that some reports remain unenacted years after their publication. Moreover, scrutiny at Westminster has often been cursory in the extreme. Scottish law reform should therefore be quicker, yet more thoroughly examined, in an Edinburgh Parliament. Some limitations on the available possibilities will have to be recognised, at least for the time being: Schedule 5 to the Scotland Act 1998 excludes from the competence of the Parliament some important areas affecting private law, such as the law of business associations, their insolvency, competition, intellectual property and consumer protection.

The possibility of going further than reform and codifying the law was specifically recognised in a provision of the original Scotland Bill which has not survived in the final Act.[2] Nevertheless, there is certainly interest in this, albeit not universal enthusiasm, in Scotland,[3] and Schedule 4, paragraph 7 to the Scotland Act 1998 allows for the possibility of an Act of the Scottish Parliament to "restate" the law. The Scottish Law Commission already has a statutory duty to consider the codification of the law.[4] Much of its work has tended in this direction, and the Commission has indicated support for such efforts, although its "current workload and . . . scarcity of resources" preclude the devotion of any time to such a substantial project as codification of the whole of private law.[5] The work of the Commission, the completion of the 26-volume *Laws of Scotland: Stair Memorial Encyclopaedia*, and

1 Scotland Act 1998, s 126(4); see further ss 28–30.
2 Scotland Bill, clause 28(9).
3 See for an early statement of intent E M Clive, "A Scottish civil code", in H L MacQueen (ed), *Scots Law into the 21st Century* (W Green, Edinburgh, 1996). Contrast however in the same volume A D M Forte, "If it ain't broke, don't fix it: on not codifying commercial law".
4 Law Commissions Act 1965, s 3(1).
5 See the Scottish Law Commission's *Sixth Programme of Law Reform* (Scot Law Com No 175, 1999), para 1.33, and its *Thirty-Fourth Annual Report 1998–99* (Scot Law Com No 179, 2000), paras 2.9–2.11.

a massive growth in research and writing on Scots law, mean that much of the basic research on the current position of the law has been done.

However, the Members of the Scottish Parliament will be pursuing political agenda rather than those of reformers of private law as such, and a codification project may lack the voter appeal to commend it as a legislative priority. An alternative possibility is a private initiative along the lines of the Lando Commission, producing what would be in effect a "restatement" of Scots private law which would test the feasibility of a code, offer a model up for substantive criticism and development, and, in whole or in part, provide material which, if found acceptable, could in due course be enacted by the Scottish Parliament. Such an initiative is already under way at the Edinburgh Law School, under the leadership of Professor Eric Clive and with a degree of official encouragement from the Scottish Law Commission and the Scottish Executive.[1] It might even be best left outside positive law, as a restatement would be more capable of adjustment over time and would avoid the rigidity and inflexibility associated with formal codes.[2]

Another benefit which such a restatement could bring, enacted or not, is to make Scots law more accessible to comparative study. As a system based on a jumble of statute and judicial decision, and in which textbook writing has focused principally on a domestic audience, Scots law has not lent itself to study by outsiders, nor has it been easy for insiders to broadcast its merits beyond the jurisdiction. That a code can change this picture is well demonstrated by the European attention attracted to a draft codification of the Scots law of unjustified enrichment compiled by Eric Clive in a private capacity when a Scottish Law Commissioner and published by the Commission in 1996.[3] Presenting other areas of Scottish private law in codal form might well prove similarly attractive for comparative study. An example that comes to mind is the law of trusts, which has developed in Scotland despite the absence of the divide between law and equity which is supposed to be the lifeblood of the institution in the system of its origin, England.[4] In the recently produced

---

1 See E M Clive, "Current codification projects in Scotland" (2000) 4 ELR 341. There is also a Criminal Code project, involving not only Professor Clive but also Professors Ferguson (Dundee), Gane (Aberdeen) and McCall Smith (Edinburgh), as well as Sir Gerald Gordon Q C.

2 Professor Clive would dissent from this view, however.

3 The draft code appears as an appendix to Scottish Law Commission Discussion Paper No 99, Judicial Abolition of the Error of Law Rule and its Aftermath (February 1996). Other versions of the text may also be consulted in F D Rose (ed), Blackstone's Statutes on Contract, Tort and Restitution 1997–8 (Blackstone Press, London, 1997) pp 444–451, or in E M Clive, "Restitution and unjustified enrichment", in A S Hartkamp et al (eds), Towards a European Civil Code (2nd edn (Kluwer, Dordrecht, London and Boston, 1998), pp 383–396.

4 The Scots law of trusts gives ownership to the trustee and confers a personal right upon the beneficiary with certain privileges. The concept goes back to the early modern period, and English influence has affected its development less than might be expected. These points are expounded in depth in two important articles by G L Gretton, in "Scotland: the evolution of the trust in a semi-civilian system" in R H Helmholz and R Zimmermann (eds), Itinera Fiduciae: Trust and Treuhand in Historical Perspective (Duncker & Humblot, Berlin, 1998) (also in a revised version in Reid and Zimmermann (eds), History of Private Law in Scotland, vol 1, pp 480–517); and "Trusts without equity" (2000) 49 International and Comparative Law Quarterly 599.

Principles of European Trust Law, the introduction, written by one English and two Dutch lawyers, states:

> "The experience of two legal systems is especially interesting. Scots law and Roman-Dutch law in South Africa both provide examples of civilian systems which have been exposed to heavy English influence. Neither knew the institutional separation of law and equity. Both have a law of property based on Roman concepts. Both Scots law and South African law have today a vigorous law of trusts, recognizable as such and named as such despite being in some important respects different in detail from the English law. However, though on each case the influence of English case law is undeniable, both Scots law and Roman-Dutch law see their law of trusts not as an artificial implant from an alien system, but as part of a civil law inheritance. In large measure we are witnessing the revivification of the familiar Roman institutions of *fiducia* and *fideicommissum*. In the present volume, the Scottish National Report may prove to be of particular interest to civilians considering the implementation of the trust in their domestic law."[1]

The Lando Commission has nearly completed its work on Contract; but what we have discovered, as we work on such matters as assignation, prescription, plurality of debtors and creditors, and illegality, is that increasingly we are straying beyond the boundaries of contract into property, delict and unjustified enrichment. From within the Group has therefore come a move to work towards a European Civil Code, which has now commenced as a project at Osnabruck in Germany and at Utrecht, Tilburg and Amsterdam in the Netherlands. Funding has come from the German and Dutch equivalents of the British research councils; these and other British funding bodies have so far shown no willingness to join in, unfortunately. I find myself on the project's Advisory Board; so far as I know, the only other Scots lawyer involved is John Blackie of Strathclyde, in the Delict group. Its first full meeting was at Utrecht in December 1999, with a second in Rome in June 2000, a third in Salzburg in December 2000, and a fourth in Stockholm in June 2001. The project is exciting and hugely ambitious; perhaps over-ambitious. Grand projects for European unity or harmonisation are not getting, or perhaps always deserving, a good press at the moment. Yet the beauty of this being an academic project, rather than for real, like monetary union, may be that a model will be created which can be tested and criticised, and then put into use should the time ever seem ripe to do so.

What can Scots law contribute as Europe's only mixed legal system? If there is ever to be a European Civil Code, whether as positive law or in "restatement" form, it will have to be equally accessible to the Common and the Civil Law traditions; in other words, it will have to be "mixed". The possibility that a more acceptable model could be provided by the

---

1   D J Hayton, S C J J Kortmann and H L E Verhagen (eds), *Principles of European Trust Law* (Kluwer, The Hague, 1999), pp 3–4. The National Report for Scotland is by K G C Reid and is at ibid, pp 67–84.

only existing "mixed" system in Europe is surely one which deserves to be put to the test.[1] But we Scots must put our house in order, both in terms of making our law accessible to those who would examine it from the outside, and of reforming it to the standards which are now being set by deliberations in Europe and around the world. We need also to be more aware than we have been as to what it means to be mixed: what elements have gone into the mix, and why; and what other mixed and mixing systems have done and are doing.[2] It is a challenge to which our judges, legislators, law commissions and, perhaps above all, our academics must rise as Scots law enters the twenty-first century. If we do, then perhaps we will at last be able to say, with Lévy-Ullmann, that Scots law does indeed give us a picture of the law of the civilised nations.

---

1 As an example, a group from the Edinburgh and Strathclyde Law Schools has recently begun work to form a Trusts team contributing to the European Civil Code project.
2 A point made with particular force in du Plessis, "The promises and pitfalls of mixed legal systems: the South African and Scottish experiences" (1998) 3 *Stellenbosch Law Review* 338 at 344–349.

5 Old and Foreign: History, Historiography and Comparative Law

John Blackie

INTRODUCTION

It is not common for commentators on the law to link a consideration of what is "foreign" with what is "old". By contrast, quite often historians and historiographers in Britain do make some connection between these ideas. In such writing, an insight into the two ideas is frequently summed up by quotation, still memorable, though in danger of losing its force from too frequent use: "the past is a foreign country: they do things differently there."[1] Many comparative lawyers are also legal historians working in the history of the development of legal rules. The overt reason why comparative lawyers, therefore, make a link between studying the old and the foreign is particularly to consider the development of doctrines in different legal systems over time as a necessary part of understanding the nature and role of these doctrines, and also sometimes to consider their interactions. That literature is one where, for particular academic intellectual reasons, a connection is made quite consciously between the old and the foreign. However, the thought that there may be some common ground between the way these two things impact on us, is also relevant in considering a particular type of primary material that is a central feature of the way that law is carried out and carried forward in any legal system. This is in the use of sources. This issue could be considered from this point of vantage with regard to the work of law reform, but it is in the use of case law by courts that the matter is most apparent and can be studied over a longer time span.

The issue is coming to be of greater practical importance in Scotland in particular, because there is more foreign material being cited to the courts than there has been for centuries. In the last decade, especially, there has been a revival, at least in cases on major points of law, of the use of material from fairly far back in time. At the same time, the question of the general use of material from at least the nineteenth century has remained constant. The use of more foreign material has recently attracted interest as demonstrating the functional uses of comparative law.[2] It is normally now

---

1 L P Hartley, *The go-between* (1st edn) (Hamish Hamilton, London, 1953) 1.
2 See E Örücü, "Comparative Law as a Tool of Construction in Scottish Courts" (1999) 4 *Juridical Review* 27 where all the case law of the Court of Session, the High Court of Justiciary and the House of Lords in Scottish appeals for five years in the 1990s is examined in detail.

argued that its use is desirable where appropriate—though some are wary of English material,[1] or suggest that it requires varying degrees of care in its use.[2] The present essay, however, seeks to explore the different question of what Scottish judges have considered "appropriate" over a relatively long time span, both with respect to the "foreign" and the "old". It seeks to do this principally by looking at ways in which the Court of Session and the High Court of Justiciary have, over the last three centuries or so, considered this question.[3] The purpose is to study an aspect of the nature of Scots law as a doctrinal system over time rather than to seek to argue normatively for what the system should do in the future, or to comment favourably or unfavourably what has been done up until now.[4] In this way, it is hoped to throw some light on what it has meant to be engaged in judging on points of law within this legal system as opposed to any other, and to consider how that has evolved over time.

It is statistically inevitable that, unless there were to be some rule against it, more cases from relatively far back in time will be cited in a small juris-diction such as Scotland than in a large legal system. This is the more so because the law is not codified, and many of the statutory areas relate to statutes that came into force quite some time ago. The idea that there is something in common between the old and the foreign also prompts a consideration of what it is about a decision being "old" and what it is about a decision being "foreign" that at different times and in different contexts has been relevant to its use in the Scottish legal system. A number of questions follow. First, are there common elements that have guided judges in the Scottish courts both in the consideration of the question of the age of any given legal material and the question of the "foreign"? Second, is there anything about the fact that material is "old" or "foreign" that has resulted in particular Scottish approaches to that? Third, if there is, is it or is it not, because "they do things differently there"?

Before getting on to these questions, the terms "old" and "foreign", of course, themselves need further examination.

---

1 See C McDiarmid, "Scots Law: The Turning of the Tide" (1999) 3 *Juridical Review* 156.

2 As argued by Niall Whitty and the present writer in J Blackie and N Whitty, "Scots Law and the new *Ius Commune*" in H L MacQueen (ed), *Scots Law into the 21st Century: Essays in Honour of W A Wilson* (W Green, Edinburgh, 1996), pp 77–78.

3 Seventeenth- and sixteenth-century material is referred to below to some extent. But it is outside the scope of this essay to consider in depth the use of the wide range of *ius commune* contemporary material that was routinely used in both Scots civil, and Scots criminal courts up to a point around the end of the first third of the eighteenth century. For this generally in the sixteenth century see the transcript of Sinclair's *Practicks* by G Dolezalek, available on the internet at http://www.uni-leipzig.de/~jurarom/scotland/dat/sinclair.htm. For the seventeenth century in the law of *injuria*, including with respect to its criminal aspects, see J Blackie, "Defamation" in K Reid and R Zimmermann (eds) *A History of Private Law in Scotland* (Oxford University Press, Oxford, 2000) (Vol 2)—*Obligations* pp 641–652, 662–667 and 675–678.

4 For that different topic see in particular E Örücü, "Comparative Law as a Tool of Construction in Scottish Courts" (1999) 4 *Juridical Review* 27 and further work of the same author, and others, referred to there. Some of the present writer's views can be found in J Blackie and N Whitty, "Scots Law and the new *Ius Commune*" in H MacQueen (ed), *Scots Law into the 21st Century* (W Green, Edinburgh, 1996).

WHAT IS MEANT BY "FOREIGN"?

"Foreign" seems to be the easier idea. To some extent, all legal systems have rules for this as the issue arises in cases that themselves involve a foreign element, that is cases raising issues of private international law. The rules are part of the law of evidence. Looked at in that context, "foreign" is a class of matter that is not within judicial knowledge. Foreign law, as a matter of the native law of evidence and procedure requires to be proved,[1] and international private law contains rules for determining this question of what is foreign law. But for any consideration of "foreign" law within the legal system it is clear that this has now to be widened, at least to include material of a European origin that is mediated through Scotland being within the supra-national legal order of the European Union, and also because the legal order of the European Convention on Human Rights now forms part of the domestic law of the jurisdiction.[2]

However, the rules of private international law, even when supplemented in these two ways, do not tell us when something that has become part of judicial knowledge by previously having formed part of the decision of a case in a Scottish court has actually "gone native". This, however, is a central matter in seeking to explore the nature of Scots law over an extended period of time. For this task, it is necessary to keep as candidates for being included in a category "foreign", those aspects of legal material that have technically become part of our law in the sense that they do not require evidence and proof. So, for present purposes, the meaning ascribed to "foreign" is: any aspect of law which under our rules of private international law requires vidence and proof, together with any aspect of law which once would have been considered under that test, but has "gone native" in Scotland.

This assimilation of foreign material has occurred at different times, and is obviously part of the way that the mixedness of a legal system is not a static thing. The frequency, for example, with which the decisions of Friesland, collected by the Dutch early seventeenth-century jurist, Johannes Sande, are cited in the reports in Morison from that time until around a hundred years or so later, when compared with citations in those reports from other collectors of decisions from other jurisdictions, suggests something of the sort had happened with that source in that period.[3] Examples are clear in the late twentieth-century developments in the law of duty of care and negligence, where it is the Australian case law that has gone native in England and in Scotland.[4]

---

1 For a succinct discussion of this and also how it applies to English law see E Örücü "Comparative Law as a Tool of Construction in Scottish Courts" (1999) 4 *Juridical Review* 27 at 29.

2 The use of case law of other jurisdictions to throw light on aspects of the law of Scotland that arise by way of legislation based on international conventions is another route in which in a sense foreign case law can go native. For examples in the reported case law of the 1990s see E Örücü "Comparative Law as a Tool of Construction in Scottish Courts" (1999) 4 *Juridical Review* 27 at 33–34.

3 References can be found until at least the early years of the eighteenth century as in *M'Dougall v Maxwell* (1706) Mor 1248.

4 The leading case on the general principles to be applied to determine whether a duty of care is capable of arising, *Murphy v Brentwood District Council* [1991] 1 AC 398 is directly inspired by the Australian decision, *Sutherland Shire Council v Heyman* (1985) 60 ALR 1.

WHAT IS MEANT BY "OLD"?

The difficulty of defining "old"

The notion of the "old" and the "new" is not so readily fixed. Even when there is a direct statement by a judge referring to a case as "old", that does not necessarily mean anything more than that he or she feels that it was decided some while ago. The problem is, of course, that by definition all decisions referred to by courts are decisions from the past, even if the past is only yesterday. The meaning of "old" cannot be fixed by definition. Writers on the law, as opposed to judges, often quite confidently assume that somehow there is a divide, that everyone knowing about these things would recognise, between what one might call "today's law" and the law of the past. Today, more often than not, textbooks have a history chapter at the beginning. This itself is a development in the form of legal writing in the twentieth century, since writers on Scots law in the late nineteenth and early twentieth century do not routinely have these history chapters in their work.[1] This suggests a change of perspective on the "old" on the part of later twentieth-century writers.

Sometimes the divide simply reflects an individual's age or psychology. That, too, however, may tell us something about the nature of Scots law. It is part of the folk memory of those who studied the law of trusts and succession at the University of Edinburgh in the late 1960s and early 1970s that the lecturer[2] would refer to things like "a recent case, 24 Rettie ...", a volume of law reports published three quarters of a century earlier. Another, and probably more accurate, part of that folk memory is that the Professor of Scots Law in the late 1960s showed a preference for not only the "old", but, indeed, the superseded, by continuing to expound the pre-1964 law of intestate succession, ending that exposition with the cryptic phrase, "the Succession (Scotland) Act 1964 falls to be considered".[3] The fact that the folk memory is itself very possibly based on a fiction, or at least inaccurate in detail, does not affect the point. As one gets older one tends to lengthen backwards one's feeling for what is the present and become less confident about where its boundaries in the past lie.[4] Judges are usually over 50 years of age, and for most of the nineteenth century and the first quarter of the twentieth century were usually over 60.[5]

---

1 For example, there is none in Gloag and Irvine, *Rights in Security* (W Green, Edinburgh, 1897) nor in Gloag, *Contract*, 2nd edn (W Green, Edinburgh, 1929). Compare the leading work on Scots contract law today, W McBryde, *Contract* (W Green, Edinburgh, 1987) paras 1–13 to 1–24.

2 The late G Campbell H Paton.

3 Professor George Montgomery.

4 Cf. the use the phrase "contemporary times" in C McDiarmid, "Scots Law: The Turning of the Tide" (1999) 3 *Juridical Review* 156 at 157.

5 There was more variation in the eighteenth century. Bankton was appointed at the age of 70 in 1750 (see W M Gordon, "Introduction" to Bankton *An Institute of the Law of Scotland*, Vol 3, Stair Society Vol 43 xiv–xv). Lord Justice Clerk Sir Gilbert Elliot, his almost exact contemporary, was appointed at the age of 33 (as Lord Minto) (see Jane Blackie's article on Sir Gilbert Elliot, Lord Minto (1693–1766) in H G C Mathew *et al* (eds) *New Dictionary of National Biography* (Oxford University Press, Oxford, forthcoming)).

The idea of the "old" may thus change over time. It may change, too, from one context to another. What is seen as an "old" case in one area of law may be of an age that would not be considered "old" in another. However, the prevalence of references to "old" or "early" or "recent" or the like in case law entails that the idea has some meaning. These terms are not just random labels.[1] It is possible to look at what has been meant by "old" in different situations in our law by analysing the use of such words in the judgments of judges over time, and in that way build a table of the meanings and import that judges have given to them. In carrying out this task, various categories are explored in more detail below.

"Early" and the relative length of the "chronology" of case law

The phrase, "an early case", or "the early case of X" may or may not suggest a set of ideas relating to relevance and usability that is distinct from those ideas associated with the phrase an "old case". A reference to an "old" case or an "early" one can, indeed, be to something that in chronological terms is not that far away in time relative to the whole chronology of Scots case law. The chronology from the present, as far as the record of printed reported decisions is concerned, extends back to the fifteenth century in civil cases.[2] The first civil case available in a printed report seems to be one from 1470.[3] For practical purposes the earliest printed report of a criminal case is exactly 200 years later.[4]

It should not surprise that judges should fix their sense of "early" by reference to points in time which differ from those points that general historians would use. Nor should it surprise that judges in different legal systems, in different contexts, and at different times, would use different chronological points of reference. The word "early", it may be noted as background, is quite mobile, too, in its use today amongst professional historians. For, example, a period of history taken as starting around 1500 is now routinely described as "early modern". That suggests that it is a

---

1   They can come to be almost that in books. See, for example, the title of memorial festschrift for the late Professor Sir Thomas Smith, D L Carey Miller and D W Meyers (eds) *Comparative and Historical Essays in Scots Law* (Butterworths/The Law Society of Scotland, Edinburgh, 1992) where the "Comparative and Historical/" is broad enough to include anything before the day on which it was completed, and includes a range of outstanding essays not only on aspects of doctrinal legal history and comparative law but also on aspects of the law of Scotland as it currently stood.

2   It does not seem to have been researched what is the earliest case cited in a reported Scottish case. One mentioned by W A Wilson (in his essay, "Dealing with Decisions" in *Introductory Essays on Scots Law* (2nd edn) (W Green, Edinburgh, 1984) p 78) from 1546 is illustrative of the fact that "some of the early reports are short and pithy": (1546) *A v B* Mor 3828.

3   *Steuart v Weir* (1470) *Balfour's Practicks* 470 (the date of 1420 in the Table of Cases to P G B McNeill (ed), *Balfour's Practicks*, Stair Society Vol 21, xcv is a typographical error).

4   *HMA v Weir* (1670) MacLaurin 1. This was not printed until over a century later (1774). It is an exciting start—the topics are listed in the reporter's catchwords as "Venus nefanda, Incest, Adultery, Fornication, and Sorcery". There are in fact printed reports of two Scots treason cases from the 1630s, but these reports were published even later and for British political campaigning reasons at the time of publication, rather than expressly for use by Scots lawyers: *HM Advocate v Lord Uchiltrie* (1631) 3 Cobbett's State Trials 426; *HM Advocate v Lord Balmerino* (1634) 3 Cobbett's State Trials 591.

subdivision of another, larger, period called "modern". But even that is not clear, since the phrase "modern history" typically carries with it a resonance of having to do with a period that starts much more recently than around 1500. One can contrast this usage of "early modern" by general historians with a rather different label used by historians of western music. For them the music that was played and composed in the period that general historians call "early modern", is in fact "early music", without the "modern".[1] Modern music is very recent, though there is a counter tendency to see all the innovative music of the last 100 years as "modern".

An express reference to the fact that a case is "early"[2] is sometimes a statement that it is the beginning of what is seen by the person using it as something that is new. This is not in the sense of the length of the relative chronology of all the cases on the subject, but in the sense of a "new start". It carries with it an implied view that there has been a gap at some point.

As a matter of language, therefore, such words of description do not of themselves tell us what the user means, as a preliminary to utilising it. In fact, in some situations the concept, "early case" seems quite distinct from that of "old case".

Legal rules relating to the use of "old" material

Naturally, many common law and statutory rules depend for their operation on the passing of time, for example the law of prescription. But rules of that type do not result in only case law from a period in the past being relevant, or in giving a special place to such case law. There appear to be only three rules in Scots law that definitely entail such consequences. One is a common law rule that "ancient writings" are to be interpreted as they would have been at the time of their creation,[3] which could potentially limit discussion to cases solely from that time. The other two apply only to statute law. These are the *contemporanea expositio* rule applying to the interpretation of Scots Acts passed before 1707, and the rule that codifying statutes are generally to be interpreted without reference to case law decided before the codifying statute was passed. Additionally, in the case law there is a difference of opinion as to whether there is another directly relevant rule— whether or not it is presumed that with consolidation statutes the legislature took into account the existing case law on the provisions now consolidated. The view that there is no such rule has been expressed in the later twentieth century by modernising judges, with the lead taken in England. This indicates an attitude to the past that gives it a lower status.[4]

---

1 Indeed, this is the title of the leading British academic journal devoted to historical musicology *Early Music* (1973 to date). A glance at its pages shows that the term "early" there is extending in that context ever later. Articles can there be found, for example, on the performance practice between the two world wars, and even in the 1950s.
2 See *Dick v Douglas* 1924 SC 787 at 791, per Lord President Clyde.
3 The rule that famously prevented a word of neutral gender in the sixteenth-century statutes of the University of Edinburgh from permitting the granting of degrees to female students: *Jex-Blake v Senatus of the University of Edinburgh* (1873) 11 M 784.
4 For detailed discussion of this in the context of the vexed question of the ranking of floating charges in insolvencies in Scotland, see S Wortley, "Squaring the circle: revisiting the receiver and 'effectually executed diligence'" (2000) 5 *Juridical Review* 325.

It is linked to an approach that treats the matter as being about the law responding to changing circumstances, which is not as such an idea that depends on contrasting the "old" and the "new".[1]

The first of these rules relating to statutes, like the rule about ancient writings, provides a "cut off point". So does the rule about codifying statutes. By contrast, if the rule for consolidation statutes exists, that rejuvenates the existing case law. All these phenomena, "cut off points", "fresh starts", and "rejuvenation" are encountered also more generally. So these legal rules are considered further below under those headings.

There may also be a further relevant rule of law, applying both to areas of law based on common law and areas of law based on or involving statute law. Whether there is or is not depends on whether there is a legal rule, *cessante ratione legis cessat lex ipsa* within our law regulating binding precedent, and on what form that rule takes. It is thought that the "weak form" of such a rule is all that we have, and that does not depend for its operation on any sense of the "old"; it depends only on the fact that the circumstances to which a common law rule is applied change over time, as a continuous matter.[2] On the other hand, in so far as some of the case law that has been used to pursue the debate on these questions does separately tell us something about the idea of "old", these cases, rather than the legal rule and its form, are relevant to this study.[3]

Old as authoritative on its own

The first, and much the least commonly encountered, phenomenon of this nature is where the relative age of a case is referred to as raising a question of whether a particular precedent is binding or not. There are two special factors in the Scottish context that play a part in this form of the idea. First, the Court of Session and the High Court of Justiciary are "collegiate courts". Some 200 years ago they were even more clearly that. Second, it is the case that the notion of binding precedent has itself changed from one where a "tract of decisions" achieved an effectively permanent and fixed rule on a point, to a situation where a single decision from a level up the hierarchy of appellate courts can be binding. It has been suggested by one commentator that the fact that a decision dating from the period when the former was the position (and when in fact also our higher Courts were more clearly colle-giate) should not be treated as binding in the same way as other precedents.[4]

---

1 *Fitzpatrick v Stirling Housing Association Ltd* [2001] 1 AC 27, and, in a specifically Scottish context though on UK legislation, *MacDonald v Ministry of Defence* [2001] ICR 1 (at the time of writing on appeal from the Employment Appeal Tribunal to the Court of Session).

2 G Maher and Sir Thomas Smith, "Judicial Precedent", 22 *The Laws of Scotland: Stair Memorial Encyclopaedia* (the view of G Maher).

3 See in particular the discussion of *Hyslops v Gordon* (1854) 2 Sh App 451 in A Rodger, "The Strange Demise of *Hyslops v Gordon*" in A J Gamble (ed) *Obligations in Context* (W Green, Edinburgh, 1990) 1–12 (see also further below).

4 S Styles, "Antique judgments and modern judges" 1989 SLT (News) 393. The particular situation considered was a fairly extreme one: whether it was right to hold that the rule established in an eighteenth-century case that where, as in a transaction relating to land, the transaction had to be in a signed writing, if it was a peer of the realm who signed he or she should do so in a peculiar form.

There should at least be a willingness to examine today's context, especially if there has been statutory change to the surrounding rules. At the present time there is some evidence that the approach to precedent is in practice, if not as a matter of law, becoming somewhat more flexible again, through the creative use of the idea of *obiter dicta* and so on.[1]

Another question linked to this is the extent to which the length of time that a precedent of an appellate court has existed is to be taken into account in decisions where the Court, in a new case, has power to overrule that precedent. There have been three prominent contexts where this arises in Scots law since the reform of the structure of the Court of Session in the early nineteenth century. One (in civil matters) is the exercise by the House of Lords of its power to overrule its own former decisions.[2] The second is the ability of larger than normal bench of judges in the Inner House of the Court Session and in the High Court of Justiciary to overrule a previous decision of smaller appellate bench. The third is the more general situation where a Court is considering whether or not to follow a persuasive decision. In respect of the first of these contexts there has been a tendency not to overrule decisions of long standing. However, the longest standing House of Lords decision to be overruled in this way is a Scottish decision overruled in a Scottish case.[3] The age of the decision was considered as a factor that could (depending on the balance of other factors) point in the direction of not overruling. But in the event the old case was killed off by the process of "premature ageing", and is explored under that heading below.

Old as the only cases that can be relevant—"cut off points"

This form of "old" as authoritative arises with the rule that in interpreting pre-1707 Scots Acts the approach must be *contemporanea expositio*, i.e. the meaning must be that which contemporaries at the time of passing the statute would have given it. It also arises in relation to the common law rule that ancient writings have to be interpreted according to the meaning that they had at the time they were created. Neither of these rules, of course, are confined to limiting the range of case law that can be used. But they can have that effect. The rules for interpreting pre-1707 Scots statutes are a particularly strong version of this, in that they relate to a precise date, and this stands in sharp contrast to the general rule in statutory interpretation that changing circumstances can be taken into account. A further factor, that tends to reinforce this, is the fact that in the last 100 years or so there have been very few cases relating to the interpretation of pre-1707

---

1 See, for example, the case of *Barnes v HM Advocate* 2000 SCCR 995 which sorts out and makes understandable the famously difficult statutory rules on the extent of the protections given to an accused who gives evidence from some of the situations where it is sought by the crown or those acting for a co-accused to lead evidence of his or her previous convictions, etc. The previous leading case of *McCourtney v HM Advocate* 1977 JC 68 was got round by this technique.
2 Practice Direction [1966] AC 1.
3 See *Darling v Gray & Sons* (1892) 19 R (HL) 31; *Dick v Burgh of Falkirk* 1976 SLT 21 at 24, per Lord Wilberforce.

statutes, except in the area of bankruptcy law, where the wider statutory context had been altered by a series of statutes beginning in 1772 (up to a complete statutory change in 1985), and conveyancing, where repeated statutory change in the nineteenth and twentieth centuries had largely overlaid the pre-1707 statutes. The rule itself may have its origin in the standard law relating to statutory interpretation in the *ius commune* of the seventeenth century. If this is so, then, the preference for the "old" was created by that world itself.

It is worth noting that it may go against the grain in our legal system to have artificial "cut off point" rules, where they do not link to some other idea such as the true old law (see further below). Even then, the rule that statutes seen as codifying an area of law are not to be interpreted by reference to cases decided under the former law has often been honoured in the breach rather than the observance. Well-known examples are the sale of goods legislation and the legislation governing bills of exchange.[1]

Old as not authoritative unless rejuvenated

The law has changed

The sense of "old" can be of something that is not at all far back in the past. This is true where there has been radical change in an area of the law, for example through a change from a common law basis to a statutory basis, or a change from one statutory basis to quite another in an area of law in, say, the last decade.[2] As suggested above, "old" signals a qualitative shift rather than the passage of time.

Rejuvenation by other native material

The process of self-conscious rejuvenation has the effect that, irrespective of how short its distance back in time, the rejuvenated line of case law will be described as "old".[3] The last of the line of cases, which is now rejuvenated, may then be seen as "early" even if it is not that distant chronologically. The use of the procedure of having a "tutor" appointed to look after the whole range of decision-making for an adult, not himself or herself capable of understanding and taking decisions, provides a clear example of this. The beginning of the line of case law in fact goes back to the early sixteenth century. There had been no case since 1924.[4] There was then a "revival", as is reflected in the article in the *Scots Law Times* that gave renewed currency to the practice on the basis of an unreported case in 1987.[5] But at the moment of "revival", the last case before is seen as

---

1 See *Bank of England v Vagliagno Brothers* [1891] AC 107 for the official position.
2 A prominent example is in the law relating to parents and children in Scotland. See A B Wilkinson and K McK Norrie, *Parent and Child* (2nd edn) (W Green, Edinburgh, 1999) where "Developments since 1991" appear (in addition to in other contexts) in Ch I: Historical Introduction, at para 1.09.
3 M Aziz, "The Regulation of Research Involving Human Subjects" (unpublished PhD, Edinburgh University, 1997).
4 See *Dick v Douglas* 1924 SC 787.
5 A Ward, "Revival of Tutors Dative" 1987 SLT (News) 69.

"early", even though in the whole series it may be chronologically quite late relative to the rest. The case law rejuvenating it may then come to be seen against that backdrop as "recent" for quite a while.[1] But if a case occurs that considers the point in some wider frame of reference, the "early" case may well be transformed into one seen as (relatively) "recent". In the mid-1990s, little more than five years after the "revival", this happened with the case law on tutors for adults. The wider frame of reference was needed to consider for the first time end of life decision-making in respect of someone in a persistent vegetative state.[2] The Court of Session had to consider whether it had a general *parens patriae* jurisdiction. To consider that wider point, and incidentally to locate the law relating to tutors for adults within that framework, material from as far back as the sixteenth century was explored.[3] So, the case of 1924 that had been in 1987 seen as "early" came only a few years later to be part of the "recent" through the process of rejuvenation being completed in every respect.

Premature Ageing

This is the opposite phenomenon. The simplest version of this in fact results in premature death. This is where a case is buried in a set of law reports that writers on the law, or lawyers in a later leading case never visited. An extreme example of a case prematurely aged and suffering death that way is a sheriff court case that on its facts is identical to the leading late twentieth century Scottish case on the relationship of the law of "nuisance" to the law of negligence.[4] The case that was missed was a case which, though chronologically younger than at least one of those referred to, suffered from premature ageing by being found only in an extremely rarely visited set of reports.[5] Where death occurs by not being mentioned in a later leading case, especially where the dead case is from the lower courts, it is likely to be final.

In a similar way, a case that is known about, but does not have any effect on how people order their affairs, may be treated as prematurely aged. This was the main reason given for it being possible for the House of Lords in a case in the 1970s to overrule a decision of its own from the late nineteenth century.[6] The one Scottish judge in this case in the House of Lords stated:

> "it cannot be said that this is the class of case in which persons may have acted in reliance on old-established law; no prospective liability could possibly have been calculated, either by an employer or his underwriters, according to the contingency of whether a hypothetical injured man would or would not have instituted proceedings before his death."[7]

---

1 For a writer using precisely these words see M Aziz, "The Regulation of Research Involving Human Subjects" (unpublished PhD thesis, Edinburgh University, 1997).
2 *Law Hospital NHS Trust v Lord Advocate* 1996 SLT 848.
3 The starting point was *Balfour's Practicks* 114 and 254.
4 See *RHM Bakeries (Scotland) Ltd v Strathclyde Regional Council* 1985 SLT 214.
5 *A Orr Ewing and Company v Board of Police of Glasgow* (1875) Guthrie's Select Cases in the Sheriff Courts 475.
6 See *Darling v Gray & Sons* (1892) 19 R (HL) 31, overruled by *Dick v Burgh of Falkirk* 1976 SLT 21.
7 *Dick v Burgh of Falkirk* 1976 SLT 21 at 29, per Lord Kilbrandon.

Moreover, unlike the other judges, who agreed with him on this main point, he trumped the "prematurely aged" case with material from further back— in the form of some early nineteenth-century cases, Stair, and, on one point, Heineccius (which he conveniently found quoted by Lord MacMillan in another case).[1] The prematurely aged was thus killed off at the hand of the chronologically older, which were to some extent thereby rejuvenated.[2]

Old with characteristics that make it unapproachable

This need never occur if sufficient effort is given to interrogating an old case and its background. However, it is sometimes the case that there is a lack of accessible literature or time for a court to work out what the case was really saying. This is also shown by instances where a later court has rushed in confidently and taken a view of the historical background that is different in some ways from that that an academic historian could have taken.[3] Another reason may be that the later court is determined to clarify for itself the law on the point and is impatient with having to go back to a case or cases where there was or were a variety of conflicting views.[4] Or it may simply be that the "old" is seen as intractable. That impression may be totally unjustified and based on a misunderstanding of an aspect of the world in which the old case was decided. For example, an "old" case often referred to in later cases on the law relating to vesting, *Frog's Creditors*, has suffered from being scorned as a ridiculous old thing, because it said that to avoid a particular result the word "allenarly" must be used.[5] In fact that word was just the word for "only" at the time *Frog* was decided, a word without fusty technical overtones. Indeed, it might have been thought extraordinarily technical and obscurantist to use the word "only" at that time. No Scots lawyer ever seems to have used it then.[6]

INTERACTIONS BETWEEN THE USE OF "OLD" AND THE USE OF "FOREIGN"

An important theme in any consideration of the state of Scots law is the extent to which the legal system, or aspects of it, are backward- or forward-

---

1 *Recitationes* Lib. IV. Tit. IV. Para. mcxi; *Stewart v London Midland and Scottish Railway Co* 1943 SC (HL) 19.

2 But they did not have that status for long. Two years later the whole lot were made of no importance by a new statutory scheme for the law regulating death claims in the Damages (Scotland) Act 1976.

3 Compare the discussion of the history of kindly tenancy within Scots law as found in the case concerning the rights of the king's kindly tenants of Lochmaben in *The Royal Four Towns Fishing Association v Assessor for Dumfriesshire* 1956 SLT 217 with the wider frame of reference in the work of historians as Margaret Sanderson, *Scottish Rural Society in the Sixteenth Century* (John Donald, Edinburgh, 1982), pp 58–63.

4 As happened in the case that established in the mid-nineteenth century that truth is always a defence in a defamation action, *Mackellar v Duke of Sutherland* (1859) 21 D 222.

5 *Frog's Creditors v His Children* (1735) Mor 4262.

6 "Allenarly" was the standard word for "only" from at least as far back as the early sixteenth century for all contexts, including ordinary descriptions, as in the "pupil was, at the time of his father's decease, in his father's power allenarly": *The King v Oliphant* (1528) Mor 16216. It gradually went out of use, and was replaced by "only" in standard usage from the middle of the eighteenth century on.

looking.[1] It does not follow, however, that it would inevitably be only by looking forward that the system would be encouraged to look sideways at the foreign. One way in which "old" and "foreign" have been connected in the developing experience of the Scottish legal system is that looking at the "old" has stimulated looking at the "foreign". In Scots private law, this is a feature that has, to different degrees and at different times, prevented looking backwards from getting in the way of moving forwards.

Old as inward looking—Old as outward looking

As part of Scottish culture the law reflects two views of the vision of an older Scotland. On the one hand the "old" is "John Knox ... an embittered man. He could never be at ease with the gay French Queen".[2] On the other hand, it is "a European capital, the city of Hume and Boswell".[3] There are examples where there has been a clear preference in a judgment for enjoying the old and quirky, if not embittered. But these examples are rare. As noted in the previous section the opposite sometimes happens, and the "old" may occasionally get dismissed as unapproachable—but even in the twentieth century, where there seems to be a higher incidence of revelling in the old as quirky, there do not seem to be many examples of this. They are confined to contexts where there is some other connecting factor with that sort of old Scotland, as in the obscure corners of conveyancing, as dealing with the King's kindly tenants of Lochmaben,[4] or with interpreting the language of pre-1707 Scots Acts, where, as already noted, *contemporanea expositio* is the rule. The language of those statutes continued right to the end to be a form of Scots that for formal legal purposes had already otherwise gone out of use. So, there is with them an additional cultural connecting factor of a language that is peculiarly of Scotland, and exclusive of others. A late twentieth-century example reinforces that by not only calling on St Luke's gospel (as good, from a Scots point of view, an old Presbyterian source as any), but even Burns' *Tam O'Shanter*[5] to interpret what range of people a farmer was strictly liable to for damage done by straying livestock under the now repealed Winter Herding Act 1686.[6] Burns there throws light on the range of perhaps less or not always religiously inclined, the counter-culture of old Scotland, the "drouthy neebors". To some extent this is being "ornamental".[7] But it is not only

---

1 See for the development of criminal law in the last 250 or so years as affected by a study of our law that is characterised as having "turned inwards and backwards", L Farmer, *Criminal Law, Tradition and Legal Order: Crime and the Genius of Scots Law 1747 to the Present* (Cambridge University Press, Cambridge, 1997), p 37 ff.
2 M Spark, *The Prime of Miss Jean Brodie* (first published 1961) (Penguin Press, Harmondsworth, 1965 edn) p 33.
3 *The Prime of Miss Jean Brodie*, p 43.
4 See *The Royal Four Towns Fishing Association v Assessor for Dumfriesshire* 1956 SLT 217, and note 3 an page 85 above.
5 *Farquharson v Walker* 1977 SLT (Sh Ct) 22 at 23, per Sheriff Kermack.
6 By the Animals (Scotland) Act 1987.
7 A word used in E Örücü, "Comparative Law as a Tool of Construction in Scottish Courts" (1999) 4 *Juridical Review* 27, for a way that foreign material is sometimes used.

that. Where a judge quotes from a work of Scottish literature it is a sure sign that a special Scottish flavour is intended.[1] A quotation from English literature is, by contrast, almost certainly purely ornamental.[2] A late flowering of this indulging in a Scottish flavour can be seen in the amendments to pre-1707 Scots Acts in recent legislation on land law being done in their Scots language (which is additionally justified by the goal of consistency).[3]

Only the "latest foreign" is useful

It is clear at all times over the last four or so centuries in Scotland, that when foreign is used it is the normally latest foreign material. There are some examples where this is not the case, but these have typically been where "old foreign" juristic literature is referred to rather than "old foreign" case law.[4] Lawyers at all periods show themselves much more likely to identify a potentially useful foreign case if it is fairly new. In Scotland, at least, this has meant that the "functional" use of comparative law has not had the rich texture of the use of "old" native law. The tendency to use the latest "foreign" is in itself one of the reasons why sometimes the "old" native and the new "foreign" are have been used together in decisions.

The intellectual reasons why the "old foreign" has not typically been used have probably varied in Scotland over time. In the sixteenth and seventeenth centuries there was no linguistic barrier to exploring the whole range of continental European literature, including case law. It was readily available, at least to lawyers practising before the courts in Edinburgh,[5] and there would not have been any great fear of misunderstanding the material. It is clear, however, that in that period, too, it was the latest "foreign" *ius commune* material that counsel deployed in prefer-

---

1 For an example by an English judge in a twentieth-century Scottish House of Lords case see the reference to Mrs Grant of Rothiemurchus: *Memoirs of a Highland Lady 1797–1827* in *Wills' Trustees v Cairngorm Canoeing and Sailing School Limited* 1976 SLT 162 at 194, per Viscount Dilhorne.

2 As in the quotation from Milton "they also serve who only stand and wait" by an English judge in the Northern Irish House of Lords case on vicarious liability, in *Century Insurance Insurance Co Ltd v Northern Ireland Road Transport Board* [1942] AC 509 at 514, per Viscount Simon LC. I am indebted to my colleague, Scott Wortley, for drawing my attention to this.

3 I am indebted to my colleague, Scott Wortley, for drawing my attention to this.

4 As in *Caledonia North Sea Ltd v London Bridge Engineering* 2000 SLT 1123 at 1140, per Lord President Rodger referring to Pothier, *Coutumes des Duché, Builliage et Prevôté d'Orleans*. Pothier is cited in a number of twentieth-century Scots cases. But in the previous Scots cases where he is cited, all the examples had been to his famous works on contract and specific contracts, for example to illuminate the meaning of "warrandice" in transfers of heritage his work on Sale: *Clark v Lindale Homes Ltd* 1994 SLT 1053.

5 The extensive holdings of not only juristic literature but case law from continental jurisdictions in the sixteenth and seventeenth centuries in Aberdeen University Library, and even more so in Glasgow University Library, indicate that this may well have been the case for lawyers in provincial centres as well. (For Aberdeen see G R Dolezalek, "An Account of Antiquarian Legal Literature at Aberdeen", available on the internet at http://www.abdn.ac.uk/~law113/library/). The history of when such items were acquired by these libraries has not yet been researched.

ence to such material from further back.[1] The reason was that the world of the *ius commune* at that period was decidedly forward looking. Accordingly, what mattered was to engage with the latest material. In that material the disputes on what the law was on a point were carried on in both juristic writing and case law in courts all over Europe, as in Scotland. The *ius commune* was the very opposite of static, and the very opposite of uniform. From after the first third or so of the eighteenth century this ceased in Scotland to be perceived as still being the case. A long drawn out re-orientation of much Scottish legal thinking then occurred. An idea of Britain became an impulse for some use of new "foreign" material in the form of English material.[2] Examples have been discussed in recent academic literature in the fields of criminal law,[3] the law of defamation[4] and insurance law.[5]

During the nineteenth century it continues to be the new "foreign" that is used, but the background developed. The new context was the British Empire and the wider English-speaking world, which was seen by Scots lawyers at the time as their world, as Lord Rodger has demonstrated.[6] This was certainly the position from the middle of the nineteenth century until at least the end of the Second World War. However, there was another reason, both in the early interactions with English material during the eighteenth century and later against this imperial background, for not looking at "old" foreign. With "old" material from England, and the wider English speaking world, it was relatively difficult for a Scots lawyer to be sure that it had been properly understood. At the same time, the huge development of English law itself through the nineteenth century meant that even in England the "old" English material was being referred to less commonly.

---

1 For the preference for recent *ius commune* in the sixteenth century see the transcript of Sinclair's *Practicks* by G R Dolezalek, available on the internet at http://www.uni-leipzig.de/~jurarom/scotland/dat/sinclair.htm For its impact on Scottish law reform legislation in the sixteenth century see J Cairns "Historical Introduction" in K Reid and R Zimmermann (eds), *A History of Private Law in Scotland* (Oxford University Press, Oxford, 2000) (Vol 1)— *Introduction and Property* 101. For the preference for seventeenth-century recent *ius commune* literature on the law of *injuria*, including with respect to its criminal aspects see J Blackie, "Defamation" in ibid (Vol 2)—*Obligations* pp 641–652, 662–667 and 675–678. For the phenomenon in connection with formation of contract, see G Lubbe in ibid (Vol 2) at 9 ff. Numerous other contributions to both volumes of *A History of Private Law in Scotland* show more generally the impact of the *ius commune*.
2 How far that evidences the correctness of the general historical analysis found in the seminal work, L Colley, *Britons—Forging the Nation (1707–1837)* (Yale University Press, New Haven, 1992) or supports some modification of that as has been explored by a number of historians more recently is not yet clear.
3 J Cairns, "Hamesucken and the Major Premiss in the Libel (1672–1670)" in R F Hunter (ed) *Justice and Crime: Essays in Honour of the Right Honourable Lord Emslie* (T & T Clark, Edinburgh, 1993).
4 J Blackie, "Defamation" in K Reid and R Zimmermann (eds), *A History of Private Law in Scotland* (Oxford University Press, Oxford, 2000) (Vol 2)—*Obligations*, pp 657–660.
5 A Forte, "Insurance" in *A History of Private Law in Scotland* (Vol 2)—*Obligations*, pp 339 ff.
6 "[There was] ... a tendency [on the part of lawyers in Scotland] to see themselves as part of a larger English-speaking family of lawyers scattered throughout the Empire and the United States of America": A Rodger, "Thinking About Scots Law" (1996) 1 *ELR* 3 at 18.

Another intellectual reason for preferring the new "foreign" has been, at least in the later twentieth century, that such material has been deployed in connection with points of law that relate to major issues, central to cultural life, economics and questions of ethics. A prominent example in the 1990s is in *Macfarlane v Tayside Health Board*.[1] In that case, for better or for worse, the judges of the House of Lords, using a variety of analyses, held that a parent could not get the cost of bringing up a child where the conception of that child only occurred because of negligence on the part of a health professional to advise that a sterilisation is not always one hundred per cent effective. In this they overturned in part the decision of the Inner House, and *de facto* overruled the law of England as established in a series of Court of Appeal decisions. One line of new foreign material was preferred, while another line, a variant adopted by some but not all American courts, was considered.

The Scottish experience has been, however, that the preference for the new when using "foreign" material is not solely based on intellectual considerations. Lawyers are strongly pragmatic, and there may be other pragmatic reasons for following a certain course. Sometimes it is even possible to show that a lawyer grabbed opportunistically at something new and foreign that had caught his or her eye. This has occurred ever since there have been newspapers or periodicals in Scotland reporting material from Courts elsewhere.[2] The great increase throughout the nineteenth century in the number and size of newspapers, and the development of legal periodicals in Scotland over the same period especially promoted this.[3] One example of opportunistic use of the "foreign" by a such a route deserves particular mention, because it occurred in a case that was on all fours with the important 1980s Scots House of Lords case on the relationship of nuisance to negligence, but was not cited there.[4] In this case a doctrine not explored in the important 1980s case, that there was a difference between the position of a public authority defender and other defenders when a sewer overflowed, was applied. This was based in part on a case from India.[5] The date of *The Times* newspaper report of that case is in the same month that the sheriff at first instance pronounced decree in the case in which it was cited.[6] It must have been seen by the lawyer who relied on it in the newspaper for the day or for a day shortly before that on which he argued the case.

There are pragmatic dangers, however, in always going for the new foreign. It may be that the not-quite-so-new is mistaken for the really new. It may be that the really new turns out, after the event, to have been not

---

1 *Macfarlane v Tayside Health Board* 2000 SLT 154.
2 The Scots Magazine in the eighteenth century was one way in which lawyers were alerted to English cases: see J W G Blackie, "The use of English Case Law by the Court of Session in the Eighteenth Century" (forthcoming).
3 The attention given to American material in the early volumes of the *Juridical Review* in the 1890s may be a reason for the fashion around that time in Scotland for using cases from courts in the United States, for which see in particular Rankine, *Law of Landownership in Scotland* (1st edn, 1879) (4th and last edn, 1909) (both published by W Green, Edinburgh).
4 *RHM Bakeries (Scotland) Ltd v Strathclyde Regional Council* 1985 SLT 214.
5 *Madras Railway Co v Zemindar of Carvetinagarum* The Times 6 July 1874 (Privy Council).
6 29 July 1874.

quite the same in its import, or even dramatically different. There are examples where Scots courts have followed what they thought was the position in some other jurisdiction, only for it to transpire later that that was wrong and the position in that other jurisdiction had already changed. Examples from the twentieth century include the law of consent to medical treatment,[1] the question of duty of care for negligence in the context of an illegal activity,[2] and the remedies available where a person is in default on a hire purchase contract.[3] That this can be shown to have occurred even as often as this has something to do with the relative lack of really comprehensive libraries, at least in the twentieth century and at present.

Where the new foreign helps out the old native

Rejuvenation

In this the past is, in part at least, made a less foreign country by updating it with the help of a real foreign country. It is a form of rejuvenation that is inspired by a particular view of where Scotland and the legal system at the time lies in the world, which, as we have seen also plays a role in the reasons for preferring the latest "foreign". The process has been particularly apparent in a tendency to look for the true old and authoritative law. It has been marked in decisions dealing with major points of private law in the last decade. In these cases it is also notable that much foreign material has been cited. Three decisions in particular stand out. One is the leading case in the 1990s on end of life decisions,[4] where the "old" is accompanied by reference to a Canadian decision (not followed as such) from 1986.[5] Another is the leading decision from the same decade on the recovery payments made under error of law, where eighteenth-century Scots material is combined with a large range of overseas material.[6] A third is the leading decision from the year 2000 on the law of subrogation, where "a tract of authority stretching back beyond the time of Stair" made an appearance in the company of overseas material in which "a number of

---

1 See *Craig v Glasgow Victoria and Leverndale Hospitals Board of Management* (Inner House) unreported 23 March 1976—reference to an out-of-date edition of a Canadian case book not including the more recent cases from the Supreme Court of Canada.
2 See *Winnick v Dick* 1984 SLT 185 referring to *Smith v Jenkins* (1970) 44 ALJR 78, but not to *Jackson v Harrison* (1978) 138 CLR 438 which is used in *Weir v Wyper* 1992 SLT 579 at 582, per Lord Coulsfield. Counsel in the latter case may have been alerted through an article by A H Hudson, "Crime, tort and reparation: an English solution" 1990 SLT (News) 193 to the fact that this Australian case had already, before *Winnick*, modified the position in the Australian case cited there. For comment on *Weir* by A H Hudson see his article "Crime, Tort and Reparation: A Common solution" 1992 SLT (News) 203 and see also the later case, *Taylor v Leslie* 1998 SLT 1248.
3 See *Granor Finance Ltd v Liquidator of Eastore Ltd* 1974 SLT 296. But this (and others can be found of this sort) was a self-conscious decision not to follow the newer material: 1974 SLT 296 at 298, per Lord Keith.
4 *Law Hospital NHS Trust v Lord Advocate* 1996 SLT 848 ranging back to sixteenth-century material and even the medieval text *Regiam Majestatem*: 1996 SLT 848 at 863, per Lord Clyde.
5 *Re Eve* (1986) 2 SCR 388.
6 *Morgan Guaranty Trust Co of New York v Lothian Regional Council* 1995 SC 151.

discoveries" were made by counsel who in their search for authority no longer "stop[ped] at the shores of the United Kingdom".[1] To some extent the prevalence of this type of combination may reflect a development that is ongoing in our legal culture. But it is part of a way of looking at law in a case law based system, which has a particular type of rigour. It is associated with a view that the courts require all material that helps the formulation and understanding of the principles.[2]

Resurrection

It may be that only one example of this can be shown. But it is likely that this phenomenon may occur more frequently in the future, because of the building of computer databases, accessible worldwide. The one example that this writer has been able to identify occurred before that development began. It is a striking instance of the way that the "foreign" may be used to renew the "old". It shows that the right sort of "foreign" material can revivify even the "prematurely aged". The once dead case is a Scots case from shortly before the First World War, *Main v Leask*.[3] In current terms it is about duty of care in negligence in "pure economic loss" cases. (It was a successful claim by share fishermen for loss of their shares of the profits they would have earned when the boat that they used but did not own was out of action having been damaged by the defender's negligence). The case was in the Scots books, but under another heading, remoteness, which correctly reflected the classifications within the law of delict at the time the case was decided. But the changing of the classifications was tantamount to death and burial.[4] Exhumation was carried out in a PhD at the University of London,[5] and given prominence by the same writer in a journal article published in Canada.[6] The Canadian exhumation was followed by resurrection, in Australia, due to the exceptional thoroughness of the High Court there in using the Canadian periodical literature.[7] From thence the case of the Scots share fishermen finally got back alive to the United Kingdom. Its first reappearance in a Scots reported case, in which it was distinguished, was in 1984.[8] More recently, it has made an appearance south of the border where it was also distinguished.[9] Presumably the courts would rather it had remained decently buried.

---

1 *Caledonia North Sea Ltd v London Bridge Engineering* 2000 SLT 1123 at 1136, per Lord President Rodger.
2 See for this in particular Lord Rodger of Earlsferry in, "Savigny in the Strand" (1993–1995) 28–30 Irish Jurist 1.
3 *Main v Leask* 1910 SC 772.
4 See Walker *Delict* (2nd edn) (W Green, Edinburgh, 1981), pp 273 and 277.
5 C Harvey, "The Duty Concept in Negligence: Liability for Infringement of an Economic Interest" (PhD, University of London) 580. The discussion of *Main v Leask* 1910 SC 772 is at 587.
6 C Harvey, "Economic Losses and Negligence: 'The Search for a Just Solution'" (172) 50 *Can Bar Rev* 58.
7 *Caltex Oil (Australia) Pty Ltd v Decca Survey Australia Ltd (The Willemstad)* [1976–1977] CLR 528 at 529, per Gibbs J.
8 *Blackburn v Sinclair* 1984 SLT 368.
9 *Bellefield Computer Services Ltd v E Turner and Sons Ltd* [2000] BLR 97.

More generally

Obviously it may be that a lawyer might seek to use the "foreign" to help out the "old" when it is not sought to rejuvenate or resurrect it. An instance of that is found in a case reported in 1980 concerning the law of "fraudulent" preferences, where an insolvent person or business prefers to assist one creditor over others.[1] The law goes back to the seventeenth-century, and seventeenth-century statutes, but the court did consider, rather inconclusively, material on a completely different regime from an Australian province. There are doubtless other examples, but their rarity suggests that the interactions between the old native and the foreign normally have depended on some other factor being necessary.

Where the old triumphs over some of the foreign

This is another clear point of intersection between the two ideas. Two different variants of it can be found in Scots material. The first of these does not seem to have arisen in the last two centuries. But the fact that it can be found in the eighteenth century, and then disappears, is evidence that in these matters general cultural change is also important. This first variant was to categorise some foreign law as tyrannical. For instance, in a case in the early eighteenth century it was argued that certain authorities were inappropriate material because they dated from a time before "the principles of liberty and property against the ancient Langobardick servitudes were more asserted."[2] In fact, there is a whole class of foreign material, including foreign case law, that was abandoned *en bloc* on this ground— the late sixteenth- and seventeenth-century continental European material on criminal law. Hume, who, if he did not cause this to occur, made certain that it was not gone back on, disguises his reasoning by saying that such material as it is foreign is "very absurd to look into ... for an exhibition of the practice of Scotland, which those foreign authors could know nothing about".[3] As for any idea of using these writers on general topics, "they teach nothing more than any man of plain sense, with a little attention to the subject, will readily, and to as good purpose, make out for himself". But the real reason for their being confined to a dustbin in Scotland is apparent elsewhere. This is in Hume's willingness, though without a "superstitious admiration" to use English law at times, as it is "a great body of written and practical reason, recommended by the example of a free and an enlightened people".[4]

---

1 *Nordic v Scotprint Ltd* 1980 SLT 189. The equivalent since the Bankruptcy (Scotland) Act 1985 is an "unfair preference".
2 *Governors of Heriot's Hospital v Alves* (1707) M 15994—a case on the now obsolete law of multures.
3 Hume, *Commentaries on the Law of Scotland Respecting Crimes*, Vol 1, p 17. The first edition, under the title, *Commentaries on the Law of Scotland respecting the Description and Punishment of Crimes*, was published in 1797.
4 Hume, *Commentaries on the Law of Scotland Respecting Crimes*, Vol 1, p 13. For the extent to which Hume borrowed from England, and for the need of further research on that see L Farmer, *Criminal Law, Tradition and Legal Order: Crime and the Genius of Scots Law 1747 to the Present* (Cambridge University Press, Cambridge, 1997) 37, 43 and 50.

The other variant is an approach that classifies some non-Scots material that has been used before as now being too foreign, because it is now seen as having distorted the true original doctrine of our law on some topic or other. By relying on rediscovering "law before the fall", what had seemed, in some contexts even for centuries as being foreign but helpful now becomes foreign and unhelpful. The most prominent example of this in the last decade is, as is widely known, the "rediscovery" that payments or other transfers, made under an error of law are recoverable in an action within the law of unjustified enrichment, just as much as payments or other transfers made under an error of fact are. The "old" case that was shown to support this, *Stirling v Earl of Lauderdale*, dates from the early eighteenth century.[1] As a decision it had long been considered to fall into the category of "old and so obscure that we cannot understand". However, rejuvenation was achieved by looking at the papers of counsel in the case obtained "thanks to the industry of the pursuers' counsel."[2] It appears to be unique to Scotland that this way of rejuvenating what has been seen to be old and fusty can take place. It is only possible because up to the early nineteenth century in our civil procedure counsel had to put their detailed legal argument, and indeed the facts, into written form for consideration by the Court.[3]

Where the old native shows why some of the foreign is useful

One model of history that crops up in various contexts is that if one goes back far enough everything is the same. The history of languages such as the romance languages, is an example of that in a non-legal context. This way of looking at the past has played a role in some Scottish legal material and creates a peculiarly direct link between the use of old and foreign material. A very clear example of this is to be found in the leading twentieth-century case on our law relating to what sorts of rivers give rise to a public right of navigation.[4] A preliminary move was to rejuvenate the "old" Scots case law by going back to the papers that lay concealed behind the law report, a process involving "a vast amount of diligence and research".[5]

---

1 *Stirling v Earl of Lauderdale* (1733) Mor 2930.
2 *Morgan Guaranty Trust Co of New York v Lothian Regional Council* 1995 SLT 299 at 313, per Lord President Hope.
3 Another set of the pleadings in *Stirling* (obtained by Ross MacDonald, University of Dundee from the Scottish Record Office) can be found—"Recovery of Benefits Conferred under Error of Law"—in Scot Law Com Discussion Paper 95 (1993), Vol 2, Part 1, Appendix 19–22. Use of the papers that formed part of an earlier decision is now quite common in academic writing, too. There are other examples in work of the Scottish Law Commission as in "Diligence on the Dependence and Admiralty Actions" Scot Law Com Discussion Paper 84 (1989) paras 3.147 ff—case from 1808 and 1811 (papers collected by Hume referred to). I am indebted to Niall Whitty for this reference.
4 *Wills' Trustees v Cairngorm Canoeing and Sailing School Ltd* 1976 SLT 162. For the background of this case and those cited in it and the extent to which "old" law was abandoned at various times in connection with a number of issues relating to public rights in rivers see N Whitty, "Water Law Regimes" in K Reid and R Zimmermann (eds), *A History of Private Law in Scotland* (Oxford University Press, Oxford, 2000) (Vol 2)—*Obligations* 420 at 438 ff.
5 *Wills' Trustees v Cairngorm Canoeing and Sailing School Ltd* 1976 SLT 162 at 188, per Lord Wilberforce. This case revived *Grant v Duke of Gordon* (1782) 2 Pat App 582 (House of Lords); Mor 12820 (Court of Session).

Whether or not it was successfully rejuvenated gave rise to a difference of opinion. The majority thought so, but one judge found aspects of the case still "very puzzling."[1] Here the point was not to triumph over the foreign. Instead, the process involved a range of foreign material being directly referred to. This even included material from one codified continental European system, albeit found by way of a Canadian decision from Quebec on appeal to the Privy Council,[2] noted as a "judgment that contains a number of interesting citations from French authors—notably Dalloz".[3] In fact there is direct reference to Article 538 Code Civile (in French), though again got at by way of a Quebec case on appeal to the Privy Council.[4] But it is a particular view of the "old" as an original where everything was the same that prompts this. It thus takes the reference further back to "other [i.e. here earlier] streams [that] existed in French jurisprudence long before the compilation of the Code Napoleon". Then US material[5] gets used, and from thence, suitably for these purposes, "[old] English authorities including Hale, *De Jure Maris*". This all leads to an absolutely express statement of this particular model of history that once all was pure and the same as being the reason for the foreign material being relevant in this context:

> "I have referred to these cases drawn from differing systems of law, to support the existence of a rule, which is really one of the common law of nations, resting ultimately upon facts and needs not confined to any one place or time, that the use of a river, according to its natural quality and capacity, for downstream floating is recognised by the law; and to support the use of broad and liberal principle for the statement and application of the rule."[6]

Another of the judges put it in a slightly different way, but still linking the "old" and the "foreign" in a positive sense: "I derive considerable support for my opinion by the analogy and reasoning of the old French writers".[7]

Where the foreign trumps the old native

This is similarly uncommon and seems to be confined to where the "old" is in fact not very far back in time. One area where it has happened is in the law relating to the situations in which the accused, if he or she chooses to give evidence, is protected from cross-examination that tends to show him or her to be of "bad character".[8] There was some assistance from English

---

1 *Wills' Trustees v Cairngorm Canoeing and Sailing School Ltd* 1976 SLT 162 at 194, per Viscount Dilhorne, referring to the manuscript notes that were on the papers as to what the judges said.
2 *Bell v Corporation of Quebec* (1879) 5 App Cas 84.
3 *Wills' Trustees v Cairngorm Canoeing and Sailing School Ltd* 1976 SLT 162 at 190, per Lord Wilberforce.
4 *Maclaren v A-G for Quebec* [1914] AC 258.
5 *Morgan v King* (1866) 35 NYR 454.
6 *Wills' Trustees v Cairngorm Canoeing and Sailing School Ltd* 1976 SLT 162 at 191, per Lord Wilberforce.
7 1976 SLT 162 at 203, per Viscount Dilhorne. He then quoted nine lines of French without translation.
8 *Leggate v HM Advocate* 1988 SCCR 391, 1988 SLT 665.

material in enabling the Court to overrule a larger than normal bench case[1] of only a year or so earlier and disapprove of *dicta* in a mid-twentieth-century Scots case[2] where they were in the judgment of a judge of particularly high authority.[3] But here there was a further factor pointing towards the foreign, in that the law, although based on a Scottish statute, has its origin in the late nineteenth century in statutes passed for both jurisdictions. They had meanwhile gone their separate ways to some extent in case law. Although it is not easy to reconcile all the *dicta* in the English cases, it seems clear that the approach to this problem in the two jurisdictions is now substantially the same.[4]

Where the foreign is used instead of the old native

This is something that can be identified at times in twentieth-century Scots case law. But it was never common and it perhaps no longer occurs. The conditions fostering its occurrence are: a lack of accessible literature leading to the old native, and/or the old native being in a form that is off-putting. Two cases on aspects of the law of intentional delict point to the contrast. In a case in 1999 a judge carefully expounded for the first time the Scots law of "molestation" in relation to workplace bullying.[5] He carefully avoided having to rely on some rather confused English case law on "harassment". When the question of intentional causing of economic harm on the part of an officer of a public body arose in 1983[6] the Court, in quite the opposite spirit, adopted as a whole the English tort of misfeasance in a public office, without looking at relevant Scots cases. They do exist. But none are later than the early nineteenth century and they would need some development to produce a law adapted to the world of the late twentieth century.[7]

CONCLUSION: HISTORY, HISTORIOGRAPHY AND COMPARATIVE LAW

It is clear that there are links between the approaches that have been taken by Scottish judges to both the "old" and the "foreign". Some of this is obviously about the functional use of legal material. Legal history can be functionally used in exactly the same way as comparative law can be. Recently it has been usefully emphasised that "decisions must be read against the background of the law as it was at the time they were pronounced and of subsequent doctrinal development ... A fragment of law cannot be detached from the world in which it was created without

---

1 *Templeton v McLeod* 1986 SLT 149.
2 *O'Hara v HM Advocate* 1948 SLT 372.
3 Lord Justice-Clerk Thomson.
4 *Leggate v HM Advocate* 1988 SLT 665 at 671.
5 Lord Reed in *Ward v Scotrail Railways Ltd* 1999 SC 255.
6 *Micosta S A v Shetland Islands Council* 1983 SLT 483.
7 Relevant cases can be found collected together in J W G Blackie, "Scotland" in J Bell and A W Bradley (eds), *Governmental Liability: A Comparative Study* (UKNCCL, London, 1991), pp 44–60.

violence to its meaning and significance."[1] However, the nature of approaches to "old" and "foreign" that have been taken by judges in cases in Scotland over the last three or more centuries, and the interactions between them have a bearing on another type and use of legal history as well.

An aspect of doctrinal legal history is that it is a subset of the history of ideas. It carries that investigation out by, amongst other things, considering what has been said in judgments in cases for "consumption and use by careful 'targetted' readers".[2] It, therefore, can play a further role, as can comparative law, to throw light on what those users have considered "appropriate", and how that has been reflected in the creation of this source of material. That is an aspect of the "state of Scots law" over time. It is "what was once possible".[3] The meanings at different times and in different contexts given by judges in Scotland to the idea of the "old" and the "foreign", as with the use of sources generally, highlights the fact that the "state" of Scots law has always been one of flux. That is not only for the obvious reason that ideas change, but because the sources that are considered to matter have constantly been reselected. Doctrinal legal history does not have the luxury of many areas of the history of ideas studied by intellectual historians of "a very limited number of classic texts written by a handful of authors".[4] Nor is there a "canon" of case law growing steadily over time. On the other hand, the material used in any decision looks like a temporary "canon" and has the feature of being reactive to material from earlier in time, especially when it is "old" or "foreign".[5] In that case the use of the "old" and the use of the "foreign" in Scotland have frequently raised the same or similar issues, and in various ways have interacted. What the process seems to show is not so much anything about whether the system is or is not civilian, nor about its "style" as a legal system.[6] It shows the way in which judges within it, against the background world of their times, have dealt, and will, it is anticipated continue to deal, with the challenge of judging on points of law within a small legal system that has had no absolute points drawn barring looking backwards or looking sideways.

---

1 K Reid and R Zimmermann, "The Development of Legal Doctrine in a Mixed Legal System" in Reid and Zimmerman (eds) *A History of Private Law in Scotland* (Vol 1)— *Introduction and Property* 11.

2 M de Certeau, "Histoire et mystique" (1973) (trans A Goldhammer *et al*) in J Revel and L Hunt (eds), *Histories—French Constructions of the Past* (The New Press, New York, 1995) p 444.

3 M de Certeau, "Histoire et mystique".

4 R J Evans, *In Defence of History* (Granta Books, London, 1997) p 85, considering the current debate amongst historiographers and historians as to the importance of or lack of validity of the use of documentary sources.

5 Even the minority of scholars of literature who argue of a constant and growing canon of literary works emphasises that it reacts to earlier material. (H Bloom, *The Western Canon* (Macmillan, London 1994) at pp 11–12: "The Western literary Canon is primarily manifested as the anxiety of influence that forms and malforms each new writing that aspires to permanence".)

6 For consideration of the wide divergences of opinion with regard to Scots law viewed from these angles see N Whitty, "The Civilian Tradition and Debates on Scots Law" (1996) *Tydskrif vir die Suid-Afrikaanse Reg* 227 at 227 ff.

6 Scottish Self-Government and the Unitary Constitution

Neil Walker*

THE CONSTITUTIONAL DIMENSION OF SELF-GOVERNMENT

Arguments for Scottish legal and political autonomy take many forms. As it has waxed and waned since the Union of 1707, the case for independence or lesser forms of self-government in Scotland, like many similar movements in the modern age, has drawn upon a diverse combination of factors—economic, administrative, political and cultural.[1] Economic considerations typically point to the wealth of national resources, as well as to the advantages of economic management on a smaller scale. Administrative considerations tend to embrace the logistical, representative and participatory benefits of more local and more responsive systems of public administration. Political considerations indicate the distinctiveness of the broad balance of political preferences within the national *demos* and the appropriateness of dedicated institutions to reflect these preferences. Cultural considerations remain the deepest well-springs of nationalism, and the most difficult to illuminate. They have to do with national self-consciousness as a constituent of personal and collective identity, whether such self-consciousness is conceived of in "thick" ethnic terms—treating the nation as a community of fate, or in "thin" civic terms—concentrating on the sense of belonging of those who share civic institutions and are members of the same civil society.[2]

---

* I would like to thank participants at seminars in the Universities of Aberdeen and Edinburgh, and in University College, London, as well participants in the Glasgow seminar, for their comments on earlier versions of this article. The usual disclaimer applies. Later sections of the present contribution draw upon parts of my "Beyond the Unitary Conception of the United Kingdom Constitution?" [2000] PL 384.

1 See e.g. T Devine, *The Scottish Nation: 1700–2000* (Penguin, London, 1999) Chs 23–25; N Davies, *The Isles: A History* (Macmillan, London, 1999) Ch 10; T Nairn, *After Britain: New Labour and the Return of Scotland* (Granta, London, 2000); N Walker, "Constitutional Reform in a Cold Climate: Reflections on the White Paper and Referendum on Scotland's Parliament" in A Tomkins (ed) *Devolution and the British Constitution* (Key Haven, London, 1998) p 61.

2 For an interesting exchange on whether and to what extent the civic/ethnic distinction can be maintained, see M Ignatieff, "Benign Nationalism? The Possibilities of the Civic Ideal", pp 141–148, and R Fine, "Benign Nationalism? The Limits of the Civic Ideal", pp 149–161 in E Mortimer (ed) *People, Nation and State: The Meaning of Ethnicity and Nationalism* (Tauris, London, 1998).

When we move from the abstract to the concrete, it is evident that the particular mix and balance of these large forces changes from context to context and from time to time. In particular, the watershed in Scottish self-government represented by the establishment (following a long and uneven history of administrative devolution)[1] of a devolved Scottish Parliament in the Scotland Act 1998 reflects the growing post-war salience of the argument for economic nationalism; the cumulative disillusionment of an increasingly social democratic political community with the long unbroken period of Conservative Government at Whitehall; a more general conversion to the benefits of "subsidiarity" in the management of a complex modern polity in which the "suprastate" level of the European Union becomes an ever more prominent factor;[2] and an (internationally resonant) resurgence of national self-consciousness,[3] in its Scottish context[4] increasingly but by no means exclusively drawing upon civic rather than ethnic considerations.

Clearly, too, the weight and significance attributed to these factors differs depending upon perspective and strategy. For example, amongst other significant differences, advocates of independence place greater emphasis than those who are inclined towards lesser forms of self-government upon the importance of issues of cultural identity. Indeed, no matter how complex and wide-ranging their other supporting arguments, it tends to be a basic article of faith for those committed to independence that these basic identity aspirations cannot be satisfied short of self-determination and the successful assertion of national sovereignty.[5]

We shall return to this point shortly, as it informs a distinction central to the discussion below. First, though, we need to introduce a further feature of the argument for Scottish self-government, one which provides the focal point of this chapter—namely the *constitutional* dimension. The constitutional dimension provides a general structuring framework for the various particular themes within the self-government debate mentioned above: cultural, political and—less immediately but still highly pertinently— economic and administrative. With regard to these themes the UK constitutional framework provides a set of constraints and opportunities, the diverse and controversial understanding and evaluation of which both informs the distribution of positions along the spectrum of self-government—from the devolutionary *status quo* through federalism to independent sovereign statehood—and conditions the strategies of those associated with these positions.

---

1 See e.g. C R Munro, *Studies in Constitutional Law* (Butterworths, London, 1999), Ch 2.
2 See e.g. N MacCormick, *Questioning Sovereignty: Law, State and Practical Reason* (OUP, Oxford, 1999), Ch 9.
3 See e.g. M Guibernau, *Nations without States: Political Communities in a Global Age* (Polity, Cambridge, 1999).
4 See references in note 1 on page 97 above.
5 This claim is in some ways complicated by the move towards "postnational" constitutionalism and "post-sovereignty" referred to in the penultimate section of this chapter. Some sophisticated nationalists (see, e.g. MacCormick, *Questioning Sovereignty: Law, State and Practical Reason*, esp. Chs 10–12) now assume that autonomy and state sovereignty in the territory of the EU is more or less compromised and qualified by membership of the EU. However, even within this approach sovereignty retains currency as the claim to independence, autonomy and formal equality *vis-à-vis* other states—for these purposes bracketing off the European Union and its claims to sovereignty.

Two features of the UK constitutional framework are of particular significance in structuring the self-government debate. The first is the pivot of the entire constitutional framework, namely the doctrine of the sovereignty of Parliament. The fundamental "rule of recognition"[1] of the British Constitution places the Queen in Parliament in a position of unimpeachable authority. To be sure, the detailed meaning and scope of this rule remains controversial, particularly in the light of British membership of the European Union and the growing willingness of British judges to countenance the overriding authority of the EU legal order in circumstances of conflict with the domestic order.[2] Of more direct concern, there is a well-known strain of thinking in the Scottish courts,[3] and—much more explicitly and forcefully—in Scottish academic circles,[4] which has sought to argue that the British Parliament was "born unfree,"[5] the Union legislation of 1707 setting out as constitutive (and so constitutional) conditions of the Union the protection of various Scottish institutions against future Westminster legislative override. Nowadays, however, even those who would wish it otherwise, and who would continue to argue that the best interpretation of the source material is that it *should have been* otherwise, would concede that the dominant, and to all intents and purposes, settled position is the traditional Diceyan one[6]: that the Union was effectively an *incorporating* Union, in which the founding principles of the old English constitutions continued to prevail, including the capacity of the Westminster Parliament to repeal all earlier legislation, not least the Union legislation itself.

For advocates of an independent Scotland, this conclusion, however unpalatable in principle, at least clarifies matters. It means that, regardless of the *political* claims to the sovereign right of the Scottish people made from time to time, recently most prominently by the Scottish Constitutional Convention as it assumed a leading role in the campaign for a Scottish Parliament,[7] there is no scope for the *legal* accommodation of that claim in any shape or form within the extant framework of the British constitution. In a sense, that is the end of the matter for strong nationalists. If the identity claim is fundamental to their case, and if this cannot be satisfied short of sovereignty,[8] then the British state is incapable of meeting

---

1 HLA Hart, *The Concept of Law* 2nd edn (OUP, Oxford, 1994) Chs 6 and 10.
2 See, e.g. *R v Secretary of State for Transport, ex p Factortame Ltd* [1990] 2 AC 85; *R v Secretary of State for Employment, ex p Equal Opportunities Commission* [1995] 1 AC 1. See also P Craig, "Britain in the European Union" in J Jowell and D Oliver (eds) *The Changing Constitution*, 4th edn (OUP, Oxford, 2000) p 61.
3 See e.g. *MacCormick v Lord Advocate* [1953] SC 396; *Gibson v Lord Advocate* [1975] SLT 134; *Robbie The Pict v Hingston (No 2)* [1998] SLT 1201.
4 See e.g. J D B Mitchell, *Constitutional Law* 2nd edn, (W. Green, Edinburgh, 1968) pp 93–98; N MacCormick, "Does the United Kingdom Have a Constitution?" (1978) 29 NILQ 1.
5 See Mitchell, *Constitutional Law*, p 69. See also C R Munro, *Studies in Constitutional Law* (Butterworths, London, 1999), p 137, and E Wicks, "A New Constitution for a New State? The 1707 Union of England and Scotland" (2001) 117 LGR 109.
6 See e.g. N MacCormick, *Questioning Sovereignty: Law, State and Practical Reason* (OUP, Oxford, 1999), p 59.
7 See e.g. N Walker, "Constitutional Reform in a Cold Climate" referred to in note 1 on page 97 above.
8 See note 5 on page 98 above.

their aspirations, or even of providing a constitutional context through which their aspirations may be pursued with any prospect even of partial or long-term success. The only option is constitutional rupture—in Kelsenian terms[1] a legal revolution—and the autochthonous foundation of a new Scottish state.

But it is by no means the end of the matter if we take instead the broader spectrum of self-government claims and the wider range of themes under-girding these claims. If the continuing sovereignty of the British state is *not* the key concern, as is the case for many advocates of self-government, attention then turns to how the British constitution might accommodate various other candidate versions of Scottish legal and political autonomy. Indeed, even for strong nationalists, the broader constitutional back-ground remains relevant in so far as it may affect the weight of the supporting package of arguments for independence in terms of which they seek to convince others (and perhaps reassure themselves).[2]

This brings us to a second—and, for the purposes of this chapter cen-tral—structural feature of the British constitution, namely its unitary qual-ity. Elsewhere I have argued at some length[3] that there is a deep and resilient distinction between those who view the British constitution atomistically and those who view it holistically—between, on the one hand, those who perceive its almost uniquely unwritten—or non-documentary[4]—status as endowing it with a formless, protean character, exhibiting little or nothing by way of unifying principle or design, and, on the other hand, those who discern beneath the formless surface deep-rooted values and perennial pre-occupations and so a broad normative and structural coherence. The mean-ing and implications of the unitary idea of a constitutional order with a single, unrivalled agency or institutional complex of ultimate legal compe-tence in the sphere of government is crucial to this debate for the simple reason that it is the one structural feature of the constitutional order which is undeniably resilient even from the most implacably atomistic perspec-tive. That is to say, the unitary character is a *necessary* structural inference from the "top rule"[5] of parliamentary sovereignty.[6] As such, it provides a

---

1   H Kelsen, *General Theory of Law and State* (trans A Wedberg) (Harvard University Press, Cambridge, Mass, 1945).
2   Think, for example, of the vigour with which the Scottish National Party pursued its "Doomsday scenario" prior to the General Elections of 1987 and 1992. The essence of its argument was the starkly political point that if, as then seemed plausible, the Conservative majority in the UK seemed likely to continue for the foreseeable future, the equally firm social democratic majority in Scotland would become effectively disenfranchised; see e.g. T Devine, *The Scottish Nation: 1700–2000* (Penguin, London, 1999), Ch 25.
3   N Walker, "Beyond the Unitary Conception of the United Kingdom Constitution?" [2000] PL 384–389.
4   Munro, *Studies in Constitutional Law*, p 3.
5   H W R Wade, "The Basis of Legal Sovereignty" [1955] CLJ 172 at 187–189.
6   The converse does not, however, hold. That is to say, it is possible to have a unitary consti-tutional order without a top rule which vests power in a single agency or institutional complex. Instead, as Wheare points out, the top rule might dictate the supremacy of a written Constitution, which in turn might allocate ultimate legislative and governmental power to a single agency or institutional complex: K C Wheare, *Modern Constitutions*, 2nd edn (OUP, Oxford, 1966), pp 19–24.

key battleground in the deeper debate, the atomists seeking to deny, and the holists to assert, its deep structuring power.

In turn, the atomism/holism debate and the implications of the unitary constitution hold the key to a whole series of linked questions about the entire New Labour constitutional reform programme ushered in since 1997; whether the programme is properly viewed as radical or cosmetic; if radical, whether it is beneficially transformative of an ossified institutional morality or dangerously destructive of a precious legacy; if cosmetic, what it would take to achieve a truly transcending "constitutional moment". More pertinent to our present concerns, the debate also promises to unlock the meaning of that particular part of the constitutional reform programme concerned with devolution and the aspiration towards self-government—a "rolling programme"[1] which has already delivered legislative and executive institutions to Northern Ireland[2] as well as to Scotland and a deliberative and executive Assembly to Wales.[3] In simple terms, a holistic reading of the constitution and a correspondingly strong interpretation of its unitary disposition would imply a rigid constitutional culture and one in which a devolution programme such as contained in the Scotland Act could deliver only a modest measure of self-government in Scotland and in the other nations and regions. Conversely, an atomistic reading of the constitution and a correspondingly weak interpretation of its unitary disposition would imply a malleable constitutional culture and one in which the devolution settlement promises, or at least permits, a more radical measure of self-government.

The reading of the British constitution urged below is one which is closer to the atomistic than to the holistic end of the spectrum. It suggests, accordingly, that the unitary conception places only modest impediments in the way of Scottish self-government. It is argued, first, that the unitary conception of the constitution is actually a very flexible notion, capable of embracing a wide range of different constitutional structures and political visions.[4] Second, however, although within the particular field of self-

---

1 See e.g. R Brazier, "The Constitution of the United Kingdom" (1999) 58 CLJ 96, R Hazell and B O'Leary, "A Rolling Programme of Devolution: Slippery Slope or Safeguard of the Union?" in R Hazell (ed) *Constitutional Futures: A History of the Next Ten Years* (OUP, Oxford, 1999); C R Munro, *Studies in Constitutional Law* (Butterworths, London, 1999), Ch 2; H Elcock and M Keating (eds), *Remaking the Union: Devolution and British Politics in the 1990s* (Frank Cass, London, 1998); V Bogdanor, *Devolution in the United Kingdom* (OUP, Oxford, 1999); M O'Neill, "Great Britain: From Dicey to Devolution" 53 *Parliamentary Affairs* 69; J Bradbury and J Mitchell, "Devolution: New Politics for Old?" (2001) 54 *Parliamentary Affairs* 257.

2 Northern Ireland Act 1998.

3 Government of Wales Act 1998.

4 Indeed, although Wheare's discussion of the subject has been influential in the modern acceptance of the centrality of the unitary theme to an analysis of the UK constitution, he himself was at pains to emphasise its flexibility: "The class of unitary Constitutions is so wide and varied, the degree and method of decentralisation in practice in unitary Constitutions is so diverse, that a good deal more must be known about a Constitution described as 'unitary' before we can feel that we know what it is like": Wheare, *Modern Constitutions*, 2nd edn (OUP, Oxford, 1966), p 21.

government there *are* nevertheless certain fundamental limits set by the unitary conception, even these fundamental limits are less constraining than is often assumed. Third, in any event these fundamental limits are unlikely to be directly challenged, in large part because of the development of multi-dimensionality within the sphere of public law. Where once there prevailed a monist conception of public law, of state constitutions as the single and largely unrivalled sources of public legal authority within the world order, in the post-Westphalian order the state is increasingly in competition with other authoritative sites. This more pluralist environment militates against the transformation and transcendence of the unitary conception of the state in a double sense; in strategic terms it makes such a transformation of the British state more difficult to deliver, but also in normative terms it makes such a goal less directly significant and less immediately relevant to the fate of communities. The unitary conception of political community can now be transcended, not by transcending the unitary conception of the (British) constitutional state, but by transcending the constitutional state itself. In other words, the new pluralism *of* legal orders to some extent compensates for the limits of pluralism *within* a particular legal order.

THE FLEXIBILITY OF THE UNITARY CONCEPTION

The key to understanding the flexibility of the unitary constitutional conception of the British state lies in acknowledging that there are two separate discourses associated with the unitary theme, one narrowly legal/constitutional and the other more broadly political. If that distinction is made, we can appreciate that the unitary state, as defined in legal terms, can accommodate much of what is excluded by a unitary political discourse and embraced by political pluralism. Partly, and most obviously, the distinction between legal and political conceptions is about different types of power associated with the two discourses. The legal conception concerns the type of order and of authority that may be generated through the specialised form of "institutional normative order"[1] associated with law. The political conception of unitary order, on the other hand, concerns *de facto* political power in all its forms and manifestations and the type of order that may be produced through its operation.

Associated with these different power claims, the legal and political conceptions of unitary order may also be distinguished in terms of their overall discursive field. Each discourse involves counterposing unitary order to a different conceptual opposite. Within legal discourse, the unitary constitutional state is opposed to the state in which ultimate legal authority is not vested in any single institutional centre, a category typically limited in the relevant literature to the federal constitutional state.[2] While this limitation

---

1   MacCormick, *Questioning Sovereignty: Law, State and Practical Reason*, Ch 1.
2   See e.g E Barendt, *An Introduction to Constitutional Law* (OUP, Oxford, 1998) Ch 3; Wheare, *Modern Constitutions*, pp 19–24.

may be unnecessarily restrictive,[1] the federal state is certainly by far the most significant manifestation of a legally non-unitary state, and in the context of a discussion of self-government is in any case the primary focus of our concern. Although the precise legal definition of federalism is elusive,[2] in basic terms, legal authority under a federal constitutional order is distributed in separate parcels between central (federal) legislatures and governments on the one hand and provincial (state) authorities on the other, and in such a manner that neither sphere of authority is (entirely) free to trespass upon, override or remove the competence of the other. As noted above, the unitary legal state, in contrast, has a single centre of authority from which all other authority flows, in the British case the Queen-in-Parliament. Within political discourse, on the other hand, the conceptual opposite of the unitary conception(s) of the political order, is/are the myriad pluralist conception(s) of the political order. Pluralism for these purposes provides a broad umbrella covering both any explanatory thesis accounting for the political order in terms of a diversity of authorities and influences and any normative thesis advocating a diffusion of power between different groups, mechanisms or sites of authority.[3] The unitary conception of political authority, on the other hand, like its legal counterpart, identifies and/or advocates one dominant centre of political power.

The referential field of the political opposition between unitary and pluralist conceptions of order is clearly far more expansive than the referential field of the legal opposition between unitary and federalist approaches. Granted, the political opposition embraces within its terms

---

1 Strictly speaking, since the relevant literature sets up unitary and federal as conceptual opposites with mutually dependent meanings, logic precludes the search for non-unitary forms of order other than federal. However, if we are interested in constitutional forms which challenge unitary order in a manner or on a scale similar to federalism, then a broader picture begins to emerge. For example, an entrenched and justiciable charter of rights may pose a challenge to, and impose limits upon, the ultimate authority of any single complex of legislative and executive power, as in Ireland. Equally, a "diarchical" constitutional arrangement in which primary law-making powers are divided between the legislative and the executive, as in France, involves a challenge to unitary order, more broadly defined. Even strong versions of the separation of powers doctrine, as in the US, pose a challenge to unitary order, although in this case legislative competence is not directly challenged but balanced by the other organs and functions of government. Of course, if this broader, multi-faceted, notion of non-unitary order is developed, the UK constitution still falls within the unitary definition. Indeed, the top rule of parliamentary sovereignty necessarily rules out rights entrenchment, diarchical division of legislative authority or rigid separation of powers just as it rules out federalism, since all such arrangements presuppose rules of institutional design which are not within the control of Parliament. However, for the sake of argument, even if this more broadly exclusionary conception of unitary legal order is conceded, it does not weaken my case for the inherent flexibility of the unitary form. Rather, it simply shifts the emphasis to the second limb of my argument, developed in the text below, concerning the compatibility of a wide variety of visions and designs of pluralism, *politically* defined, with unitary legal arrangements.

2 See e.g. Brazier, "The Constitution of the United Kingdom" (1999) 58 CLJ 96 at 125–126; Barendt, *An Introduction to Constitutional Law*, Ch 3.

3 For an explicit opposition between unitary and pluralist political theory, see P P Craig, *Public Law and Democracy in the United Kingdom and the United States of America* (OUP, Oxford, 1990) Chs 1–6; on the varieties of pluralism, see also D Miller and M Walzer (eds), *Pluralism, Justice and Equality* (OUP, Oxford, 1995); R Bellamy, *Liberalism and Pluralism: Towards a Politics of Compromise* (Routledge, London, 1999).

the aspirations associated with a territorially-based cultural pluralism, or multi-culturalism. In turn, these aspirations map onto the kind of institutional pluralism that we associate with federalism and other forms of sub-state self-government with which we are concerned.[1] But this association with self-government and territorial identity politics by no means exhausts the scope of the unitary/pluralist opposition within wider political discourse. Paul Craig, for instance, identifies a rich variety of different socio-political constellations and normative projects or dispositions within and between the two political orders of the United States and the United Kingdom which might count as species of the genus pluralism.[2] In the United States, perspectives as divergent as Dahl's conception of countervailing group power[3] and Buchanan's public choice theory[4] register on the pluralist scale. The family of pluralisms in the United Kingdom is just as extended, and again a basic distinction lies between, on the one hand, those pluralisms which look to civil society and the framework of government itself for their diverse centres of authority, and on the other, those pluralisms which look to the operation of the market-place as an alternative form of ordering and interest representation.[5]

It should come as no surprise that pluralism within a wider political discourse is such a broad church. After all, the variables that pluralism is concerned with, namely the accommodation of a diversity of values and institutional forms within a polity, often operate at a point fairly removed from the foundations of any particular substantive political theory. Thus, as with the tradition of Fabianism, guild socialism and, more recently, "associative democracy",[6] institutionalised respect for a diversity and balance of interests and values may be predicated upon a basically redistributive and socialist ethic. Similarly, as already noted, pluralism may be consistent with a strong free market-orientation. In particular, much of the theory and practice of the New Right in the 1980s is about the reassertion of a kind of pluralism, as a backlash against, and direct challenge to, the perceived corporatist hegemony of the post-war years, with its emphasis upon the incorporation of hierarchical and non-competitive forms of interest representation into the framework of government.[7] Indeed, many of the new institutional forms and themes which we associate with the

---

1 Indeed, this link can be seen in the intellectual foundations of the US Constitution—the first federal constitution—where Thomas Madison in *The Federalist Papers* develops certain pluralist lines of thought to argue for the comprehensive framework of checks and balances, including the federal division of power, that we associate with the foundation settlement: see Craig, *Public Law and Democracy in the United Kingdom and the United States of America*, pp 57–58.

2 Craig, *Public Law and Democracy in the United Kingdom and the United States of America*, Chs 3–6.

3 R Dahl, *A Preface to Democratic Theory* (University of Chicago Press, Chicago, 1958).

4 J M Buchanan and G Tullock, *The Calculus of Consent; Logical Foundations of Constitutional Democracy* (MIT Press, Ann Arbor, 1962).

5 See Craig, *Public Law and Democracy in the United Kingdom and the United States of America*, Ch 5.

6 P Hirst, *Associative Democracy* (Polity, Cambridge, 1994).

7 See Craig, *Public Law and Democracy in the United Kingdom and the United States of America*, pp 153–157.

development of public law and public administration over the last 20 years are linked to this new market-based pluralism. The "hollowing out"[1] of the state through the transfer of functions outwards to private and other non-state agencies and the "new public management" which seeks to introduce private management techniques, disciplines and incentive structures are the twin poles of a strategy which aims both to transfer decision-making and functional authority from public bureaucracy to private enterprise and to reshape public bureaucracy in a manner which involves greater responsiveness to the consumer and greater internal competition over access to resources, the development of policy and the provisions of services. Privatisation, contracting-out, the development of Next Steps Agencies, the proliferation of Ombudsmen, the introduction of internal markets and new forms of public audit: these are all points on that new policy continuum.[2]

In other words, pluralism should be thought of not as a doctrine, but as Marquand suggests, as "a disposition, a mentality, an approach" consistent with a number of different doctrines, and, "like most approaches to politics ... a matter of feeling as well as of belief."[3] It follows that at the other side of the divide, unitary theories within political discourse, too, are internally diverse, cut across different substantive doctrines, and are as much a matter of disposition and feeling as of belief. Craig, again, points to Dicey's important contribution to the unitary theory of the state.[4] Dicey developed a theory of unitary, self-correcting democracy within which the dominant political authority of Parliament was justified through a bottom-up conception of representative democracy, the central legislative institution liable to electoral correction if it passed questionable laws. Dicey combined this somewhat naive commitment to Parliament as the paradigm of representative democracy with a conservative political outlook, in particular a fear of class legislation and a distaste for state welfarist intervention.[5] A unitary conception of the political order is also compatible with some conceptions of modern conservative thought. Those who are less apt to see the pluralist strain in the Thatcherite New Right programme, who are more inclined to view the renewed prominence of market allocation as against state distribution in terms of a pattern of deepening economic inequality rather than as a pluralist challenge to the state monolith, have preferred to label the type of statecraft it represents as

1   See R A W Rhodes, *Understanding Governance: Policy Networks, Governance, Reflexivity and Accountability* (Open University Press, Milton Keynes, 1997), esp. Ch 1.
2   See e g I Harden, *The Contracting State* (Open University Press, Milton Keynes, 1992); T Daintith, "The Techniques of Government" in Jowell and Oliver, *The Changing Constitution*, 3rd edn (OUP, Oxford, 1994) p 209; D Oliver, *Common Values and the Public-Private Divide* (Butterworths, London, 1999) Chs 1–2; P Birkinshaw, *Grievances, Remedies and the State* (2nd edn, Sweet & Maxwell, London 1994).
3   D Marquand, "Pluralism v Populism" *Prospect* 42, June 1999, 27 at 29.
4   Craig, *Public Law and Democracy in the United Kingdom and the United States of America*, Ch 2. See A V Dicey, *An Introduction to the Study of the Law of the Constitution* (10th edn, Macmillan, London, 1959).
5   See e.g. M Loughlin, *Public Law and Political Theory* (OUP, Oxford, 1992) Ch 7.

authoritarian individualism,[1] or even authoritarian populism.[2] On this view, a strong unitary state is required to preserve order in the face of social unrest and indiscipline and to guarantee liberty and property against individual jealousy and collectivist encroachment. At the other side of the ideological divide, however, those who champion a relatively unitary conception of the political order also include democratic collectivists,[3] committed to an inclusive and egalitarian socialist or social democratic vision.[4]

Clearly, therefore, the distinction within political discourse between unitary and pluralist conceptions of the state is porous, elusive and uneven. The relationship between the two is graduated rather than dichotomous, more-or-less rather than either-or. It is a matter of contested interpretation where some perspectives are situated on the continuum. And neither unitary nor pluralist discourses tracks the course of any substantive political doctrines. Instead, they both cut across the major doctrines.

This helps to explain why the unitary conception of the state within legal discourse can be so accommodating towards such a diversity of political discourses. The unitary legal conception, based upon the doctrine of parliamentary sovereignty, is *formal* rather than *substantive*, and so does not imply any particular set of reasons why Parliament should be said to be sovereign.[5] A wide range of political discourses can sustain and be sustained by the doctrine of parliamentary sovereignty. Many members of the ecumenical church of political pluralism, their only common credential that they preach some degree of diversity of institutions and authorities— political, civic or economic—are thus not incompatible with a legal doctrine whose only imperative is the vesting of indivisible authority in a particular agency *in the final analysis*.

Neither is this a recent development. It is not a case of new models of political pluralism wearing the old-fashioned and ill-fitting clothes of parliamentary sovereignty. Constitutionalist political discourse in Britain has always been a "palimpsest of sometimes discordant myths, understandings and expectations, reflecting the changing values of succeeding generations".[6] One enduring faultline has been the collision between unitary and pluralist political theories, vying for ascendancy in providing the better interpretation, the more attractive ideological foundations of our constitution. As we saw, one canonical figure in our constitutional heritage, Dicey, articulated a unitary conception of our constitution. Another equally canonical but even earlier figure, Blackstone, set out a very different justificatory theory which focused on the contemporary

---

1 D Marquand, *The New Reckoning: Capitalism, States and Citizens* (Polity, Cambridge, 1997, Ch 10).
2 S Hall and M Jacques (eds), *The Politics of Thatcherism* (Lawrence & Wishart, London, 1983).
3 Marquand, *The New Reckoning: Capitalism, States and Citizens*.
4 See, e.g. K D Ewing "Human Rights, Social Democracy and Constitutional Reform", in C Gearty and A Tomkins (eds) *Understanding Human Rights* (Mansell, London, 1996) p 40.
5 See P P Craig, "Sovereignty of the United Kingdom Parliament after *Factortame*" (1991) *Yearbook of European Law* 221 at 234.
6 Marquand, "Pluralism v Populism", at 27.

eighteenth-century notion of the balanced constitution and which contained clear pluralist elements—parliamentary sovereignty on this view supplying a pluralist institutional bulwark against the absolutist pretensions of the executive monarch.[1]

So there is only the loosest of coupling between a unitary political discourse and the unitary legal theory of the state. There is patently a lack of correspondence in the strong sense of a unitary approach providing the necessary and exclusive grounding in political theory for the unitary legal conception. Even once the lack of strict correspondence is conceded, it is not even empirically true that the best historical justifications for the unitary legal order have been always or preponderantly unitary political justifications. Such a state of affairs would have left a highly skewed legacy of constitutional doctrine sustained by a unitary orthodoxy. But in some of the most revealing discursive battlefields of our constitution that has not been the case. For example, in recent years, the unitarian position that judicial review of administrative action is best justified by reference to interpretation of the will of the sovereign Parliament and the linked doctrine of *ultra vires* has been strongly resisted by those who would seek deeper justifications in our constitutional heritage for holding the executive branch to account.[2] Equally, against the prevailing orthodoxy, a renewed common law constitutionalism has recently sought to ground the protection of human rights in something more substantial and less fickle than the intention of the legislature.[3]

What is true of these examples, both of which involve arguments primarily within the judicial sphere and thus tied closely to sources and restricted to forms of reasoning which tend to stress continuity and coherence—that is to say, to a method which would tend to reinforce whatever holistic qualities the constitution might possess—is even more emphatically true of broader constitutional topics where the primary constitutional actors are political or administrative and so less tied to narrow concerns of jurisprudential integrity. Most pertinently, this wider category clearly includes most of the spheres of action and mechanisms of constitutional practice (e.g. the election of this (socialist) or that (conservative) government; the establishment and monitoring of this or that scheme of administrative or functional devolution; the setting of this or that mechanism for (re)distributing wealth[4] or for acknowledging regional needs in

---

1 See Craig, "Sovereignty of the United Kingdom Parliament after *Factortame*" at 234–237.

2 See e.g. P P Craig, "Competing Models of Judicial Review" [1999] PL 448; and "*Ultra Vires* and the Foundations of Judicial Review (1998) 57 CLJ 63; J Jowell, "Of Vires and Vacuums: The Constitutional Context of Judicial Review" [1999] PL 448; C Forsyth, "Of Fig Leaves and Fairy Tales: The *Ultra Vires* Doctrine, The Sovereignty of Parliament and Judicial Review" (1996) 55 CLJ 122; M Elliot, "The Demise of Parliamentary Sovereignty? The Implications for Justifying Judicial Review" (1999) 115 LQR 119; and "The *Ultra Vires* Doctrine in a Constitutional Setting: Still the Central Principle of Administrative Law" (1999) 58 CLJ 129; D Oliver, "Is the *Ultra Vires* Rule the Basis of Judicial Review?" [1987] PL 543.

3 For a balanced assessment of the emergence of this new jurisprudence in and beyond the courts, see M Hunt, *Using Human Rights Law in English Courts* (Hart, Oxford, 1997).

4 On the flexible use of the Barnett formula for allocating public expenditure to Scotland, see I McLean, "Yes, Yes! Begone With Scotland!" (1997) *New Statesman*, 22 August, 18.

economic management or investment[1]) through which many of the substantively political, administrative and economic aspirations and options associated with various intermediate positions along the spectrum of self-government can be accommodated. In other words, there is simply no structural force operating within the British constitutional framework which would exclude or strongly prejudice those parts of a broader pluralist menu that are conducive to various intermediate forms of self-government or that reflect the ambitions of those who pursue these forms of self-government.

ACCOMMODATING TERRITORIAL DIVERSITY

If many pluralist themes—including those invoked in support of broader visions of national or regional self-government—can be reconciled with the formal institutional constraints of parliamentary sovereignty, this is not true of federalism. Yet, federalism is incompatible with a unitary legal conception of the state on technical grounds rather than substantive grounds. It is simply not possible to generate the type of entrenched institutional pluralism necessary for federalism on the basis of the formal concept of the indivisible sovereignty of Parliament. That legal incompatibility does not, however, mean that federalism has been a repugnant idea within the political discourse of constitutionalism which has provided the long-term cultural accompaniment to the legally unitary British state. Federal union rather than incorporating union, indeed, was the preferred option of the Scottish negotiators prior to the Treaty of Union of 1707, although the lack of a historical prototype and the weakness of the Scottish leadership ultimately precluded such a solution.[2] Federalism also figured prominently as a candidate solution to the problem of accommodating Irish demands for autonomy in the nineteenth century, advocated at different times by both Home Rule and Unionist interests.[3] Moreover, British politicians, civil servants, academics and interest groups have been active in promoting federalist ideas in contexts other than the internal structure of the United Kingdom, including the integrity of the British empire, the organisation of the international order, the internal structure of decolonised states, and, more recently, Britain's relationship to Europe.[4]

---

1   It is instructive in this regard that one of the subjects of the new Constitutional Concordats dealing with those aspects of the devolved settlements which are nor easily reducible to permanent legislation is inward investment; see *Memorandum of Understanding and supplementary agreements*, Cm 4444, October 1999, Concordat on Financial Assistance.

2   See e.g. N MacCormick, *Questioning Sovereignty: Law, State and Practical Reason* (OUP, Oxford, 1999), pp 55–60; A A Olowofoyeku, "Decentralising the UK: The Federal Argument" (1999) 3 *ELR* 57 at 66; J Kendle, *Federal Britain: A History* (Routledge, London, 1997) Ch 1.

3   Principally by Isaac Butt on the Home Rule side in the 1870s and by Joseph Chamberlain on the Unionist side in 1886. See Olowofoyeku, "Decentralising the UK: The Federal Argument", at 66.

4   See generally, Kendle, *Federal Britain: A History*.

None of this gainsays the fact that the legal sovereignty of Parliament continues to constitute a fundamental impediment to the institutional design of federalism within the present UK constitutional order. However, matching the endurance of an active political discourse concerning federalism is the resilience of the type of substantive political debate about identity, recognition and mutual accommodation of diverse communities which typically underpins federalism.[1] These arguments, and the territorially-rooted cultural pluralism they embody, are in principle no more abhorrent to parliamentary sovereignty than the other types of pluralisms we have considered. This is important, since it underpins the argument to follow that the exclusion of federalism from a unitary framework implies nothing about the acceptability of other methods of accommodating territorial diversity.

We can formulate two propositions which seek to demonstrate that, even in the context of the present escalation of demands for constitutional recognition of regional and national identity within the United Kingdom, the unitary conception of the constitution remains a flexible instrument to accommodate diversity. As with our earlier discussion of other types of pluralism, the distinction between legal and political discourses on the unitary constitution is axiomatic.

In the first place, if federalism is viewed within a broader political discourse it appears as a graduated state of affairs rather than, as in the legal discourse, one which is basically[2] conceived in either/or terms. Viewed as a graduated affair, there are many positions which contain federalist elements, sometimes labelled "quasi-federal".[3] Yet, viewed in legal terms, these quasi-federal positions, not being federal in the classical sense, are perfectly compatible with the unitary constitution. That is to say, although within political discourse we can recognise a range of positions which are proximate to—bear a family resemblance to—classical federalism, they are not, in legal terms, contaminated by that proximity.

Consider the new devolved assemblies designed for Scotland itself, and also for Northern Ireland,[4] separately and, *a fortiori*, in combination, the most ambitiously conceived in this or any previous constitutional reform initiative in the United Kingdom. On the one hand, there remains clear water between these schemes and a legal definition of federalism. Unlike a

---

1 The development of territorially and otherwise-defined cultural identity politics, often couched in terms of claims for constitutional recognition, is of course a world-wide phenomenon—one which has attracted a voluminous literature. See e.g. W Kymlicka, *Multicultural Citizenship* (OUP, Oxford, 1995); D Miller, *On Nationality* (OUP, Oxford, 1995); J Tully, *Strange Multiplicity: Constitutionalism in an Age of Diversity* (CUP, Cambridge, 1995).

2 Although even K C Wheare, whose discussion was highly influential within legal academic circles, kept the term quasi-federal for borderline cases: *Modern Constitutions*, 2nd edn (OUP, Oxford, 1966), p 20.

3 See e.g. V Bogdanor, *Devolution in the United Kingdom* (OUP, Oxford, 1999), Ch 8; R Hazell, "Reinventing the Constitution: Can the State Survive?" [1999] PL 84; Wheare, *Modern Constitutions*, p 20.

4 For comparative analysis, see B Hadfield, "The Nature of Devolution in Scotland and Northern Ireland: Key Issues of Responsibility and Control" (1999) 3 *ELR* 3; A J Ward, "Devolution: Labour's Strange Constitutional Design" in J Jowell and D Oliver (eds), *The Changing Constitution*, 4th edn, (Oxford University Press, Oxford, 2000) p 111.

properly federal arrangement, there is no attempt to entrench the status of either devolved body against the abolitionist instincts of a future Westminster Parliament, although in Northern Ireland there is an attempt to entrench—at least politically if not legally—the answer to the wider question of statehood by reference to a referendum procedure.[1] Equally, there is no attempt to prevent the Westminster Parliament encroaching on the devolved sphere of authority in either case; on the contrary, the sovereign authority of Westminster to legislate even in transferred matters is explicitly preserved.[2] Nor is there any attempt to establish a new constitutional court as federal umpire, charged with policing the jurisdictional boundaries of the settlement on all sides. Instead, we have a very old court—the Judicial Committee of the Privy Council—monitoring the compliance of the devolved but not the central body.[3]

On the other hand, in broader political terms these new settlements are significantly closer to the federalist end of the continuum than their predecessors in the Northern Ireland Act 1920 and the abortive Scotland Act 1978. In both new settlements the transferred powers are defined residually rather than enumerated[4] or subject to a general limitation,[5] a device used in many federal arrangements to enhance the flexibility of the local jurisdiction. Again unlike their predecessors, neither settlement allows the centre any *general* power of veto over local legislation,[6] which limitation on central power is an additional feature of federal balance. In another echo of federal arrangements, the Scottish settlement, though not the Irish, allows a modest tax-varying power to the devolved executive and Parliament.[7] Finally, and returning to the question of entrenchment, it is noteworthy that the absence of legally watertight entrenchment of either settlement is not defended as a political insurance policy for the centre, as a longstop power of unilateral rejection of the devolved arrangements. Clearly, that remains legally possible, but in both settlements the framer's intent[8] was to link the new institutions to the consent or otherwise of the constituencies affected, a provision made explicit in the more complex transnational circumstances

---

1   Northern Ireland Act 1998, s 1 and Sch 1.
2   Northern Ireland Act 1998, s 5(6); Scotland Act 1998, s 28(7).
3   Northern Ireland Act 1998, ss 11, 79 and Sch 10; Scotland Act 1998, ss 33, 98 and Sch 6. Nevertheless, the Court of Session remains well placed under the 1998 Act to influence the general constitutional jurisprudence of the new order. On its early case law under the Act, see S Tierney, "Constitutionalising the Role of the Judge: Scotland and the New Order" (2001) 5 ELR 49.
4   As they were under the Scotland Act 1978, s 63 and Sch 10; see now Scotland Act 1998, ss 28–29.
5   As they were under the "peace, order and good government" provision of the Government of Ireland Act 1920, s 4(1); see now Northern Ireland Act 1998, ss 5–6.
6   Although the specific powers of veto of the devolved legislature and executive retained by central Government are greater under the Northern Irish scheme than the Scottish scheme; compare Northern Ireland Act 1998, ss 10, 14 and 25, with Scotland Act 1998, ss 35–58. Nevertheless, according to one set of commentators, even the provisions of the Scotland Act remain sufficiently wide to allow their critics "to evoke ... the spectre of the Secretary of State as Governor General"; C M G Himsworth and C R Munro, *Scotland Act 1998*, Current Law Statutes, 46/35.
7   Scotland Act 1998, ss 73–80.
8   Which, of course, does not necessarily bind a future Parliament of the UK.

of the Belfast Agreement and the Northern Ireland Act 1998,[1] and expressed as a background assumption in the context of the Scotland Act 1998.[2] The key point is that the British state has come closer than ever before to conceding that its retention of legislative omnicompetence in the context of a devolution process is a matter of legal form rather than political substance. Ritual deference continues to be paid to the legal theory of the unitary state, but the developing culture of negotiation and balanced settlement reflects, or at least portends, a rather different political understanding.

A second proposition which underpins the accommodating nature of the unitary legal conception relates to its exclusive concern with the federal alternative. The unitary legal conception does not recognise forms of institutional accommodation of territorial difference which may be just as pronounced as federalism, if not more so, but which cannot be adequately captured within a strict unitary/federal opposition; and in failing to recognise these different forms the unitary legal conception refrains from ruling them out. In particular, the unitary conception does not adequately capture the linked ideas of the "union state"[3] and of "asymmetrical government."[4] The union state is one, such as the United Kingdom, Canada or Spain, in which parts of the territory have been incorporated by agreement, which agreement allows variation in governmental arrangements as they affect the incorporated territory or territories. The union treaties with Scotland and Ireland in 1707 and 1800 are clear examples of these foundation agreements.[5] The constitutional character of the union state, however, cannot simply be read off from its foundation parchments. Instead, they provide points of departure for continuous renegotiation or variation in the light of changing social, economic and political circumstances. The union state, therefore, provides a key historical pathway towards a more general model of asymmetrical government, in which a heterogeneity of governance arrangements between regions becomes a normal and persistent feature of a state. Clearly, the present rolling programme of devolution, with distinctive blueprints and timetables of reforms for different parts of the territory, fits the model of enduring and dynamic asymmetry. Seen in that light, indeed, the muddied waters over the future of regional government in England—whether Regional Chambers, Regional Assemblies or city mayors—represent the

---

1 Northern Ireland Act 1998, s 1.
2 For the development of the idea of consent in the context of the debate about entrenchment within the Scottish Constitutional Convention and in the early days of the New Labour administration, see J McFadden and W Bain (eds) "Strategies for the Future: A Lasting Parliament for Scotland?" in T St J Bates (ed) *Devolution to Scotland: The Legal Aspects* (T & T Clark, Edinburgh, 1997).
3 S Rokkan and D Urwin, "Introduction: Centres and Peripheries in Western Europe" in S Rokkan and D Urwin (eds) *The Politics of Territorial Identity: Studies in European Regionalism* (Sage, London, 1982) p 11.
4 M Keating, "What's Wrong with Asymmetrical Government?" in H Elcock and M Keating (eds) *Remaking the Union: Devolution and British Politics in the 1990s* (Frank Cass, London, 1998) p 195.
5 Although the former contained far more guarantees of enduring institutional distinctiveness than the latter.

unfolding of a new, but essentially continuous chapter, in a long and familiar constitutional narrative.[1]

In certain respects, then, particularly in its eschewal of the idea of a uniform and symmetrical division of powers, the union model may be even more accommodating of diversity—of plurality—than the federal model. But the point is precisely not to attempt to place the union/asymmetrical model on the same scale as unitary and federal models. That is to make a category mistake. The unitary/federal opposition within a specialist legal discourse recognises nothing beyond that dichotomy. Ideas of the union state and asymmetrical government are more appropriate to a broader political discourse, where positions are more graduated and less one-dimensional. The union state is not an alternative to the unitary or federal state, but merely the product of a different way of categorising and measuring institutional homogeneity or diversity within states. So union states can, in a narrower legal sense, be *either* unitary states, as in the United Kingdom, or federal states, as in Canada. Their character is not adequately captured by either legal category, and so, as in the domestic example, they may both be compatible with the formal terms of the unitary state but institutionalise elements of diversity more profound than are found in many federal states.

THE UNITARY STATE AND BEYOND

In this final section I depart from the internal perspective and look at the character and durability of the unitary state from an external perspective. At the end of a century in which states, as the primary political actors on the international stage since the Treaty of Westphalia of 1648, gathered and exercised unprecedented levels of power, a burgeoning literature charts the emergence of new forms of power and authority beyond the state and challenging the long-standing political hegemony of the state.[2] Within public law,[3] the new emphasis is on the development of multiple sites of authority set beyond yet operating alongside the "law-state",[4] whose historical claims to internal and external sovereignty have been articulated through constitutional law and international law respectively. The new approach seeks to make sense of the idea of "constitutionalized" power beyond the state—where constitutional power has traditionally nested—

---

1 R Hazell, "Reinventing the Constitution: Can the State Survive?" [1999] PL 84 at 90–92; "Loose Ends" *Prospect* 56, October 2000. See also Regional Development Agencies Act 1998; Greater London Authority Referendum Act 1998; Greater London Authority Act 1999; Local Government Act 2000.
2 This literature, which some attempt to unite around the portmanteau theme of "globalization", refers to a complex mix of legal, political, cultural, economic and technological processes, with different disciplines centring different strands. For an overview, see D Held, A McGrew, D Goldblatt and J Perraton (eds), *Global Transformations* (Polity, Cambridge, 1999).
3 See esp. N MacCormick, *Questioning Sovereignty: Law, State and Practical Reason* (OUP, Oxford, 1999); J H H Weiler, *The Constitution of Europe* (CUP, Cambridge, 1999).
4 MacCormick, *Questioning Sovereignty: Law, State and Practical Reason*, p 9.

and also to examine the relationship between the various overlapping authoritative sites or putatively authoritative sites—national and "post-national"[1]—within this new multi-dimensional, or plural, legal space.

In briefly examining the implications of these developments for the relationship between Scottish self-government and unitary conception of the UK state, I invoke a *meta*constitutional framework of analysis I have developed elsewhere.[2] The prefix "meta" is chosen because it stands in relation to the activity denoted by the concept prefixed as "a higher science of the same nature but dealing with ulterior problems."[3] Cosmopolitan metaconstitutionalism refers to a range of authoritative legal discourses emerging as part of the post-Westphalian order, which have the same general object of reference as state constitutional law—namely, the framework of public authority—but which, unlike the latter, do not look to the state as their fundamental source of validity. Rather, metaconstitutional discourse claims a separate and often a higher normative authority than state law, even though this tends in turn to be challenged by the state through its traditional constitutional discourse and representations of sovereignty.[4] Metaconstitutional discourse, even though its *historical* and institutional origins lie in the decisions and actions of sovereign states, purports to authorise, instruct, influence, supplement or supplant state law or state public authorities, and in so doing conceives of its own *contemporary* authority as original and irreducible.

There are a variety of different but interrelated forms of metaconstitutional discourse operating at different levels and occupying different sites, some of which are relevant to the present inquiry.[5] As intimated earlier, my contention is that the existence of such sites makes the perseverance of the unitary state in the face of the demand for Scottish self-government more rather than less likely, on both strategic and normative grounds. We can deal with the strategic grounds by examining the most basic form of metaconstitutionalism, the one least abstracted from the constitutional state.

This first type of metaconstitutionalism seeks to reshape the traditional intra-constitutional law sphere of the relations between different groups within the state—whether national, ethnic, territorial, religious, linguistic or functional—in a manner which goes beyond those forms of legal "identity politics",[6] such as claims to mutual respect, to multicultural citizenship

---

1 D M Curtin, *Postnational Democracy* (Universiteit Utrecht, 1997); J Shaw, "Postnational Constitutionalism in the European Union" (1999) 6 *Journal of European Public Policy* 579; D Chalmers, "Postnationalism and the Quest for Constitutional Substitutes" (2000) 27 *Journal of Law and Society* 178.

2 See N Walker, "Flexibility within a Metaconstitutional Frame: reflections on the future of legal authority in Europe" in G de Burca and J Scott *Constitutional Change in the EU; From Uniformity to Flexibility* (Hart, Oxford, 2000), p 9. See also N Walker, "Sovereignty and Differentiated Integration in the European Union" (1998) 4 *European Law Journal* 355.

3 *The Shorter Oxford English Dictionary.*

4 On the centrality of the idea of sovereignty to the representation of a polity *qua* polity, see H Lindahl, "The Purposiveness of Law: Two Concepts of Representation in the European Union" (1998) 17 *Law and Philosophy* 481.

5 For a fuller development, see Walker, "Flexibility within a Metaconstitutional Frame", pp 17–21.

6 See references at note 1 on page 109 above.

or, most relevantly to us, to the distinct political institutions we associate with federalism or other forms of devolved (symmetrical or asymmetrical) government, which can be accommodated within the existing framework of state authority. Instead, it proceeds to question and challenge the constitutional integrity of the state itself through secessionist or quasi-secessionist claims. For the most part this is necessarily a *counterfactual* legal discourse. Unlike the forms of metaconstitutionalism considered below it is not anchored within an institutional site or sites which can make a plausible current claim to possess fundamental law-making authority. On the other hand, as explored below, this form of metaconstitutionalism may be sustained and supported through its relationship to these other, more state-removed metaconstitutional sites which *do* possess plausible claims to fundamental legal authority. Yet, as long as the integrity and internal distribution of authority of the state which it challenges remains intact, then, secessionist or quasi-secessionist discourse clearly can be no more than aspirational. That does not mean, however, that it is merely a form of constitutional law-in-waiting. It is *meta*constitutional in the sense that while its ultimate purpose may be the creation of a new state, and thus a new constitutional order, the process by which the transformation is sought addresses matters of fundamental political authority through arguments—historical, ethical or pragmatic[1]—of sufficient depth and breadth to pose a challenge to the *general* claim of constitutional law to ultimate authority.

This type of counterfactual metaconstitutionalism also has an indirect impact upon existing state constitutional law. In the moulding of primary constitutional discourse, political prudence may demand or dialogic openness may encourage the taking into account of secessionist or quasi-secessionist discourse, often with consequences which escape the intentions of those who make the accommodation. In the current climate, British constitution-builders do so in the knowledge that institutions to which they have recently applied their official constitutional *imprimatur*, such as devolved assemblies and local referenda, may have a meaning and a role within alternative metaconstitutional discourses. So, the new Scottish Parliament is on one view the cement of the Union, on another a stepping-stone to independence.[2] The referendum which preceded was on one view a healthy exercise in local democracy within an increasingly "federalist" constitutional pattern, on another a prefigurative assertion of the popular sovereignty of the Scottish people. Clearly, too, the new institutions created under the Belfast Agreement and the Northern Ireland Act, and the procedures by which these are ratified and legitimated, have

---

1 See, for example, the rich mix of arguments used on behalf of the secessionist case in the Quebec Secession Reference; *Reference by the Governor of Canada pursuant to s 53 of the Supreme Court Act, concerning the secession of Quebec from Canada* [1998] 2 SCR 217. See also M D Walters, "Nationalism and the Pathology of Legal Systems: Considering the *Quebec Secession Reference* and its Lessons for the United Kingdom" (1999) 62 MLR 370.

2 For a stimulating account of the symbolic constitutional politics of devolution, including the important "constitutive" (p 273) role of the new Scottish Parliament, see T Nairn, *After Britain: New Labour and the Return of Scotland* (Granta, London, 2000).

different and contested meanings between unionist and nationalist communities.[1]

Strategically, then, this type of metaconstitutionalism provides the context for a kind of constitutional shadow-boxing, a bargaining in the shade of the possibility of a radical constitutional alternative. Critically, what this strategic context also does is militate against a fundamental constitutional resettlement of the existing state of the type required to move beyond the unitary model. Just as the current debate on whether the European Union needs, deserves or is likely to receive a constitutional baptism in the form of its own new model constitution cannot sensibly be joined without acknowledging that for some such a move would credit the European Union with a legitimacy as an independent polity that they are not prepared to concede, so an appreciation of similar sentiments of "constitutional denial"[2] should inform consideration of the prospect of a new constitutional order for the United Kingdom. As Brazier concludes, it is likely to "be those who champion local rights most strongly who would oppose a federal structure for the United Kingdom the most vigorously".[3] Strong nationalists are bound to be wary of a process which would so "freeze" and endorse an arrangement to preserve the integrity of the state whose very legitimacy they challenge.

Moving on to the normative considerations for treating multi-dimensionality as supportive of a unitary conception of the state, we should recognise that there are two opposite strands to this, and that together they tend to squeeze out the option of a federal arrangement at the UK level as an expression of national self-government . On the one hand, multi-dimensionality can be seen as a counterweight to excessively unitarian elements within the constitutional order, as a way of acknowledging, making concessions to and ultimately containing or absorbing fragmentary pressures and separatist aspirations. On the other hand, the existence of other metaconstitutional sites may provide a more supportive and attractive context, and so a significant mobilising force, for movements for constitutional independence, thus by comparison making the middle option of accommodation within a more diversified federal polity less attractive.

This normative point is vividly exemplified as we move to higher metaconstitutional sites.[4] A second type of metaconstitutional discourse seeks

---

1 See *Agreement reached in the Multi-Party Negotiations*, Cm 3883, (HMSO, London, 1998); B O'Leary, *The British-Irish Agreement: Power-Sharing Plus*, (Constitution Unit, London, 1998); B Hadfield, "The Belfast Agreement, Sovereignty and the State of the Union" [1998] PL 599; D O'Donnell, "Constitutional Background to and Aspects of the Good Friday Agreement—A Republic of Ireland Perspective (1999) 50 NILQ 76.

2 N Walker, "European Constitutionalism and European Integration" [1996] PL 266 at 278.

3 R Brazier, "The Constitution of the United Kingdom" (1999) 58 CLJ 96 at 127.

4 It can, however, also be seen at work at the first level of metaconstitutional authority. Thus, one of the consequences of constitutional shadow-boxing in the Irish context is the acknowledgement in s 1 of the Northern Ireland Act that if a majority in a referendum vote that the North should cease to be part of the UK and instead form part of a United Ireland, such a wish will be respected and acted upon by the British Government. In other words, it raises "a statutory doubt" (R Brazier, "The Constitution of the United Kingdom" at 113) about the continuance of the union between Great Britain and Northern Ireland, one that provides a beacon of hope to nationalists.

to shape and instruct the traditional intra-state constitutional law sphere of the basic rights and duties of the individual *vis-à-vis* the state. The paradigm case here is "international" human rights law.[1] Mainly through Treaty law promulgated at both regional and local level, but backed by peremptory norms of international law (*ius cogens*) and the general framework of international customary law, this area of law expanded exponentially in the wake of the Second World War. It is a movement which has challenged the premise of untrammelled state sovereignty preventing the traditional framework of international law from addressing individuals as well as states themselves as the subjects, rather than the mere objects, of its legal rules. As well as the development of a substantive state-transcendent human rights jurisprudence,[2] this form of metaconstitutionalism has been increasingly underscored by a constellation of non-state courts and tribunals within which such rights may be vindicated, including most prominently the European Court of Human Rights under the auspices of the Council of Europe. It is instructive in this regard that both Irish and Scottish devolution settlements presume a central role for the European Convention and its jurisprudence, effectively entrenching its provisions against local repeal or amendment.[3] In the context of Scottish self-government, this entrenchment may be something of a double-edged sword. For some, its imposition by a British state unprepared, under the Human Rights Act 1998, to bind its own Parliament in the strict sense that it binds its devolved legislatures,[4] it smacks of residual imperialist arrogance—not to say hypocrisy.[5] For others, however—indeed for some of the same constituency viewing entrenchment through a different lens—it is a sign of constitutional maturity, of the Scottish polity (absence of sovereignty

---

1 See e.g. H J Steiner and P Alston, *International Human Rights in Context; Law, Politics, Morals* (OUP, Oxford, 1996).

2 This jurisprudence is increasingly influential in the national courts even of those states, such as the UK, which retain a basically dualist approach to international law, and so remain reluctant to endorse international law as domestic law without domestic legislative instruction. A landmark decision in this regard is *R v Bow Street Metropolitan Stipendiary Magistrate, ex parte Pinochet Ugarte (Amnesty International intervening) (No 3)* [1999] 2 WLR 827, in which the House of Lords, drawing upon both domestic law and customary international law, held that a former head of state enjoys no immunity in extradition or criminal proceedings brought in the UK in respect of the international crime of torture; see H Fox, "The Pinochet Case No 3" (1999) 48 ICLQ 687.

3 Scotland Act 1998, ss 29(1)(d), 57 and Sch 4, para 2(f); Northern Ireland Act, ss 6(2)(c), 7(1)(b) and 24(1)(a). See also the establishment of a Northern Ireland Human Rights Commission under ss 68–72. In the Irish context, the establishment of a human rights regime under a European umbrella is particularly relevant to the question of the acceptability of the two extremes of the unitary *status quo ante* or a new all-Ireland state. That is so because the recognition of the ECHR and the introduction of a Human Rights Commission are an integral part of a strategy of "double protection" in which both unionists and nationalists are guaranteed a minimum floor of citizenship rights *regardless* of who holds the sovereign power in the North. See R Hazell and B O'Leary, "A Rolling Programme of Devolution: Slippery Slope or Safeguard of the Union?" in R Hazell (ed) *Constitutional Futures: A History of the Next Ten Years* (OUP, Oxford, 1999), p 30.

4 A Lester, "Human Rights and the British Constitution," in J Jowell and D Oliver (eds) *The Changing Constitution* 4th edn (OUP, Oxford, 2000) p 89.

5 See e.g. C M G Himsworth, "Rights Against Devolution" in T Campbell, K Ewing and A Tomkins (eds) *Sceptical Approaches to Entrenched Human Rights* (OUP, Oxford, 2001, forthcoming).

notwithstanding) acquiring some of the familiar, but hitherto unavailable, institutional wherewithal of responsible self-government.

A third type of metaconstitutional discourse shapes relations between states in ways which supplement and modify the internal constitutional structure of those states. Again, the current metaconstitutional conversation between Britain and Ireland provides a good example. The Belfast Agreement provides for a new permanent institutional complex embracing both East-West structures (British-Irish Council and British-Irish Intergovernmental Conference)[1] and a North-South Ministerial Council[2] as a means to endorse and to stabilise an element of power-sharing between the two states. This new edifice provides an additional point of constitutional reference, an intermediate site of contestation, interest representation and identity formation to dilute the significance of the sovereign state. In the Scottish context, there are connected developments—albeit without the trans-state complexity—which again hint at structural mediation between the sovereign centre and Scottish institutions. The British-Irish Council—more evocatively dubbed "the Council of the Isles"—also includes representatives from the other devolved areas, and so was heralded by some as a new and advanced form of quasi-federal institution for the United Kingdom *as a whole*. Even if the restriction of its jurisdiction to matters with an Irish dimension rather belies that particular claim,[3] the somewhat belated creation of a cross-executive Joint Ministerial Committee on Devolution[4] supplies a more promising candidate for innovative institutional design of this sort.

Finally, this type of arrangement shades into a fourth type of metaconstitutional authority, which in addressing relations between states develops an institutional structure with sufficient depth and scope of authority to constitute a non-state polity. Of course, the extent to which an institutional structure constitutes a separate polity is a matter of degree. Clearly the Good Friday structures, for now at least, fall short, but the GATT/WTO structure and the North American Free Trade Association, to take but two examples, are less clear-cut cases, as also are some of the regional international organisations.[5] At the other end of the spectrum, and most relevant to our inquiry, is the supranational legal framework of the European Union. Originally conceived of as a means to regulate certain fundamental economic relations between states and designed with the orthodox tools of international law, the European Union, as is well-known,[6] gradually developed its own claim to sovereign authority within

---

1 Cm 3883, *Strand Three.*

2 Cm 3883, *Strand Two.*

3 R Hazell, "Reinventing the Constitution: Can the State Survive?" [1999] PL 84 at 90. The Council also includes representation from the Channel Islands and the Isle of Man.

4 See Hazell, "Reinventing the Constitution: Can the State Survive?". See also *Memorandum of Understanding and supplementary agreements*, Cm 4444, October 1999, Concordat on Financial Assistance.

5 See B Laffan, *Integration and Co-operation in Europe* (Routledge, London, 1992). See also N Walker, "The EU and the WTO: Constitutionalism in a New Key" in G de Burca and J Scott (eds), *The EU and the WTO: Legal and Constitutional Aspects* (Hart, Oxford, 2001).

6 See e.g. S Weatherill and P Beaumont, *EU Law* (3rd edn, Penguin, London, 1999) Ch 12.

a limited sphere. Indeed, as the European Union has attracted a complexity of institutional structure and a range of legal competences which begins to rival those of the state, then it has come to represent a particularly developed form of metaconstitutional law. It provides a crucial additional dimension in legal identity formation which may significantly modify the implications of membership of any particular state polity.[1] Of course, it is a question of great complexity and controversy whether and to what extent large states, small states and devolved or federalised parts of states may be advantaged by the existence of the supranational theatre of the European Union. In particular, as Scottish devolution settles there is a vigorous debate between nationalists and pro-European unionists (increasingly focusing upon the authorship and status of those post-devolution constitutional innovations, namely "constitutional concordats",[2] which address, *inter alia*, relations between central and devolved government in the treatment of EU matters, and also upon the specific institutional mechanism—the aforementioned Joint Ministerial Committee on Devolution—and substantive norms through which these relations are in fact addressed) as to whether Scotland can have greater influence as a small but autonomous state or as a modest and sometimes unheard voice within a larger state.[3] The instant point is not to answer that question, but to acknowledge that it produces alternative institutional projections, alternative ways of imagining and modifying the sense of political community provided by the unitary state. For those who make these projections, the unitary state—British *or* Scottish, (or, indeed, Irish, English or Welsh) takes its place as an integral part of the overall picture, but it no longer frames the picture.

CONCLUSION

None of what I have said in this article is intended to eulogise the unitary constitution, or to apologise for the *dirigiste* political culture and authoritarian political projects which have often flourished under its name, strong traces of which remain as a telling counterweight to the ostensibly radical constitutional agenda and rhetoric of New Labour.[4] If I have shown that the unitary constitution of the United Kingdom is a more flexible affair than is often imagined in the context of Scottish self-government and other

---

1 Consider, for example, the symbolic impact of the SNP's adoption of the "Independence in Europe" slogan at its 1988 annual conference: see T Devine, *The Scottish Nation: 1700–2000* (Penguin, London, 1999), p 608.

2 See *Memorandum of Understanding and supplementary agreements*, Cm 4444, October 1999, Concordat on Financial Assistance. See also R Rawlings, "Concordats of the Constitution" (2000) 116 LQR 257.

3 See G Clark, "Scottish Devolution and the European Union" [1999] PL 504; M Happold, "Independence: In or Out of Europe? An Independent Scotland and the European Union" (2000) 49 ICLQ 15; C Jeffery, "Sub-National Mobilisation and European Integration: Does it Make any Difference?" (2000) 38 *Journal of Common Market Studies* 1.

4 In particular, on the resilience of the "Myth of British Greatness" and its close relationship with consitutional conservatism, see T Nairn, "Mario and the Magician" (2001) 9 *New Left Review* 5.

pluralist visions, and that the advent of multi-dimensionality has made it simultaneously more difficult to transform but less central to the overall public law framework, these are not reasons for complacency. Equally, there should be no room for complacency at the other side of the divide, if the argument for sovereign autonomy wins the day and beckons a new state co-extensive with the Scottish nation—but one most likely still unitary in a strict legal sense. Rather, the insufficiently acknowledged normative openness of the unitary constitution in the British tradition coupled with its resilience make it all the more important that we attend to the task of developing a more appropriate and fuller normative language for that unitary constitution or its successors.[1] Against this backdrop, the acknowledgement of the flexibility and durability of the unitary state and of its gradual de-centring within a wider cosmopolitan configuration of public law is but a modest staging-post in the journey towards local constitutional self-understanding.

---

1 A task already taken up in recent years and in different ways by, *inter alios*, P P Craig, *Public Law and Democracy in the United Kingdom and the United States of America* (OUP, Oxford, 1999); M Loughlin, *Public Law and Political Theory* (OUP, Oxford, 1992); T R S Allen, *Law, Liberty and Justice: the legal foundations of British constitutionalism* (OUP, Oxford, 1993); R Brazier "The Non-Legal Constitution: Thoughts on Convention, Practice and Principle" (1992) 43 NILQ 262; T C Daintith, "Political Programmes and the Content of the Constitution" in W Finnie, N Walker and C M G Himsworth (eds) *Edinburgh Essays in Public Law* (Edinburgh University Press, Edinburgh, 1991), p 41. See also in the context of an independent (and unitary) Scottish state, N MacCormick, "An Idea for a Scottish Constitution" in Finnie, Walker and Himsworth, p 159.

7 Transitional Jurisprudence in the UK: a very Scottish Coup?

Scott Veitch

"Know that we have divided
In three our kingdom: and 'tis our fast intent
To shake all cares and business from our age;
Conferring them on younger strengths, while we
Unburthen'd crawl toward death."

King Lear, Act 1, Scene 1.

Inquiry into the nature of societies in transition has increased dramatically in recent years, to the point where a newly-minted -ology has arrived: transitology. Of course, societies are always, and always have been, in some form of transition; but it is the range and density of recent events and the global conditions within which they take place that have provided the impetus and the varied foci for transitologists. Needless to say, lawyers and legal sociologists have cottoned on to this, and the notion of "transitional jurisprudence" has emerged, which looks at the role of law and legal institutions in transitional periods. Something more fundamental, it is thought, can be exhibited about law and its manifestations, when considered in periods of change or stress.

One of the key areas of study has concerned countries in transition from non-democratic to democratic regimes. Using these latter terms broadly, this has covered countries and regions as diverse as South Africa and South America to Germany and former communist Eastern Europe. Jurisprudentially speaking, this focus is not entirely new: the famous Hart-Fuller debate in the 1950s was spawned by these legal theorists responding to the needs and legal possibilities of post-war Germany coming to terms with the legacy of Nazism. But debate, as with jurisprudence generally, has broadened greatly —and beneficially—since then. The range of philosophical and political reference has increased, and with it has come the opportunity of setting legal concepts and practical developments within a framework which analytical jurisprudence would not countenance.

Certain themes have emerged in this transitional jurisprudence that I will draw on in a specific way. I will consider recent political and legal changes in the United Kingdom with a view to what has been going on in other countries, and as a way of providing a different perspective on the recent events taking place here. There are similarities and differences which are instructive to explore, both as an academic matter, but also from the point of view of an understanding of contemporary legal politics. To those ends, the main example I will use is that of Scotland's relation to the changes taking place in the United Kingdom. This provides ample material for beginning to address questions raised by transitional jurisprudence, as well as allowing for some more local reflections to come to the surface.

"WE, THE SUBJECTS OF THE BRITISH CROWN …"

Unlike the American "We, the people", "We, the subjects of the British Crown" was hardly going to be a good opening line for a modern post-revolutionary constitution. (Maybe this is why Britain never had a written constitution.) Her Britannic Majesty and Her Britannic Majesty's Government and loyal subjects have seen to it that things happen differently in Britain. A shifting mixture of the scabrous and the deferential, "we the people" never made many inroads into the sovereignty of the Crown-in-Parliament. Unwittingly following her ancestors' ethnic roots, the Queen's most Excellent Majesty managed to get her subjects to fulfil Immanuel Kant's injunction that: "A people should not inquire with any practical aim in view into the origin of the supreme authority to which it is subject."[1] The iconography of majesty may have been embodied in the Leviathan of Hobbes, but any radical potential associated with social contract theory itself quickly became an outmoded and suspect notion subsequent to the two—one real, one virtual—revolutions of the seventeenth century. Since then, institutionally the conventional has always dominated the truly consensual and "we, the subjects"—for fear of acknowledging and uttering this status too much, perhaps—have kept pretty quiet.

But things have changed and are in the process of changing. It is not quite true to say that the United Kingdom is experiencing a transition from a non-democratic to a democratic regime. But neither is it entirely false. There are different time-zones of democracy in the United Kingdom which clearly signal changing conceptions of democracy and understandings of the polity.

Some of these can be outlined briefly. First, one can see persistently non-democratic elements at the heart of the regime. Leaving aside the freakishness of monarchy, the best and most vivid example of this is, undoubtedly, the unreformed reformed House of Lords. Cogently anti-democratic, it claims an ancient lineage which reproduces forms of elites that "we, the subjects" seem understandably incapable of changing; in the modern context, its time is, most aptly perhaps, out of joint. Next, one can see the variety of existing and putative regional assemblies: in Scotland, Wales, Northern Ireland, and as is likely, England. Each of these has, or will have, its own democratic time, its own more or less predictable

---

1 I Kant, *The Metaphysics of Morals* (trans M Gregor) (Cambridge University Press, Cambridge, 1991), p 129.

rhythm, its own—more or less—difference from Westminster mean-time. These differences are manifested in all sorts of ways, from political and legal competences or their lack, to a bizarre array of actually co-existing voting systems. Finally, for now, these zones are overlaid with the difficult, but constant tempo of the European Union.

Most of these democratic times and styles have emerged relatively recently. But how are we, jurisprudentially, to make sense of this? Let me suggest two elements of analyses of societies in transition which might help. First, a hypothesis: that while the role of law and legal institutions has always been important in transitional periods, certain significant and identifiable elements of contemporary law and legal mechanisms are playing an increasing role in negotiating the current changes. Second, that the relation between transition and transformation of a society usually involves exposing a tension between the *ethnos* and the *demos*. At critical moments of social transition, appeal to ethnic and cultural groupings and differences come to the fore in ways which uphold or challenge, make secure or unstable, the commonalities and boundaries of what is to constitute the democratic community. This necessarily invokes questions of borders and limits—not just geographic—and of the existence and meaning of cultures in their temporal dimension, as drawn from the past and as projected into the future.

I will explore in turn these areas of concern, although it is highly likely that they are not truly separable. Suffice to say for now, that in the current unfolding of events in the United Kingdom, "We, the subjects" are currently involved in a transition which shakes loose older legal and political assumptions and practices, and which rests, at least in part, on conceiving a notion of "We, the people" which is new to the inhabitants of these islands.

LEGAL ASPECTS

Before coming to both the Scottish dimension and the hypothesis just mentioned, let me begin with some established constituents of transitional jurisprudence. Ruti Teitel, in an important article,[1] identifies three areas of legal activity which become key in periods of transition: the rule of law; criminal justice, and constitutionalism. I will summarise each briefly.

First, the rule of law: dilemmas arise here in relation to problems of legal continuity from the old to the new regime. Tensions arise between the value of recognition of, and adherence to, positive law, and the need to construct new versions of political justice and accountability which are required to transform the legal culture of the society. These tensions can be understood in terms of a version of natural law-positivism (as with the Hart-Fuller debate), or, more plainly, as between rival understandings of the obligatoriness or legitimacy of positive law. Teitel suggests, rightly, that the meaning of these dilemmas will vary according to how the

---

1 R Teitel, "Transitional Jurisprudence: The Role of law in Political Transformation" (1997) 106 *Yale Law Journal* 2009.

seriousness of past abuses and wrongs were, or rather are now, conceived. Amongst others we might single out two aspects which play an important role here: first, the role of international law as a body of law and potential source of transcendent norms which can be referred to in helping to overcome the dilemmas of the rule of law in the particular country; second, the role of the judiciary and in particular its relation to the legislature in the transitional period, in terms both of law creation and of the creation of a specific culture of adjudication. Here, a rule of law dilemma is played out in the context of a heightened awareness of the political nature of the judicial function, yet also in accordance with an awareness of the still-unsettled nature of the new politics and political institutional structure. These aspects will vary from place to place depending on a number of factors, including the nature of the events of the past, the current take on conflicts past and present, and the legal culture of the country.

Next, and related, the criminal law plays an important role in responding to and establishing a normative ethos with regard to both present and past. How to deal with past offenders, and on what terms, become key concerns in coming to terms with the country's past as well as in attempts to settle established standards for future conduct and legal expectations for the new regime. Here, responses have ranged from large-scale criminal trials, individual prosecutions, international prosecutions, to (in the inverse) selective or blanket amnesties administered through the use of legislation or quasi-legal institutions such as truth commissions. Deciding which of these routes to follow will depend on various factors and their combination: the ability to identify successfully who to prosecute, the reality of likely success in prosecution, the expense of trials, likely political and wider social responses to trials in terms of arguments of justice, punishment, or correction, the need to attain truth and whether criminal law is the best method for doing so, the perceived ability of criminal prosecution or amnesty in helping to achieve transitional political goals, etc. All these will no doubt have some relation to questions of the rule of law and, likewise, responses to the rule of law dilemmas will affect attitudes towards criminal prosecutions.

Finally, constitutionalism. Teitel argues that "Constitutionalism in periods of political change stands in constructivist relation to the prevailing political order. Transitional constitutionalism not only is constituted by the prevailing political order, but is also constitutive of the perception of political change."[1] Again contingent on locality, the general claim she is making is that constitutionalism in the transitional phase is intimately bound up with the conditions for a transformative politics: as well as being responsive to political needs, constitutionalism can provide a secure space within which politics can take place. The element of political risk—that politically everything may be up for grabs at the one time—is simultaneously reduced and made available through constitutional (or perhaps meta-constitutional) arrangements. Here, we may again

---

1 Teitel, "Transitional Jurisprudence" at 2052.

encounter questions of transcendent norms—for example, international human rights law—as well as the significance of the judicial role. Importantly, we likewise encounter a heightened sense of the awareness of the political role of law and, specifically, constitution-making and adjudication, in their relation to democratic legitimacy, sovereignty, and legality. Perhaps even more than in the other two aspects, the approach adopted in relation to constitutionalism will vary depending on the specific transitional and other needs of the particular country.

The problems of transition in the United Kingdom are in some respects totally different from those facing other countries. Fortunately, the United Kingdom does not face—as do places such as Rwanda, Cambodia, and former Yugoslavia—a legacy which amounts to genocide and other crimes against humanity. Nor does it face having to come to terms with systematic and widespread gross violations of human rights perpetrated by a regime on a civilian population. In this sense, the components of transitional jurisprudence just identified must be treated carefully when thought about in the UK context so as not to trivialise the very real terror experienced by people in other countries.

One might in particular think that the criminal justice dimension has no bearing on UK developments, and this is largely the case. Nonetheless, the war in Northern Ireland does provide examples where, over a period of some time, the question of definitions of crime v political action has been fought over (recall Mrs Thatcher's line on terrorism: "a crime is a crime is a crime") and where the question of the political status of prisoners has been a constant source of antagonism. Moreover, the true position of the UK state has now been made clear by the putting in place of an amnesty procedure as a way of aiding the transition towards peace. The early release scheme—put into place by the Northern Ireland (Sentences) Act 1998—is undoubtedly a feature commonly found in other societies in transition as a means of attempting to curtail violence and begin a process of reconciliation. The issue of gross human rights violations has also arisen in this context—murder, torture, shoot to kill policies—and the international human rights dimension has also had some impact.

At this point, however, I want to return to a hypothesis I mentioned earlier in order to start thinking through the UK context, and more specifically some questions of law and constitutionalism as introduced by Teitel. The hypothesis was this: that certain significant and identifiable elements of contemporary law and legal mechanisms are playing an increasing role in negotiating the current changes.

Two significant elements underpin transitional developments in the United Kingdom, neither of which is indigenous. One is the European Union, the other the incorporation of the European Convention on Human Rights (ECHR) into domestic law. Both provide in their different ways a set of transcendent norms within which changing constitutional developments in the United Kingdom are taking place. Curiously, they have two effects which appear to pull in different directions. First, both limit the extent to which the "everything-is-up-for-grabs" scenario properly applies to the political transition. The former ability of independent sovereign states—in theory at least—to determine the proper limits of the exercise of sovereign legal power has been diminished within the context of the

European Union. Large-scale policy formation takes place from a different power-base, which in turn sees a certain reduction of the role of formerly sovereign parliaments to that of implementation. In this specific sense it does not matter which body—Westminster or Holyrood, say—implements policy, since effective political and economic decision-making is centred in the institutions of the European Union.

On the other hand, the institutional space this opens up inevitably weakens the old nation-state's claims to sovereignty *vis-à-vis* its component parts, and allows a flourishing of "regional" claims to emerge. But perhaps more importantly than this, and specifically with regard to the United Kingdom, the implementation into UK law of the ECHR makes available a previously unenforceable set of norms which changes the way in which sovereign power is exercised by governments. More specifically, it changes the social and legal expectations of people and their perception of their relations to law and government (one effect of which is to give courts—including especially domestic courts—a role which they have not hitherto played). Of course, it might be said that this simply brings the United Kingdom into line with the democratic conditions of many countries which have entrenched rights as part of their legal make-up. But the coincidence in timing here means not only that transitional developments in terms of devolution must be negotiated within terms which the legislature alone cannot determine, but also that the cultural spotlight has turned on legal mechanisms perhaps in a way for the first time. In both senses— limits and changing opportunities—new, at least in the United Kingdom, sources of law are playing an increasing role in the political transition in the United Kingdom.

Now there is an important caveat to this, and one which comes under the banner of constitutionalism. This has been given voice to by Tom Nairn in his recent book, *After Britain*. Nairn argues that despite the rhetoric of a modernising New Labour, Blair's project—including that of granting devolution—represents a conservative, last-ditch attempt to save the old UK state. As Nairn puts it in his inimitable style: "In practice the British state and most of its 'nation' remains in thrall to what it still cannot help apprehending as a long, even an immemorial, past. Such houses do not let themselves be abandoned so easily. They tend to possess the souls of those who inherit them, and at no time has this been plainer than in the two years since Tony Blair's government took office."[1] In other words, Blair— and his ongoing engagement with the rhetoric on Britishness would seem to bear this out—seeks not truly to modernise, but rather to retain the UK state by giving away and changing as little as possible.

The flaw Nairn sees in this is that unless the British constitution, with its rootedness in the ways of the unitary state, is fundamentally changed, it will be unable to adapt properly to the various forces regional claims throw up. The key problem with political transformation in the United Kingdom, according to Nairn, is really the *lack* of a true constitutional dimension. The Scotland Act 1998, for example, was, in law, neither

---

1   T Nairn, *After Britain: New Labour and the Return of Scotland* (Granta, London, 2000), p 22.

designed to be, nor is perceived as, anything other than a single piece of technical legislation emanating from a still-sovereign UK Parliament: that is, it is *not* a constitutional document in the sense in which that tradition is commonly understood. In this sense, then, the setting up of a Scottish Parliament does not sufficiently address constitutional issues and in fact typifies what Nairn describes as changes that are "essentially and structurally incomplete. In the normal processes of setting up regional or sub-state government a *constitution* is the foundation." As he then goes on to point out, national democracy "needs a distinct statute related to history and national identity, and (nowadays) it needs to be approved by the citizen body. In fact people become 'citizens' via such approval."[1]

Instead, what we are witnessing in the United Kingdom is a British constitution which, exemplified by the fact that its central pillars—monarchy, lords, commons—are failing to modernise, still holds on to a logic of unity and supremacy in order to reproduce the semblance of an ongoing stability. But, Nairn argues, as long as this remains the case, ultimately the regions will gather a momentum of their own, crawl out of this rotting carcass and truly modernise themselves. Transition therefore, for Nairn, requires a constitutional transformation working in tandem with the changing dynamics of political possibility (supporting Teitel's claim that transitional constitutionalism is not only constituted by the prevailing political order, but is also constitutive of the perception of political change). As far as Nairn is concerned then, constitutionalism *is* a motivating force, but one which the United Kingdom has not, yet, endorsed (except cynically to restrain it). Change will, however, he says, come as the claims of *de facto* sovereignty in the regions eventually deliver a *de jure* outcome, one in which, specifically, Scotland will generate its own political and constitutional transformation.

This is a striking diagnosis of the United Kingdom today. In terms of transitional jurisprudence, we might read this in terms of the components of the rule of law and constitutionalism, though in a different form from many other countries. For example, with regard to the former, there appears to be little debate about the meaning of legal continuity as a question of legal validity. Yet there are, nonetheless, questions about the legitimacy of law in a democratic sense, questions that are raised within a context of changing expectations of a belated shift in status from subject to citizen. These come, inevitably, to be linked to other questions around the notion of constitutionalism, in line with widely-recognised features which display a close relation with the need for constitutional settlement in times of political unsettlement.[2] And the key to understanding the role of constitutionalism lies, on this reading, precisely in the relation between the pressures of *de facto* aspirations and demands, and the *de jure* claims it confronts. Clearly, and thankfully, neither of these have to grapple with a history of violent conflict, but they do signal ways of understanding certain of the dynamics of transition we are dealing with.

---

1 Nairn, *After Britain: New Labour and the Return of Scotland*, pp 276–277.
2 In this sense, it is worth pointing out (although I will not develop it further here) that aspects of constitutionalism within the Scottish context are paralleled, though in a denser fashion, by contiguous developments in Northern Ireland.

We might pause briefly to think where the impetus for these developments might come from. Teitel drew attention to the role of the judiciary in
times of transition. Might they play a role in the United Kingdom? There
is, clearly, a sense in which the judiciary, and the public perception of the
judiciary, is changing today. The area of human rights is, and will be,
significant for this, augmenting as it does the political role of judges. In this
sense, it will be the case that the judiciary's relation to the legislature will
come under increasing scrutiny particularly where they will be called
upon to adjudicate politically sensitive matters. But as true engines for
more widespread transformation, it is unlikely the judiciary will come to
have the kind of super-role adopted by, for example, the Hungarian
Constitutional Court. The nearest in fact to a constitutional court to have
emerged here is the role given to the Judicial Committee of the Privy
Council. But, in amongst picking through death penalty appeals from the
Caribbean and long suits from other former colonies, its role in Scottish
devolution is essentially one of policing the internal frontiers of a unitary
state.

It would be surprising also if the legal profession were to play a significant role. Despite the old mantra of the separate legal system, theirs has
more usually been an approach of a "soft nationalism" and one which was
for the most part in fact quite comfortable with the constitutional set-up of
the UK state.[1] Certainly the legal elites have been largely uninspired by
any radical democratic thought. Moreover, in terms of legal practice more
broadly, it is increasingly the case that the demands of capital and interna-
tionalisation are providing the logic for engagement in such a way that
local constitutional matters will be a low priority. (That said, we can be
sure that lawyers will be benefit from any constitutional re-negotiations!)

Finally, the putative rediscovery of a distinctively Scottish constitutional
tradition has surfaced, without irony, as an argument recently.[2] This seems
to me, however, to be as outmoded as basing a UK constitutional transformation on the Magna Carta. Attempting to touch the nation's "mystic
chords of memory"—to use Abraham Lincoln's wonderfully evocative
phrase—in re-inventing a constitutional tradition worthy of a modern
democracy is indeed just that; mystical, mythic, and myopic. One picks
one's ancestors as one chooses; but it is a recipe for dodgy politics and even
dodgier historiography. It is, quite simply, unnecessary.

It may then be that the mainspring of transition will come from the
contradictions inherent in the devolution settlement as it currently exists.
The *realpolitik* of different agendas and priorities as between Westminster
and Holyrood, and in particular of different spending priorities, especially
when the political make-up of the legislatures comes into conflict, may
make clear in time the flawed and unstable institutional mechanisms we
have at the moment. When political elites realise the intractable problems
which they cannot smooth over, the voices of the voter may force a rethink.

---

1   See, for example, L Farmer, *Criminal Law, Tradition and Legal Order: Crime and the Genius of
    Scots Law 1747 to the Present* (Cambridge University Press, Cambridge, 1997).
2   For a reading of this tradition see E Attwooll, *The Tapestry of Law: Scotland, Legal Culture,
    and Legal Theory* (Kluwer, Dordrecht, 1997), Ch 3.

What we have then, to summarise, appears to be an incomplete transitional scenario. Yet, despite clear differences with other countries we may usefully see a set of questions emerging within the framework of understanding offered by transitional studies. Specifically, we find the emergence into public discussion of questions of legitimacy of law and institutions as a democratic matter in a novel way; the increased role of the judiciary and the increased public awareness of that role; and the increasing role of transcendent legal norms within which any transition is to be negotiated.

And we also find, unsurprisingly, tensions as well as obstacles, some of which indeed may work to bely the political possibilities which are arising, and even stifle some before they are able to get going. Why this might be so is a complex matter, yet it necessarily relates to unsettling questions about—and expectations of—the relation between democratic institutions and cultural and political identities. It is to this issue, therefore, that I now turn.

ETHNOS AND *DEMOS*

First let me clarify what is meant by these two terms. Seyla Benhabib has written that:

> "[a] deliberative democratic model distinguishes between the *ethnos* and the *demos*, between the ethnic, cultural, linguistic, and religious identity of a people, and the political constitution of the people as an organised, self-governing body. A *demos* can consist of more than one *ethnos*; the sovereign political community may encompass and usually does encompass more than one ethnic, religious, and linguistic community. What makes such an ethnically diverse body politic one is not some mystical act of sovereign will-formation, but the constitutional and institutional principles through which such a people enter into the world-historical arena and demand recognition from others."[1]

How might we make sense of this contrast in the context of recent developments in Scotland? The United Kingdom as a whole is witnessing an unleashing of identity questions which may be seen as a function of the potential for transformations in democratic understandings. There are a range of issues here, some old, some new. We might usefully break them down into two related sets: one concerns large-scale national/international groupings; the other, internal configurations. I will begin with the latter.

Specifically with regard to Scotland, the first year of the Scottish Parliament has witnessed some rather raw engagements with issues of identity. These were many, but there were a few prominent examples. First, and without doubt the most publicly controversial, was with regard to

---

1 S Benhabib, "Democracy and Difference: Reflections on the Meta-Politics of Lyotard and Derrida" (1994) *Journal of Political Philosophy* 1 at 19.

attitudes towards sexuality. The repeal of section 2A of the Local Government Act 1986 in Scotland witnessed a crucial, though not always sophisticated, debate over attitudes toward homosexuality. This necessarily engaged questions about the meanings of tolerance and its practice, assessments of the content of community values, and the actual and likely symbolic reproduction of both in educational institutions. (It also, in passing, gave some insights into the structures and workings of political debate: from the emerging nature of party-political allegiances to the influence of the media and the role of prominent groupings and wealthy individuals within civil society.) Second, debates over asylum-seekers have exposed tensions as to the appropriate locus of competences as between the Scottish Parliament and Westminster. More importantly, these could be seen as providing an early engagement with Scotland's role as a morally and legally responsible member of the international community. Such concerns were, moreover, addressed directly in law and in public debate with the trial and subsequent acquittal of the Faslane nuclear protestors, which saw the successful invocation of international legal norms in Greenock Sheriff Court.[1] Finally, there was strong public debate over the treatment of religious communities, and specifically of the Catholic community, in Scotland. This latter debate in particular exemplified how all such issues necessarily provoke contemporary re-assessments of historical lineages in the formation of community identities and values, and thus the necessity for public reappraisals of history for the sake of the present and the future.

What these issues all demonstrate is a combination of uncertainty and genuine debate over the significance to be attached in the first instance to understandings of relevant commonalities and differences in the community and, more importantly, over which of these differences ought to count as making a difference (in legal, political or educational terms). In this way the politics of identity have forced their way, at an early stage, to the forefront of Scottish political and legal debates. One need be neither optimistic nor pessimistic about the show so far, to realise that they form a crucial element in the forging of future democratic conditions in Scotland.

The second set of issues around the role and meanings of *ethnos* relate, as I have said, to national/international groupings. This, rather cumbersomely, refers to ongoing debates within the United Kingdom about the nature of nationality, ranging from Scottish, English and Irish, to British and, in a slightly different sense, European. These groupings, with which people variously identify, are deployed to demarcate boundaries of inclusion which, to different degrees, are necessarily linked to normative assessments of appropriate boundaries of the practice of democracy and indeed to the very constitution of the democratic unit itself. Alternative versions of these foreground or downplay the significance and content of ethnicity in so far as they link or ought to link to the element of inclusion.

---

1 For comment, see R Wallace, "How the 'Trident' sheriff got it wrong" (2000) 44(11) JLSS 18; J Mayer, "Jumping the gun" (2000) 45(1) JLSS 24; S Neff, "Idealism in Action: International Law and Nuclear Weapons in Greenock Sheriff Court" (2000) 4 ELR 74.

The connection between *ethnos* and *demos* is then currently mediated by assessing the relevance and force of the ethnic grouping as a matter of defining the relevant boundary for inclusion. It is here that a panoply of political and cultural positions is ranged, and amongst which, we must be careful to note, include positions which *resist* inclusion such as can be seen in certain attitudes to these cases: Irish-British, Scottish-British, British-European.

This is not the place to engage with a full delineation of these positions. Instead, I want to suggest that these debates arise currently in such a way as to challenge more stable understandings of legality and constitutionalism (real or putative) in the United Kingdom, for it is this dimension which deals directly with the concerns of transitional jurisprudence. Consider initially, for example, the inclusivist notion of "civic nationalism" argued for recently by Neil MacCormick, and to which he opposes the exclusivist "ethnic nationalism":

> "the nation which exercises the right of self-determination is constituted by a sense of common belonging among those who share civic institutions, with no exclusiveness towards any person or group willing to participate in them. The issue is that of acceptance of the jurisdiction of the civic institutions ... [These] are understood in broad terms to include, for example, legal norms and institutions, political representative organs, branches of public and local administration, the organisation of education, churches and religious communities in their secular aspect, and other like institutions having an understood territorial location to which they refer. Territorially located civic institutions can be objects of allegiance, understood as 'ours' by the people among whom they perform their functions. As civic institutions, they are necessarily of great political significance to the community which, to an extent, they define."[1]

To be "understood as ours" is the key phrase here. As will be well known, MacCormick argues with cogency for "ours" to be the Scottish nation, albeit conceived within a thoroughly revised and pluralist conception of sovereignty and subsidiarity existing in the context of what he calls the European Commonwealth. Such a claim is, of course, politically contested. But jurisprudentially, as MacCormick acknowledges, it clearly signals the need for legal understandings to move beyond statist notions associated with the mid-twentieth century positivist doctrines of the likes of Hans Kelsen and even H L A Hart. Allegiance by officials holding the requisite internal point of view to "whatever the Queen-in-Parliament enacts is law" is, in the current context, no longer (if it ever was) definitive of the full meaning of legal normative order within the United Kingdom. This is true with respect both to aspects of recently and more long-standing devolved powers, but also and importantly with regard to the supremacy of European Community law.[2]

---

1 N MacCormick, *Questioning Sovereignty: Law, State, and Nation in the European Commonwealth* (Oxford University Press, Oxford, 1999) p 170.
2 On the latter see *R v Secretary of State for Transport, ex p Factortame Ltd (No 2)* [1991] AC 603.

Yet it is also true in another, more forceful, sense. For "common belonging" is inextricably and now visibly bound to the notion of "the right to rights". As such, political and cultural debate over appropriate understandings of commonality feed directly into the terms of legal and democratic organisation themselves. Moreover, it is increasingly the case that local identity issues become inextricably bound to legal-constitutional sites that transcend traditional boundaries, drawing as they do on standards and rights to be found within the European Union or ECHR. What is significant is that in the contemporary UK context all these aspects are to the fore in a perhaps historically unprecedented manner. As such, and despite the devolution settlement, there appears now a political and cultural unsettlement which is simultaneously perceived as a potential for transformation, and one which will be, I suggest, increasingly insistent regardless of how it is finally realised.

The legal ramifications of this are significant since this potential attests to the fluid and provisional character of the constitutional make-up. In more settled periods, it may well be that Benhabib's argument about the relation between *ethnos* and *demos* is appropriate: "To separate the formation of identity from the constitutional and institutional issue of the seat of sovereign authority is essential."[1] Yet, it is precisely this normative stance that does not appear viable, at least for the moment in Scotland. No matter how one views the wisdom of the actual institutional machinery of the current devolution set-up, the connection between the formation and nature of identity with the possible meanings of institutional sovereignty and the appropriate demarcations for the *demos* remains for now not only necessary, but one which, with regard to its substance, remains deeply contested. Robert Cover wrote presciently that "No set of legal institutions or prescriptions exist apart from the narratives that locate it and give it meaning,"[2] and it is precisely such narratives of the varied approaches to the *ethnos* which are to the fore at the moment, and which are insistent on a reconsideration of the democratic and legal structures through which the community organises itself.

Where this is so, we are led to make a further observation—though one which is partly conjectural. That is, that whilst we can readily trace important aspects of transition there is also an important sense, perhaps still latent, of transformation taking place. This involves, I suggest, a transformation in the self-understanding of the polity that may best be understood within the context of a historical process in which the United Kingdom is now, belatedly and often reluctantly, participating and which has, as its driving force, the key impetus of nation as *ethnos*.

To explain: the German theorist Jürgen Habermas has written of the "catalyzing role" which nationalism played in the emergence of the new eighteenth-century nation-state republics. As he puts it: "the symbiotic relation between nationalism and republicanism reveals itself as merely a transitional, historical constellation. A national consciousness ... did

---

1 See S Benhabib, "Democracy and Difference: Reflections on the Meta-Politics of Lyotard and Derrida" (1994) *Journal of Political Philosophy* 1 at 18.
2 R Cover, "Foreword: *Nomos* and Narrative" (1983) 97 *Harvard Law Review* 4 at 4.

indeed transform subjects for the first time into politically aware citizens who identify with the republican constitution and its declared goals."[1] Now Habermas clearly sees this as something in the past. Indeed, like many other writers, he suggests that contemporary nationalism's credentials ought only to be thought of as having destructively negative, anti-cosmopolitan, connotations. Yet, arguably, that "catalyst" describes well what is happening in the Scotland of the present: a late-in-the-day process of modernisation (in the sense of reaching constitutional modernity, not of Blairism), and one which involves crucially, as Habermas does rightly note, the transformation of subjects into citizens.

Such a process may yet be in its infancy. That there is some catching up to do cannot be doubted, and is perhaps most symbolically attested to by one of the earliest endeavours of the Scottish Parliament, namely, the abolition of the feudal system. Nonetheless, it is precisely such potential for transformation which, unwittingly perhaps, has been unleashed.

It remains to be seen just how this process will unfold. As such I will not engage in further speculation, but stick to the more limited point that there are clear historical precedents for the outcomes of such generative conditions, and, that given the ongoing and recently growing attention to questions of nationalism and constitutionalism within Scottish debate, possibilities exist here for a transformation in democratic understandings which may not be feasible yet at the level of the UK state.

There remains one final caveat with regard to the relation between *ethnos* and *demos*: the last two decades have seen, at least according to popular and dominant conceptions, a downplaying of economic identity particularly in the form of worker participation and politicisation. Yet, in so far as we can identify a potential for transformation, and to the extent that this replicates historical developments in understandings of citizenship, the economic dimensions of citizenship cannot be ignored. Arguably, the biggest threats to political and legal self-determination (regardless of how one defines the self in any instance) are not other *ethnos* groupings but economic ones.[2] In this particular sense, one cannot differentiate the transitional scenario in the United Kingdom from more full-blooded transitions in other parts of the world. That said, this dimension is often ignored in transitional studies,[3] but, and particularly with reference to the role of the European Union, is overlooked here to the detriment of both future analysis and practical politics.

Let me now summarise these points, and in an apparently paradoxical manner. Restraints on constitutional change in the United Kingdom may

---

1 J Habermas, *The Inclusion of the Other: Studies in Political Theory*, (MIT Press, Cambridge, Mass., 1998), p 132.
2 Even Tom Nairn in his recent book surprisingly underplays this aspect, the optimism he holds out for what a written constitution can deliver appearing remarkably and ominously silent with regard not just to matters of content, but more specifically with its relation to economic organisation. See Nairn, *After Britain: New Labour and the Return of Scotland* (Granta, London, 2000).
3 But compare, for example, H Marais, *South Africa, Limits to Change: The Political Economy of Transformation* (UCT Press, Cape Town, 1998).

be seen to co-exist with the generative conditions and potential of constitutionalism as it features specifically within Scottish legal politics. This is
so particularly when we understand the legal ordering of a community as
something far more profound, intricate and constitutive than the list of
rules and regulations with which courts and parliaments deal. I have
suggested here that in order to begin to understand this broader legal field,
the constitutional tensions need to be informed by paying attention to the
contested and conflicting appearances of civic and ethnic identities, histories, and possibilities. For it is precisely these aspects which dominate
Scottish public debate, and, in as much as we remain for now within an
incomplete transitional scenario, which we can expect to have an immediate and continued impact on law and legal organisation in Scotland.

CONCLUSION

I have tried to identify some comparative markers of transition that seem
to apply to changes taking place within the United Kingdom. As far as
jurisprudential thinking is concerned, what becomes abundantly clear is
the necessity for a broad and longer-term view of the legal politics of these
developments, a perspective which is at one with the approach of the
essays in this collection as a whole.

But the substantive tensions and possibilities to which I have drawn
attention in the second part of this chapter remain in place. As a matter of
political potential, democratic legitimacy is for the moment intimately
linked to, as yet unresolved, questions of the proper boundaries and signif-
icances of commonalities and differences. It seemed important to identify
what these are, though their resolution faces ongoing blockages. Still, it
may just be that the UK state, like some old, bellowing Lear, has betrayed
through its initial kindness its power and its need, only—and inevitably—
to see that power dissipate in a way it could neither predict, nor,
ultimately, comprehend. External empires have gone, and now there is
internal break-up too. Is it just coincidence that the court of devolution
should also be the court of remnant empire?

In the end, there may be a rather drastic though understated transition
going on here and, if indeed Aristotle was right about political animals,
what we might be dealing with would look like a very Scottish coup; one
just waiting to be milked.

8 Imagined Communities, Imaginary Conversations: Failure and the Construction of Legal Identities

Paul Maharg

"Because they are large, round and bluey,
    and would look good on the top of Lady Hill.
Because their glassy depths would give local kids
    the impression that they are looking at
    the Earth from outer space.
Several Earths in fact, which encourages humility
    and a sense of relativity.

*   *   *   *   *   *   *

Because Scotland must see visions again,
    even if only through
    a marble of convenience."

"Why the Elgin Marbles Must Be Returned to Elgin".[1]

IDENTITY, CONSTITUTIONS AND LEGAL THOUGHT

How might Scottish legal thought change in the context of a Scottish Parliament? When we ask this deceptively simple question, we encounter an immediate problem. It is a problem in some ways remarkably like the situation that faced Scotland in 1707, except in inverse: nothing like this has happened before to a mixed jurisdiction with a history such as Scotland's. To explore some aspects of this question, I shall examine the subject of jurisprudential thought as an aspect of legal identity, thus taking a broad view of what constitutes legal literature; and argue for the possibility of a Scottish jurisprudence, both critical and historical.

Interdisciplinarity *within* the discipline of law is the key here. Constitutions, even what might be called subordinate constitutional legislation, such as the Scotland Act 1998, arise out of the *imperium* of governmental command: "There shall be a Scottish Parliament", the first section of the 1998 Act. But the felt need for a constitution is a complex

---

1 W N Herbert, *Cabaret McGonagall* (Bloodaxe Books, Newcastle upon Tyne, 1996), pp 36–37.

historical and cultural nexus which shapes the form of the constitutional settlement, and which arises not only from the domain of legislation ("unfinished business", democratic deficit" are key popular phrases which have expressed this), but also from a sense of identity, particularly national identity. Substantive law says little about the processes of its own formation and the change this sense of identity undergoes: to understand it better we require historical, jurisprudential and cultural perspectives.

The question of identity has recently been raised by a number of legal commentators,[1] and interdisciplinary perspectives are used to a greater or lesser extent in these and other discussions of national identity and law in Scottish legal literature. Knud Haakonssen, for instance, has argued convincingly that eighteenth- and early nineteenth-century natural law jurisprudence was a form of interdisciplinary inquiry within which there were attempts to combine "jurisprudence, civic humanism and practical ethics in a coherent moral and political outlook".[2] However, in some of the literature there is a clear separation of legal identity from other concerns. In their discussion of Scotland in the Union, for instance, Himsworth and Munro declare that:

> "[i]f the separateness of the Scottish legal system owes something to the moral force of ... considerations which were in mind in 1707, when some thought was given to maintaining its identity, there are other spheres such as education and aspects of arts and culture (such as architecture, or the press) and social and economic practice (such as patterns of domestic housing) where Scottish distinctiveness owes little or nothing to the union legislation as such."[3]

In a strict sense this view of the Union is undeniable. But it is certainly the case that the Act of Union profoundly affected almost all aspects of Scottish history, culture and law. Scottish distinctiveness from, and Scottish uniformity and conformity with, England are part of the construction of Scottish identity by means of representational signs and structures. As Stuart Hall has commented, "a nation is not only a political entity but something which produces meanings—a system of cultural representation."[4]

These words are quoted by Brown, McCrone and Paterson in their study of Scottish politics and society.[5] In their chapter on "Ethnicity, Culture and Identity" they note that in the early years, the Union "did not, by all accounts, much affect the lives of ordinary people or their immediate

---

1   See e.g. H L MacQueen (ed), *Scots Law into the 21st Century: Essays in Honour of W A Wilson*, (W Green, Edinburgh, 1996); E Attwooll, *The Tapestry of the Law: Scotland, Legal Culture and Legal Theory* (Kluwer, London, 1997).

2   K Haakonssen, *Natural Law and Moral Philosophy: From Grotius to the Scottish Enlightenment* (Cambridge University Press, Cambridge, 1996), p 5.

3   C M G Himsworth and C R Munro, *Devolution and the Scotland Bill* (W Green, Edinburgh, 1998) p 8.

4   S Hall, "The Question of Cultural Identity" in S Hall, D Held and T McGrew (eds), *Modernity and Its Futures* (Polity Press, Cambridge, 1992), p 292.

5   A Brown, D McCrone and L Paterson, *Politics and Society in Scotland*, 2nd edn (Macmillan Press, London, 1998).

masters".[1] They draw a distinction between the high politics of London and the low politics of civil society in Scotland, adding that a constitutional settlement which allowed for the continuation of the latter in Scotland would have been the only one acceptable to Scots. At first glance this view would seem to support the views expressed above by Himsworth and Munro. But they then go on to answer the key question: why, then does the Union matter so much almost 300 years later?

> "Put simply, it set the institutional infrastructure on to which Scottish national identity was grafted ... Identifying oneself as Scottish was not simply some memory trace of pre-Union independence, but a reflection of the governing structures of Scottish civil society. It both derived from, and laid the basis for, nationhood."[2]

It is in this sense that the constitutional arrangements underpinning the Scottish Parliament will gradually but fundamentally alter our sense of what it is to be Scottish, in much the same way as did the Act of Union.[3] It will do so partly because, however much we may wish it otherwise, law is, as Boaventura de Sousa Santos has characterised it, made up of "porous legality or of legal porosity of multiple networks of legal orders forcing us to constant transitions and trespassings".[4] It is significant that Santos' concept of the porosity of legal orders springs from his application of Harold Bloom's literary critical theory of misprision.[5] For Bloom, readers of poetry do not "read" a text—the word is value-neutral, and reading is anything but a value-free activity. As he put it in *A Map of Misreading*, "reading is ... a miswriting just as writing is a misreading."[6] Misprision, or the act of misreading, occurs whenever a text is read, particularly when read by a "strong" reader—that is, a reader who is implicated in various ways with the meaning the text conveys. What is true of a text is equally true of a canon for Bloom: indeed, tradition or canonicity is itself a trope within the map of misreading.[7] Thus, constitutional arrangements, which

---

1 *Politics and Society in Scotland*, p 216.

2 *Politics and Society in Scotland*, p 216.

3 J M Thomson made a similar point when he observed that there "is no direct link between the *substantive* content of the rules of private law and the Scots sense of national identity". For him, what is important is "the continuation of a separate Scottish legal system with its own court structure, procedure and judges": see "When Homer Nodded" in H L MacQueen (ed), *Scots Law into the 21st Century: Essays in Honour of W A Wilson* (W Green, Edinburgh, 1996), p 25.

4 Boaventura de Sousa Santos, "Law: A Map of Misreading" (1987) 14 *Journal of Law and Society* 279, quoted in E Attwooll, *The Tapestry of the Law: Scotland, Legal Culture and Legal Theory* (Kluwer, London, 1997), p 180. For an interesting account of trespassing as a method of cross-disciplinary research see D P Ellerman, *Cultural Trespassing as a Way of Life: Essays in Philosophy, Economics and Mathematics* (Rowman and Littlefield Publishers, London, 1995).

5 See H Bloom, *The Anxiety of Influence: A Theory of Poetry* (Oxford University Press, New York, 1973); H Bloom, *A Map of Misreading* (Oxford University Press, New York, 1975).

6 H Bloom, *A Map of Misreading*, p 3.

7 H Bloom, *Kabbalah and Criticism*, (Seabury Press, New York, 1975) p 97. As Alastair Fowler perceptively commented, there are a variety of canons existing within any single domain. He identified at least six within a *topos* of literary theory—see "Genre and Literary Canon" (1979) 11(1) *New Literary History* 97–119.

are particularly porous, are always open to misprision: examples can be found in the endlessly creative debates around the First Amendment in the USA. As legal texts, constitutional documents tend to be more open to arguments of public policy and rights-based arguments. As such, they become shaping texts which, quite apart from the legislative authority they bear, are heavily symbolic of the self-identity of a community.[1]

In one sense, a new and developing identity under a Scottish Parliament is easier to construct precisely because the identity of the United Kingdom is so weak (hence the anxious tautology of the two words), and because sovereignty does not lie with the Scottish Parliament but remains at Westminster. Both of these points require a little unpacking. UK identity is bound up with being British. But what "British" actually means is not at all clear. Many commentators, in one way or another, point to what Linda Colley has articulated in her study of Britishness, namely that UK identity was forged out of the eighteenth century wars with France and developing imperialism. The term 'Britons' is usually used to identify UK citizens in distinction to other nationalities, but as Tom Nairn rightly puts it, "there have never been 'Britons' ... any more than there were 'Austro-Hungarians' before 1917".[2] In this sense there has been a conspicuous failure since the Union to define what British-ness might actually be. Scottish, English, Welsh and Irish all have quite different defining myth-structures and narratives: their representations of national identity did not merge prior to 1707, and have not done so subsequently.

This identity weakness is apparent in the constitution itself, which requires the glue of the Crown to bind it together. As Nairn has pointed out: "Anyone who buys an elementary textbook on the British Constitution to read it (rather than pray before it) knows that the Crown is a crucial element in Constitution, Law and Government. Were it to disappear, these would require both theoretical and practical reconstruction, not a few adjustments with a spanner."[3] If Nairn is right, this is so because of the importance of the Crown as a focus for UK centralist conventions and ideologies. As the lynch-pin of these ideologies, the Crown is a bar to the development of alternative identities as these might be developed *via* constitutional reform.

The idea, of course, is not new. Over a century ago there was a similar concern with identity, first raised publicly in Gladstone's Midlothian campaign. Never one to underplay the drama of an occasion, Gladstone characterised his campaign as "a battle of justice humanity freedom law [sic], all in their first elements from the very root, and all on a gigantic scale".[4] In

---

1 See e.g. D Cole, "Agon at Agora: Creative Misreadings in the First Amendment Tradition", (1986) 95(5) *Yale Law Journal* 857–905; K Yoshino, "What's Past is Prologue: Precedent in Literature and Law", (1994) 104(2) *Yale Law Journal*, 471–511; P Gewirtz, "Remedies and Resistance", (1983) 92(4) *Yale Law Journal* 585–681.
2 T Nairn, *The Break-Up of Britain: Crisis and Neo-Nationalism*, 2nd edn (Verso, London, 1981), p 369. This quote comes from the additions to the second, expanded edition, aptly entitled "Postscript 1981: Into Political Emergency".
3 T Nairn, *The Enchanted Glass: Britain and its Monarchy* (Radius, London, 1988) p 89.
4 W E Gladstone, *The Gladstone Diaries with Cabinet Minutes and Prime-Ministerial Correspondence*, 14 vols, London, 1968–94, vol ix, 24 Nov 1879, quoted in H C G Matthew, *Gladstone 1875–1898*, (Clarendon Press, Oxford, 1995) p 41.

spite of the radical rhetoric, though, it is clear that he favoured devolution under an imperial parliament.[1] As such, his problems in framing and attempting to implement devolutionary legislation were in a number of respects similar to those faced by the drafters of the 1978 Scotland Bill and the 1998 Scotland Act.[2] That such a coincidence exists over a period of a century and more is testimony not only to the constitutional problems inherent in the Westminster model, then as now, but also of the chronic unease we have with our identity within it.

FAILURE AND RECONSTRUCTIONS

The devolution failure in 1979 presented Scottish society with a particular problem, one which affected everyone interested in the devolutionary or the independence debate. What does one do in the face of such a disappointment of expectations? What reaction could there be to the political failure of the legal solution to constitutional change in Scotland? Broadly speaking, there were two responses. The first was overtly political, and based largely on the development of ground-up initiatives, while the second was cultural, and analysed the failure of political life in Scotland. Both, I would argue, were attempts to reconstruct alternative identities; not only national identities in the cultural sense, but legal solutions to the political impasse of the eighties and early nineties.

With respect to the former, there were throughout the eighties and early nineties a number of important initiatives which enabled the debate about identity and politics to continue. Viewed broadly, these initiatives argued that there was an absence of democratic controls in Scotland, and that the current constitutional arrangements could not respond to this shortfall. The Scottish Constitutional Convention, for example, sought "a constitutional settlement in which the Scottish people, being sovereign, agree to the exercise of specified powers by Westminster, but retain their

---

1 See Matthew, *Gladstone 1875–1898*, pp 248–51. For further discussion of this and related matters in Gladstone's concept of devolved powers, see R Kelley, "Midlothian. A Study in Politics and Ideas" *Victorian Studies* 4, 1960. Dicey published a reply to Gladstone in *England's Case Against Home Rule* (John Murray, London, 1886), when the debate regarding Home Rule in Ireland was at it most intense.

2 This analogy has been made by a number of commentators. Neal Ascherson, for instance, made the following observations in his *Devolution Diary*, extracts of which were reprinted in (1986) 22 *Cencrastus* 3–14 and 49–54, and which are worth quoting in full:
    "**Tuesday 15 November 1977**
    Went to the British Museum and read the 1886 Home Rule debates. How elastic and sovereign Gladstone was, compared to politicians today! The problems were so similar. But the confidence in change and innovation was so much greater. The central doctrine of the sovereignty of Parliament was of course an obstacle to Gladstone. But I saw, as I read on, that what was only a general principle in 1886 has become a fixed taboo today, an institution as sacred and encrusted as a Coronation ceremony. Once again, it's vital to remember that things presented as immemorial British ceremonies and traditions are very often quite new and unhistorical. The 'encrusting' process, like giving false patina to a new bronze statue, is the most subtle of the techniques by which British society is managed and radical change evaded ..." (p 53).

sovereignty over all other matters".[1] All of these initiatives, to greater or lesser effect, presented alternatives to the contemporary constitutional regime, so that the case for democracy, put by many public figures in many different forums and debates, was undeniably a powerful force in the creation of the Scottish Parliament.

The alternative reaction to political and legal failure was the effort to construct imagined communities. It is now a fairly common view that after 1979, the arts and humanities played a significant part in the reconstruction of Scottish identity. In painting, music, sculpture, architecture, film, in history especially, and in literature and drama, there was sustained criticism of the status quo in British politics, and the presentation of alternative Scotlands. Douglas Dunn's collection of poems entitled *Northlight*, or Edwin Morgan's *Sonnets From Scotland* are examples of this.[2] So too is Alasdair Gray's novel *1982, Janine*,[3] an extraordinary narrative in which politics and pornography become metaphors for each other. It is recognisably a "condition of Scotland" novel, though one that bears almost no resemblance to the tradition which begins with Disraeli's *Coningsby*. In place of the English class elites of Disraeli and George Meredith, we have a Scottish middle-class security supervisor, Jock McLeish, surviving a suicide attempt, and meditating on the failures of his life and those of Scotland, the one reflecting the other, and finding redemption of a kind through the acknowledgment of his own failures and strengths.

There were similarly vigorous responses to the failure of 1979 in certain academic disciplines. The *Scottish Historical Review* recently published the papers from a symposium entitled "Writing Scotland's History", which aimed to explore recent reconstructions of Scottish history. As John Stevenson put it, discussing twentieth-century Scottish history: "Our greatest difficulty is that the narrative of current Scottish history is still dominated by the unfinished political identity of Scotland".[4] Other historians have been actively interrogating this identity. Michael Lynch's well-received one volume study of Scottish history begins by posing the question about the identity of Scots and Scottish culture. Hector MacQueen recently analysed the "modern [*ie* twentieth century] myth of Scottish legal history", that medieval law contributed "almost nothing to Scots law, which had essentially begun anew and on a Civilian basis with the writings of Stair".[5] In Enlightenment studies, the Pocockian revolution signalled by *The Machiavellian Moment* has contributed significantly to our understanding of key concepts and ideas in the Enlightenment formation of identity. In the work of John Cairns and others in recent decades, similar

---

1 Scottish Constitutional Convention, *A Constitutional Framework for Scotland* (1989), para 10.3.
2 See D Dunn, *Northlight* (Faber & Faber, London, 1988); E Morgan, *Sonnets from Scotland* (Mariscat Press, Glasgow, 1984).
3 See B Charlton, "The World Must Become Quite Another: Politics in the Novels of Alasdair Gray", *Cencrastus* (1988) pp 39–41.
4 J Stevenson, "Writing Scotland's History in the Twentieth Century: Thoughts from Across the Border", (1997) LXXVI, 1, 201, *Scottish Historical Review*, 112.
5 "*Regiam Majestatem*, Scots Law and National Identity", (1995) LXXIV, 1, 197, *Scottish Historical Review* 25.

lines of inquiry have opened up the rich detail of the history of legal education in Scotland to a remarkable extent. Other studies have revealed the astonishing sophistication of earlier sixteenth- and seventeenth-century Scottish historiographical debates.[1]

If historical commentary has provided us with valuable critiques of political culture, literary criticism has not been far behind. A number of critics have developed a sophisticated analysis of the place of Scottish literature in a British context. In an important series of articles and edited books, Cairns Craig has explored the relation of Scottish literature to the political in Scotland, and this has helped to clear a discursive space for others to explore the subject in more detail.[2] Gordon Turnbull, for instance, has interpreted James Boswell's perennial preoccupation with the characteristics of Scottish civil society in his diaries and papers as one aspect of the Scottish Enlightenment's "great revisionary interrogation of British identity and its making from the perspective of the post-Union Scot".[3] Perhaps the most influential of current critiques has been that of Robert Crawford, whose *Devolving English Literature*, and his most recent, edited collection, *The Scottish Invention of English Literature*, are archaeological investigations into the historical development of our modern concept of not only Scottish literature, but also English and British literature.[4] In its scope it is nothing less than a deconstruction of the whole notion of British literature, and as such is an investigation into the British establishment to rank alongside Linda Colley's analysis of the historical development Britishness.[5]

The literary exploration of identity Crawford undertakes provides, I would argue, one useful model for the development of a lines of inquiry into the identity of Scottish jurisprudence, and it is to his general argument that I would like now to turn. From the outset Crawford makes it clear that he is not writing a conventional chronological history of Scottish literature, but rather following a particular line of critical argument. He argues that the Scots' solution to the problems of identity and national culture posed by the Union was to "develop a 'British Literature' throughout both the eighteenth and nineteenth centuries, before a more explicitly nationalist, post-British literary consciousness came to the fore in the twentieth century".[6] In making this claim, Crawford abandons versions of the core-periphery model of cultural development in Scotland—in which the core,

1   D Allan, *Virtue, Learning and the Scottish Enlightenment: Ideas of Scholarship in Early Modern History* (Edinburgh University Press, Edinburgh, 1993).

2   C Craig, "The Body in the Kitbag: History and the Scottish Novel" (1979) *Cencrastus* 1, 18–22; C Craig, "Nation and History" (1984) *Cencrastus* 19, 13–16; *The History of Scottish Literature*, General Editor, C Craig, 4 vols, (Aberdeen University Press, Aberdeen, 1987–88); C Craig *Out of History: Narrative Paradigms in Scottish and English Culture* (Polygon, Edinburgh, 1996).

3   G Turnbull, "James Boswell: Biography and the Union" in A Hook (ed) *The History of Scottish Literature*, vol ii, 1660–1800, (Aberdeen University Press, Aberdeen, 1987) p 157.

4   R Crawford, *Devolving English Literature* (Clarendon Press, Oxford, 1992); R Crawford, *The Scottish Invention of English Literature* (Cambridge University Press, Cambridge, 1998).

5   L Colley, *Britons: Forging the Nation, 1707–1837* (Yale University Press, New Haven, 1992).

6   Crawford, *Devolving English Literature*, p 9.

ie England, dominates and oppresses the peripheral cultures at its margins.[1] Instead, he posits a more complex model where:

> "while for centuries the margins have been challenging, interrogating and even structuring the supposed 'centre', the development of the subject 'English Literature' has constantly involved and reinforced an oppressive homage to centralism. As such, English Literature is a force which must be countered continually by a devolutionary momentum."[2]

By taking a radical swerve into historical re-interpretation of sources in local and provincial centres, Crawford avoids a dualist construct of centre/periphery, English/Scottish literature: "Often what small or vulnerable cultural groups need is … a construction or reconstruction of a 'usable past', an awareness of a cultural tradition which will allow them to preserve or develop a sense of their own distinctive identity, their constituting difference."[3] This argument enables Crawford to claim that the "'provincial' energies so important to Scottish writing, and the anthropological viewpoint developed by Scottish writers, fed into American writing and into the essentially 'provincial' movement we know as Modernism".[4] It is an original approach entailing, as Crawford readily admits, a "provocative rereading of a wide variety of texts", not least in juxtapositions of figures and texts not traditionally linked—J G Frazer and Carlyle for example, or Boswell's *The Journal of a Tour to the Hebrides*, Smollett's *Humphrey Clinker*, and Scott's *Waverley*.[5] Crawford thus seeks to re-interpret for us the historical context of individual texts, and thereby to refashion the customary *gestalt* of texts in the canon. Identity and difference are thus key themes throughout his work.

We need to be cautious about drawing analogies between law and literature, but we can certainly ask how Crawford's project might contribute to our understanding of Scottish jurisprudence. I believe it could do so in at least three ways. First, it treats identity as a highly rhetorical concept. The historical complexity of constitutional thinking in and on Scotland, for example, relies on certain assumptions about identity and ways of belonging to the political whole that require close study.[6] There is, as

---

1 For the classic statement of this, see M Hechter, *Internal Colonialism: The Celtic Fringe in British National Development, 1536–1966* (Routledge & Kegan Paul, London, 1975). There have been a number of important critiques of this, notably in T Nairn, *The Break-Up of Britain: Crisis and Neo-Nationalism*, 2nd edn (Verso, London, 1981), and C Harvie, *Scotland and Nationalism: Scottish Society and Politics 1707–1994* (Routledge, London, 1994).

2 R Crawford, *Devolving English Literature* (Clarendon Press, Oxford, 1992), p 7.

3 *Devolving English Literature*, p 5.

4 *Devolving English Literature*, p 9.

5 *Devolving English Literature*, pp 9, 79. Other writers have pointed out the links between exploration, anthropology and literature in the nineteenth century. See e.g. P McCarey, "Mungo's Hat and Maxwell's Demon" (1990) 84 *Edinburgh Review* 93–113, on the influence of Mungo Park and his travel narratives on Scott's work, particularly *Waverley*.

6 And this study has been the province generally of historians rather than lawyers. See amongst many examples the work of R Finlay, *Partnership for Good? Scottish Politics and the Union Since 1880*, (John Donald, Edinburgh, 1997); M Ash, *The Strange Death of Scottish History* (Ramsay Head Press, Edinburgh, 1980); C Kidd, *Subverting Scotland's Past: Scottish Whig Historians and the Creation of an Anglo-British Identity, 1689–c.1830* (Cambridge University Press, Cambridge, 1993).

Attwooll describes it, a dialogue between "aspects of its constitutional law and the recurrence in its wider culture of certain ideas about the proper location and use of political power"[1] that needs further analysis, and Crawford's model of the place of the provincial has much to offer legal commentators in this respect. Second, it raises fundamental questions about the relationships between contemporary legal texts and their precursors. Texts such as Buchanan's *De Jure Regni Apud Scotos*, and concepts such as the community of the realm, derived from the Declaration of Arbroath and similar documents, for example, have been used in recent debates to buttress arguments for popular sovereignty.[2] Third, it leads us to question the status of a legal text. Should this include only practitioners' textbooks and overtly jurisprudential texts? Or can we expand our notion of the legal canon by considering other texts that are not at first glance overtly "legal"? We can begin to appreciate the force of this last point by considering the writings of a group of later nineteenth-century Scottish lawyers. These authors wrote upon what would now be regarded as anthropological subjects, but their writings at the same time formed an important bridge between law and ethnology.

ANTHROPOLOGY, CONSTITUTION AND LAW

The connections between jurisprudence and the historiographical traditions of the seventeenth and eighteenth centuries in Scotland did not cease in the nineteenth century. Instead, as we shall see, they mirrored the dominant cultural concepts of the time. A key figure in this process was James Lorimer whose texts, particularly his *Institutes*, reveal his interest in the historical mediation of law and legal process.[3] In his manuscript lecture notes we can discern the patterns of thought behind these and similar texts. As he put it in one lecture:

> "We live in a 'historical age' as opposed to a philos.¹· in an age, that is to say in which the main guidance to wh: men look consists in the information which they possess with reference to the results of former experience."[4]

This distinction was fairly common currency in the latter half of the nineteenth century. It is present, for instance, in the aesthetics of Walter Pater or the Hegelian approaches of John Caird to Idealism.[5] Lorimer, though, was

1 E Attwooll, *The Tapestry of the Law: Scotland, Legal Culture and Legal Theory* (Kluwer, London, 1997), p xiii, summarising esp. chapter III.
2 C Beveridge and R Turnbull, *Scotland After Enlightenment: Image and Tradition in Modern Scottish Culture* (Polygon, Edinburgh, 1997) pp 82, 86, 96
3 The full title is revealing: *The Institutes of the Law of Nations: A Treatise of the Jural Relations of Separate Political Communities* (Edinburgh, 1884).
4 J Lorimer, MSS, Edinburgh University, Gen 101.
5 See W Pater, *Plato and Platonism* (Macmillan, London, 1894); J Caird, "The Study of History" *University Addresses* (Maclehose, Glasgow, 1898), where he draws distinctions between literary history and what he terms "the science of philosophic history" (p 240). See also J Inglis, "The Historical Study of Law", (1863) *Journal of Jurisprudence* 587, which consists of extracts from an address by Inglis to the Juridical Society.

opposed to Caird's abstraction of philosophical history. For him, history in a law faculty ought to be taught in relation not to the development of constitutional government alone, but to political and social life generally.[1]

In Lorimer's lectures there is thus a wide range of historical references. The pre-classical is juxtaposed to medieval, and non-western systems are represented while the comparative and the historical are ever present. There are stadial plans drafted in notes, and elaborated in redrafted paragraphs. Reading these, and texts such as *Studies National and International,* one has the impression of Lorimer forming a typical Victorian synthesis from the rich matrices of juristic traditions. What marks his work out, however, is that he turns these comparisons to the recurrent theme of the relation between natural law and identity:

> "The literature of India furnishes innumerable monuments of the care with which the principles of natural law were elaborated into practical rules and realized in all those departments of private law wh:, in a very general way, we are accustomed to group under the head of Status, as opposed to Contract."[2]

This comparativist impulse in Lorimer's work was increasingly present in the jurists that followed him. This is a turn that Cairns Craig defines, in his essay on the "historyless" nature of much of Scottish literary narratives: "if eighteenth-century Scotland pondered the issue of how history was ordered and how it developed and where it was aimed, nineteenth-century Scotland pondered what was before history and what might never have been incorporated into it".[3] In the latter half of the nineteenth century a number of writers throughout Europe and the USA became interested in pre-classical and non-western legal systems, in the concept of what came to be known as primitive society.[4] This discipline, however, did not spring up fully-formed in the later nineteenth century, but partly grew, as ethnology, from the study of classical antiquity. The German ethnologist Jakob Bachofen, for instance, intended his seminal ethnological work *Das Mütterrecht* as an analysis of classical society. It was also partly a product of the enlightenment traditions of comparative history, whose roots in Scotland, as David Allan has so comprehensively demonstrated, lie within

---

1 See, e.g. J Lorimer *On the Sphere and Function of an Academical Faculty of Law* (Emily Faithfull, London, 1864), pp 12–13. See also the work of Galbraith Miller.
2 J Lorimer, MSS, Edinburgh University, Gen 101. Lorimer on occasion will bring the present into direct comparison with the past, in a way that Frazer does in *The Golden Bough: A Study in Magic and Religion* (Macmillan, London, 1913–15). Thus, in his lecture "Of the rise of scientific jurisprudence", Lorimer writes of Aquinas:
  "[t]he far graver questions as to the rights of private property which agitate society in our own day, and threaten to become more and more pressing, were by no means unknown to Thomas Aquinas, and it is very interesting to see how he answered them in circumstance so different from ours. He had no sweltering and festering mass of misery and disease to deal with, at all comparable to that which our manufacturing industries deposit". (MSS, Edinburgh University, Gen 101.)
3 C Craig, *Out of History: Narrative Paradigms in Scottish and English Culture* (Polygon, Edinburgh, 1996), p 45.
4 The most famous and influential of these included Bachofen, Maine, Fustel de Coulanges, P Lubbock, J F McLennan, Robertson Smith, Morgan, William Tyler and J G Frazer.

the earlier legal and historiographical traditions of the sixteenth and seventeenth centuries.[1]

In Scotland, therefore, law was a fertile source social analysis and had been for some time. David Hume's *History*, for example, dealt with changes in ownership of property, and dwelt upon the cultural shifts wrought by these changes.[2] And throughout the eighteenth century, Gilbert Stuart, John Millar, William Robertson, Lord Hailes and others had focused upon constitutional issues, an area of concern and interest in the wake of the parliamentary union with England. This interest was matched in the later nineteenth century by John Ferguson McLennan (1827–81), whose article in the ninth edition of the *Encyclopaedia Britannica* on "Law" dealt to a large extent with public and constitutional law and clearly owed debts to the Scots enlightenment tradition of historical and constitutional inquiry.

This was an approach that lies at the heart of his most influential book, *Primitive Marriage* (first edition, 1865). This book was written partly to define the concept of primitive society, and partly to correct what he regarded as Maine's mistaken view of that society in *Ancient Law* (1861). However, McLennan's interest in marriage law did not remain in the context of primitive society. In an article entitled "Marriage and Divorce: The Law of England and Scotland" published in the *North British Review* he vigorously defended what were then seen as Scotland's "barbarous" marriage customs.[3] He did so not merely by comparing the different regimes and their effects in contemporary society, but by explaining the customs as arising from historical and social dimensions. The book became a seminal text, not only for other early Scots anthropologists such as Robertson Smith (who knew McLennan, and whose own *Kinship and Marriage in Early Arabia* (1885) is indebted to McLennan) and J G Frazer, but for other early ethnologists such as Maine, William Tyler and Lewis Henry Morgan. While he studied for the Bar, for instance, Frazer read Maine's *Ancient Law*. His copy survives, peppered with arguments against Maine, and citation in support of McLennan. It is filled with insights he was later to develop in *The Golden Bough*:

> "Language, spoken or written, is a species of signs. Signs are modes of conveying thought between intelligent beings by means of sensible impressions. Signs are of two kinds: representative and symbolical."[4]

This is a remarkable passage, prefiguring Saussure, but it relies, as does the whole comparative method, upon the concept of parallel evolution. McLennan's and Frazer's ethnology and their comparative jurisprudence

---

1 See D Allan, *Virtue, Learning and the Scottish Enlightenment: Ideas of Scholarship in Early Modern History* (Edinburgh University Press, Edinburgh, 1993).
2 Hume, it will be remembered, was Librarian of the Faculty of Advocates.
3 J F McLennan, "Marriage and Divorce: The Law of England and Scotland" in *North British Review* (August 1861), pp 187, 198.
4 J G Frazer, quoted in R Ackerman, *J G Frazer: His Life and Work* (Cambridge University Press, Cambridge, 1987), p 70.

is based upon a model of comparative philology. As Robert Ackerman, Frazer's biographer, points out:

> "That the mind of man, under whatever circumstances and at whatever period, works in pretty much the same way was a conviction Frazer derived in the first instance from his empiricist forebears and in the second from Victorian evolutionary theory. His naiveté is that he applies the first to the second, as if a commonality of logical processes somehow guarantee a common course of cultural development."[1]

The anthropological writings, exotic ethnological texts at first glance, are nevertheless intriguing episodes in Scottish nineteenth-century legal thought that pose many questions for us. To what extent did anthropological inquiry influence other patterns of Scottish legal thought in the nineteenth and early twentieth centuries? How was this inquiry influenced by Darwinian and positivist ideas concerning the place of natural law and law in society? How does its treatment of legal sources and system sit beside home rule movements and imperial constitutionalism?[2] To what extent was it a product of unease about the status of Scotland and its own identity? These are some of the many questions that still require to be asked of this episode in Scottish legal thought in order to clarify its meaning for us.

The anthropological writings are a good example in law, therefore, of Crawford's project—indeed they are identified by him in *Devolving English Literature* as an important episode in the intellectual history of late nineteenth century Scotland. As Adam Kuper puts it in his study of early anthropology, "in practice primitive society proved to be [the anthropologists'] own society (as they understood it) seen in a distorting mirror ... They looked back in order to understand the nature of the present, on the assumption that modern society had evolved from its antithesis".[3] McLennan, Robertson Smith, Frazer and others wrote what came to be foundational texts for a range of disciplines; and they re-interpreted Enlightenment historical and jurisprudential theory of the origins of civil society in the context of evolutionary science and geological time. They represented to their society a narrative of the origins of law which explained, in terms which drew from traditional thought and contemporary science, how that society might have come to be what it was. Their society was deeply interested in what they had to say. In a revealing coincidence, Robertson Smith's trial for heresy in 1879, over his claims concerning the status of Biblical narratives, was covered by Scottish news-

---

1 *J G Frazer: His Life and Work*, p 73.
2 For information on the later nineteenth-century home rule movements, see Harvie, *Scotland and Nationalism: Scottish Society and Politics 1707–1994* (Routledge, London, 1994); J Mitchell, *Strategies for Self-Government: The Campaigns for a Scottish Parliament* (Polygon, Edinburgh, 1996), esp. the chapter entitled "Home Rule Pressure Groups". For an analysis of imperial constitutionalism in the Scottish context, see A Rodger, "Thinking about Scots Law", (1996) 1 ELR 3.
3 A Kuper, *The Invention of Primitive Society: Transformations of an Illusion* (Routledge, London, 1988) p 5.

papers at the same time as Gladstone's Home Rule proposals.[1] The juxta-position is extraordinarily apt as both issues were indications of shifts in self-image and identity. In Robertson Smith's trial it becomes possible for secular sciences (particularly philology) to debate with theological inquiry about the place of philosophy and religion. In Gladstone's speeches, another constitution becomes possible, though not actual. In both, there is the attempt to alter cherished sources of identity, to reveal that the encrusted text of the law (theological and constitutional) was really a palimpsest of diverse and often contradictory sources.

THE PROVINCE OF JURISPRUDENCE

The anthropological writings were of course not the only juristic literature of the period. In journals such as the early *Juridical Review* and the earlier *Journal of Jurisprudence*, in the writings of the Hegelians, and of Galbraith Miller, Dewar Gibb and others there are many different strands of legal thought. Some (especially in the journals and textbooks) are concerned more conventionally with the development of private law; but there is also much valuable jurisprudential commentary.[2] However, the question of just why, in spite of this, there was no attempt to determine the province of jurisprudence in Scotland in this crucial period is complex. It would be easy to see in the lack of definition a failure of the tradition, and a falling away from the Enlightenment precursors. But I would argue that this is not the case. As Crawford has pointed out with regard to literature, in the past provincial energies have tended to feed the metropolitan and, in the process, the complex relations of the local have remained invisible. This may be true of later nineteenth-century Scottish jurisprudence. On the other hand, it may be that the Austinian project of definition was simply seen by contemporary figures as irrelevant to a Scottish intellectual tradition that had its own constitutional dialogue, its own political alternatives, and which was constructing a prehistory to its legal foundations.[3]

However one explains it, for us in the twenty-first century there remains the need to represent and re-interpret the tradition, to ourselves and others. It is a point made by Alasdair Gray in a famous passage from *Lanark*:

---

1 The coverage of Smith's trial is extensive, and the arguments of counsel closely followed with extensive commentary. As William Donaldson reminds us, the nineteenth-century Scottish press was an accurate barometer of the pressure for social and political change—see *Popular Literature in Victorian Scotland: Language, Fiction and the Press* (Aberdeen University Press, Aberdeen, 1986).

2 As Walker has pointed out, Scottish legal text publication in the period 1880–1918 was in a relatively healthy state: D M Walker, "Legal Scholarship in Scotland" 1960 SLT (News) 10.

3 In saying this, I am not representing late nineteenth-century English jurisprudence or constitutional thinking as unitary or cohesive. I agree with Michael Lobban that there were a number of traditions, although there was "an increasing reconciliation between historical, moral and Austinian approaches": Michael Lobban, "Was there a Nineteenth-Century 'English School of Jurisprudence'?" (1995) 16(1) *Legal History* 34 at 51.

"Glasgow is a magnificent city" said McAlpin. "Why do we hardly ever notice that?" "Because nobody imagines living here," said Thaw ... "Think of Florence, Paris, London, New York. Nobody visiting them for the first time is a stranger because he's already visited them in paintings, novels, history books and films. But if a city hasn't been used by an artist not even the inhabitants live there imaginatively. What is Glasgow to most of us? A house, the place we work, a football park or golf course, some pubs and connecting streets. That's all. No, I'm wrong, there's also the cinema and library. And when our imagination needs exercise we use these to visit London, Paris, Rome under the Caesars, the American West at the turn of the century, anywhere but here and now. Imaginatively Glasgow exists as a music-hall song and a few bad novels. That's all we've given to the world outside. It's all we've given to ourselves."[1]

The situation has changed, of course, for both Glasgow and Scotland in many ways since the post-War period. Indeed, the transforming cultural energies and renaissance of historical research in the last few decades has stemmed from a determination to reverse this situation, and to represent the richness and complexity of society in Scotland both to the world and to ourselves. However, this work remains to be done in the area of jurisprudence, and its absence is increasingly felt. The continuing development of EU economic and political policies, the transforming effect of human rights legislation on many aspects of legal practice, the presence of a new legislative assembly in our midst, and above all the endless cultural and economic frontier of globalisation—all this requires from us a continual re-making of our past, a re-reading of our legal texts and institutions.

Or rather, a *mis*reading. It might be said that my case study of the anthropologists is a perverse misreading of the tradition, a few proto-anthropologists wedged into a tradition dominated by the relentless development of private law, by positivism and legal professionalisation. But I would argue that such a misreading is fundamental to the construction of our legal identity. Such "provocative re-readings" give us fresh insights into how our traditions may be constructed.

We can see this process of misreading at work in the literature on globalisation. Boaventura de Sousa Santos' recent text on the subject, for instance, uses critical categories typical of Bloom to aid in the construction of emergent paradigms in law: "[a]s there is a literary canon that establishes what is and what is not literature, there is also a legal canon that establishes what is and what is not law".[2] The canon, according to Santos, still has state law at its core, but is reproduced by "multiple mechanisms of acculturation and socialization".[3] Santos' book is nothing if not ambitious. Using the concept of "interlegality", he attempts to create forms of emancipations for globalised societies, based upon a dialogic rhetoric, and

---

1 A Gray, *Lanark: A Life in Four Books* (Canongate, Edinburgh, 1981), p 243.
2 Boaventura de Sousa Santos, *Toward a New Common Sense: Law, Science and Politics in the Paradigmatic Transition* (Routledge, London, 1995) p 473.
3 *Toward a New Common Sense*, p 473.

situated in six spaces in the world, spaces which are also rhetorical *topoi*: householdplace, workplace, marketplace, communityplace, citizenplace and worldplace.[1] His "places" are remarkably close to Crawford's view of the power of provincial energies in modern literature. These are no less than imagined communities, utopian in their projection of new legal orders within a globalised, transnationalised world system. Furthermore, as Twining has observed in his commentary on Santos' interpretation of globalisation, the "cross-cutting of normative orders puts the phenomena of legal pluralism at the centre of understanding law".[2] It is an intellectual pluralism that would not have been unfamiliar to Lorimer, McLennan or Frazer, and it is one that is essential in these first years of a new Parliament.

The phrase "imagined communities" itself is, of course, the title of Anderson's important study of nationalism.[3] For him, the nation is an imagined political community—and imagined as both inherently limited and sovereign. In a similar vein we can argue that the Scottish Parliament, even a subordinated Parliament, like the concept of the state, or of primitive society, is "not just a set of institutional arrangements but a set of purposes too".[4] Philip Allott has made similar observations: we are, he observes, ineluctably influenced by previous views of constitutional theory: Montesquieu, Kant and Hegel, Savigny, Marx, Freud and Wittgenstein have all taught us that the constitution is not historically haphazard: it "is also an organism, and programme which is also a personality. A constitution is not an arrangement of institutions. It is a dialogue between consciousness and circumstance".[5]

Consciousness and a sense of achieved selfhood, though, are hardly possible without a highly-developed sense of the past. For Scots lawyers this must involve the process of reconstructing Scottish jurisprudence— historical, comparative, critical—to place contemporary political and constitutional events within a context of Scottish legal thought and history. But as Santos, Twining and others remind us, community is more than nation alone—the phrase can be applied to any community, indeed any canon; and our sense of canon and community is predicated on our imag-

---

1   *Toward a New Common Sense*, p 484. Santos' methodology owes a lot to the literature of intertextuality. As Timothy Beal points out, "the basic force of intertextuality is to problematize, even spoil, textual boundaries—those lines of demarcation which allow a reader to talk about *the* meaning, subject, or origin of a writing": see "Glossary" in Danna Nolan Fewell (ed) *Reading Between Texts: Intertextuality and the Hebrew Bible* (John Knox Press, Louisville, Kentucky, Westminster), p 22. This is a force that Santos uses for a variety of purposes. Even the physical ordering of the text on the page embodies this—see chapter three, where the left-hand pages consist of "The Law of the Oppressed: The Construction and Reproduction of Legality in Pasargada", while the right-hand page is "chapter three-in-a-mirror", a much more personal account of "Relationships Among Perceptions that we call Identity: Doing Research in Rio's Squatter Settlements".

2   W Twining, *Globalisation and Legal Theory* (Butterworths, London, 2000), p 224. As Twining points out, he and Santos are in broad agreement on this point.

3   B Anderson, *Imagined Communities: Reflections on the Origins and Spread of Nationalism* (Verso, London, revised and extended edition, 1991).

4   N D Lewis, *Choice and the Legal Order: Rising Above Politics* (Butterworths, London, 1996), p 132.

5   P Allott, "The Theory of the British Constitution" in H Gross and R Harrison (eds) *Jurisprudence: Cambridge Essays* (Clarendon Press, Oxford, 1992).

inary conversations with the dead.[1] The conversation—talk about law as well as law-talk—must be broad enough to include the kind of multi-disciplinary inquiry proposed here. In its absence the domain of Scottish jurisprudence is still under-researched, under-theorised and under-valued.

---

1 R Rorty, "The Historiography of Philosophy: Four Genres" in R Rorty, J B Schneewind and Q Skinner (eds) *Philosopy in History: Essays on the Historiography of Geography* (Cambridge University Press, Cambridge, 1984), pp 49–75.

9 Under the Shadow over Parliament House: The Strange Case of Legal Nationalism

Lindsay Farmer

"The people of Scotland are proud of their law, although, possibly, most of them, being laymen, would find difficulty in giving an articulate explanation of their pride. The fact suggests at least that their law possesses a character so distinct that pride in it, as in any important national possession is easy to understand."[1]

THE STRANGE CASE OF LEGAL NATIONALISM

In a collection of essays on devolution and the Scottish legal system published in 1976, the editor identified a phenomenon which he termed "legal nationalism". This, he suggested, was a form of nationalism "of a slightly different type from the normal nationalism or patriotism", which was to be found uniquely in the Scottish legal profession.[2] Leaving aside the question of what is to be understood as "normal" nationalism, it is worth examining what he understood legal nationalism to be. He considered it to have four principal elements: a belief in the inherent strengths of Scots law; a belief in the exceptional character of the system; that it was a legal system ideally matched to the needs and personality of the Scottish people; and the conviction that the system should be safeguarded against those influences (principally, but not exclusively, English) that sought to dilute its identity. The distinctive characteristic of the legal nationalist, however, was that this commitment to a distinctive Scottish legal identity did not necessarily entail any support for nationalist politics.

We are all familiar with this sort of sentiment. It seems chiefly to be manifested in the pride that is taken in the achievements of Scottish legal institutions, in the claims of "It couldn't happen here" or "Our legal system is fairer", that regularly greet news of miscarriages and injustices elsewhere. On the face of it, this sort of comparison seems relatively harmless—even if it is monotonous and not especially interesting—for there is

---

1 A D Gibb, *A Preface to Scots Law* 1st edn (W Green & Son, Edinburgh, 1944), p 1.
2 J Grant (ed), *Independence and Devolution: The Legal Implications for Scotland* (W Green & Son, Edinburgh, 1976), p x.

surely nothing wrong with a little pride in the achievements of Scots law. Indeed, it might be questioned whether the Scots lawyer can be other than a nationalist in this limited sense, for the very claim to practise Scots law involves a small assertion of identity and difference. However, the phenomenon of legal nationalism goes deeper than this, suggesting a more complex understanding of the relationship between legal system and national culture. In making claims about the exceptional qualities and traditions of the law, it shades into the argument that Scots law, together with other institutions of Scottish life, has been central to the creation and preservation of Scottish identity and culture. It goes beyond a simple pride in Scottish legal institutions, to the additional claim that law has shaped national identity.[1] Moreover, as Lord Rodger has pointed out, the claims made about the Scottish legal system are not only descriptive, but are also a call to action. The assertion of superiority or difference is also, either implicitly or explicitly, a demand for the preservation or development of the system in a particular way.[2] There may be dispute over the precisely what is to be preserved—the mix of civil and common law, the relation of principle and precedent—but there is agreement that inaction is the same as indifference or neglect. The legal nationalist thus stakes out a position that places the legal system, and the tradition it represents, at the heart of Scotland's political and cultural life, and has often seemed to be amongst the most vocal defenders of Scottish culture and institutions.

However, at this point we must recall the observation made by Grant, that legal nationalism has been distinct from political nationalism. It is surely worthy of remark that, notwithstanding the claims made for the importance of Scots law as a carrier of national identity, Scots lawyers have, by and large, played little part in the development of political nationalism in Scotland.[3] Indeed, the argument is sometimes put more strongly, in the form of a claim that for all their expressions of national pride, lawyers have shown a greater interest in the preservation of the Union, and that legal nationalism is in fact deeply unionist in character. Thus, legal nationalism would seem to have a double character—nationalist sentiments laid over a secret life of unionism. Here, perhaps, we find the doppelgänger so beloved of analysts of Scottish culture: the repression that gives rise to the justified sinner; the combination of romantic nationalism with the desire to subjugate Scottishness in a larger Anglo-British identity in Scott; the strange case of Dr Jekyll and Mr Hyde. The double of the legal nationalist is the respectable unionist. If, then, we are to accept the claim that law is an institution of national identity, this must be a more

---

1　This view of the Scottish legal tradition is particularly associated with Lord Cooper and Professor T B Smith. See Cooper, *The Scottish Legal Tradition* (Saltire Society, Edinburgh, 1949); Smith, *British Justice: The Scottish Contribution* (Stevens, London, 1961). For criticism see I D Willock, "The Scottish Legal Heritage Revisited" in J Grant (ed) *Independence and Devolution: The Legal Implications for Scotland* (W Green & Son, Edinburgh, 1976).

2　A Rodger, "Thinking About Scots Law" (1996) 1 ELR 4.

3　By contrast, in one of the classic analyses of nationalism, lawyers are identified as part of the bourgeois intelligentsia whose actions led to the development of political and cultural nationalism in the nineteenth century: E Gellner, *Nations and Nationalism* (Blackwell, Oxford, 1983).

complex relationship than the conventional understanding of legal nationalism has allowed.

Of course, one response to this might simply be that the significance of legal nationalism has been overstated. It is part of the current orthodoxy that few lawyers outside a small circle of judges and academics ever shared this belief in the values and importance of the Scottish legal tradition.[1] Moreover, most lawyers are detached from politics, and it is in any case well understood that there need be no necessary connection between the demand for a national legal system and the demand for any form of political independence—even if the two things have been conflated in the writings of certain commentators. However, I think that there are two important reasons why these are not sufficient answers. On the one hand, it is clear that a full examination of the relationship between law and political and cultural identity must go beyond lawyers' perceptions of the legal system to include analysis of the role of law as a social institution. If, as Neil MacCormick has recently argued, law is a civic institution that shapes nations and national politics,[2] then this must be more than a matter of the abstract or theoretical relation between law and nation-state. It must be studied in the particular context of a Scotland where lawyers saw themselves, and were seen by others, as political and civic leaders.

An example of the way this kind of argument might be developed can be found in the work of Christopher Harvie. He has argued that, far from being detached from politics, the role of lawyers has been central to the shaping of the Scottish political character since the Union.[3] The key point he makes is that through the control of patronage and key administrative and economic functions, lawyers were not only mediators between the stunted Scottish political realm and London, but were also mediators between the political estates within Scotland. The legal profession, he argues, did not play a key role within liberationist nationalist movements in Scotland, as elsewhere in Europe, because they had an interest in maintaining a certain type of role and a certain type of identity that was very much bound up with the status quo.[4] It may even have been the case that the grounding assumptions of legal nationalism actually precluded the development of a more radical political role, given that lawyers had an interest in sustaining the existing political settlement. From this perspective, legal nationalism can be understood as nothing so much as the means

---

1 This is a point first made by Willock, "The Scottish Legal Heritage Revisited" (see note 1 on page 152 above), in drawing attention to the elitism of the Cooper/Smith position. See also A Rodger, "Thinking About Scots Law" (1996) 1 ELR 3.

2 N MacCormick, *Questioning Sovereignty: Law, State and Practical Reason* (OUP, Oxford, 1999) Chs 9, 10 and 11.

3 C Harvie, "Legalism, Myth and National Identity in Scotland in the Imperial Epoch" (1987) 26 *Cencrastus* 35; C Harvie, "The Most Mighty of Goddesses: The Scots and the Law" in *Travelling Scot: Scotus Viator: Essays on the History, Politics and Future of the Scots* (Argyll Publishing, Glendaruel, 1999).

4 A similar point is made by Colin Kidd who argues that Scottish historiography and identity, were subsumed within a larger Anglo-British identity, which was largely shaped by the Ancient Constitutionalism of the English common lawyers. See Kidd, *Subverting Scotland's Past: Scottish Whig Histories and the Creation of an Anglo-British Identity 1689–c 1830* (Cambridge University Press, Cambridge, 1993).

whereby Scots lawyers sought to defend their political position through a defence of the autonomy of the legal system. The distinctive quality of the lawyers within the Scottish legal tradition may turn out to be an ability to position themselves unerringly at the point at which political and social power intersect. At the very least this raises new questions about the relationship between legal, political and cultural identity within Scotland.[1]

This brings us to the second point, which is that we simply do not know enough about the historical development and influence of the beliefs that comprise legal nationalism. Legal nationalism is a curious phenomenon precisely because the fact of the independence of the legal system was made to carry an extra ideological burden, expressed in the form of the belief in the Scottish legal tradition. To examine this is to question the significance of the identification and survival of a separate legal tradition within Scotland, and its role as political power is devolved—which is, of course, a principal theme of this collection of essays.

However, I do not propose to take this question up in the traditional style of a weighing of the merits of one system against another, or searching for the common or distinctive characteristics of Scottish legal institutions. Instead, I am proposing a more analytical and historical examination of the case of legal nationalism. This requires a certain distance from the Scottish legal tradition, for in spite of their highly vaunted attachment to principled thought and speculation Scots lawyers have only rarely been drawn into any process of self-examination. Indeed, it is probably the case that belief in the tradition has rather hampered this process, as priority is given to action and critical analysis is seen as potentially threatening. What is required, then, is an approach that is addressed to a completely different series of questions: how did lawyers come to see themselves as the defenders of nationalism and Scottish identity?; what was the content of this nationalism and why?; and how, if at all, has it changed over time? It is only by seeking to address these sorts of questions that we can engage in the deeper analysis of the relationship between law and national identity that is necessary to the more general study of Scottish legal culture.

I will do this here through an examination of the writings and career of Professor Andrew Dewar Gibb (1893–1973), who combined a legal career as holder of the Regius Chair in Scots Law at the University of Glasgow, with a political career that included being a founder member and chair of the modern Scottish National Party. His "double life" presents an excellent opportunity to examine the phenomenon of legal nationalism, for although one might have expected Gibb's legal nationalism to be dissolved into political nationalism—thus refuting the charge that legal nationalism could not combine with political nationalism—that is not at all the case. In fact, as we shall see through an examination of his promotion of Scots law, it is his legal nationalism which colours his political nationalism and gives it its distinctive character. This, in other words, is to argue

---

1 This might also be explored from the perspective of literature. See P Maharg, "Lorimer, Inglis and RLS: Law and the Kailyard Lock-Up" (1995) *Juridical Review* 280.

that the conservative quality of legal nationalism went beyond issues of character or party to lie at the very heart of Scottish legal and political culture.

LIVING UNDER THE SHADOW: PROFESSOR ANDREW DEWAR GIBB

Dewar Gibb had an unusual academic career in the period preceding his appointment to the Glasgow chair. A graduate of Glasgow University he became a member of the Scottish bar in 1914 and the English bar in 1919— in between time serving under the command of Winston Churchill during the First World War.[1] He went on to hold posts simultaneously as a lecturer in the universities of Edinburgh and Cambridge, teaching English law in the former and Scots law in the latter. This peripatetic existence came to an end when he was appointed to the Regius Chair of Scots Law in the University of Glasgow on the sudden death of William Gloag in 1934. He seems to have been a popular and effective teacher, though in a lecture delivered on the verge of retiral in 1958 he confessed that he had never felt any enthusiasm for teaching.[2] He was nonetheless active in advocating the professionalisation of law teaching and the reform of the law degree, and the shape that the full time degree took in the 1960s seems to have been substantially influenced by his vision.[3] He died in 1973, his memorial address in the Glasgow University chapel being delivered in the warmest terms by Professor T B Smith.[4]

Politically he was conservative, beginning his political career as an unsuccessful Unionist candidate in the elections of 1924 and 1929, before becoming involved in nationalist politics in the early 1930s. When John MacCormick began, in the same period, to move the early National Party of Scotland (NPS) away from its socialist roots, Gibb was one of the influential Scots that he courted.[5] These negotiations led ultimately in 1933 to the expulsion of the extreme Celticist elements of the NPS and an amalgamation with the so-called Scottish Party, led at the time by Gibb and G M Thomson, to form the Scottish National Party.[6] Gibb was chairman of the SNP until 1940, when he resigned over the issue of the establishment of the Scottish Convention and the development of an anti-conservative position within the party. He remained active in nationalist politics throughout the 1940s, even as his influence in the party was waning. Just as significantly,

---

1 About which Gibb privately (and anonymously) published a short book: *With Winston Churchill at the Front* (London, 1924).

2 A D Gibb, "25 Years in the Faculty of Law", delivered to the Juridical Society on 7 January 1958 (NLS, Dep. 217, Box 11, folder 4).

3 See e g A D Gibb, "Reform in the Scottish Law School: A Lecture Not Yet Delivered" (1943) *Juridical Review* 152.

4 See 1974 SLT (News) 38.

5 In *Scotland in Eclipse*, published in 1930, Gibb had complained that the weakness of the NPS lay in its Socialist and pro-Irish bias (Toulmin, London, 1930), p 181.

6 On the formation of the SNP see R Finlay, *Independent and Free: Scottish Politics and the Origins of the Scottish National Party 1918–1945* (John Donald, Edinburgh, 1994), esp. Chs 3 and 4.

he was a founding member of the Saltire Society, a society for the preservation and development of Scottish culture, becoming its President in 1954. He was a close friend and associate of Thomas Cooper (later Lord Cooper) who in the same period was active in the founding of the Stair Society and the encouragement of a Scottish legal renaissance to match the self-conscious cultural renaissance being led by the charismatic Hugh MacDiarmid.[1]

His successor's assessment of his academic achievement is terse: "He wrote a good deal, but almost all of it was small".[2] However, this statement does not do full justice to his legal output which is varied, if occasionally eccentric. His main work was as the editor of standard legal works, including several editions of Gloag and Henderson's *Introduction to the Law of Scotland*, and separate treatises on the law of collisions on land and at sea. The title of one of his works, *The Trial of Motor Car Accident Cases* suggests that he was alive to contemporary problems and able to look beyond some of the traditional categories of legal writing.[3] He surely merits a special place in the affections of law students as editor of the first casebook to be published for Scottish law students,[4] and also the *Student's Glossary of Legal Terms*.[5] He also wrote *A Preface to Scots Law*, a brief popular introduction to the Scottish legal system that went through four editions between 1944 and 1964.[6]

The real interest in Gibb's writings, however, lies in a series of works which crossed the boundaries between his legal and political interests: a trilogy of political works, *Scotland in Eclipse*,[7] *Scottish Empire*,[8] and *Scotland Resurgent*[9]; a short political pamphlet on Scots law, *The Shadow on Parliament House: Has Scots Law a Future?*[10]; and, finally, a scholarly account of the relation between the House of Lords and Scots law, *Law From Over the Border: A Short Account of a Strange Jurisdiction*.[11] If we concentrate on these works, we can see that certain very strong, and rather repetitive, themes emerge.

---

1 On the founding of the Stair Society, see 1934 SLT (News) 113.
2 A comment that is perhaps more revealing about its author: D M Walker, *A History of the School of Law* (Glasgow, 1990) p 58.
3 A D Gibb, *The Trial of Motor Car Accident Cases* (London, 1930).
4 A D Gibb, *Select Cases in the Law of Scotland* (W Green & Son, Edinburgh, 1933).
5 A D Gibb, *Student's Glossary of Legal Terms* (W Green & Son, Edinburgh, 1946).
6 A D Gibb, *A Preface to Scots Law* (W Green & Son, Edinburgh, 1944). It is worth noting the rather unusual genesis of this book, prepared as a series of lectures for Polish servicemen stationed in Scotland during the Second World War. Evidence of their enjoyment of this diversion can be seen in NLS, Dep. 217, Box 3 (folder 1). I should note a couple of other curiosities: *Perjury Unlimited: A Mongraph on Nuremberg* (W Green & Son, Edinburgh, 1954); and *Judicial Corruption in the United Kingdom* (W Green & Son, Edinburgh, 1957).
7 A D Gibb, *Scotland in Eclipse* (Toulmin, London, 1930). The publication of this book led to a brief public spat with Sir Harry Lauder, over the characterisation of the Scots as mean!
8 A D Gibb, *Scottish Empire* (Maclehose, London, 1937).
9 A D Gibb, *Scotland Resurgent* (A Mackay, Stirling, 1950).
10 A D Gibb, *The Shadow on Parliament House: Has Scots Law a Future?* (Porpoise Press, Edinburgh, 1932).
11 A D Gibb, *Law From Over the Border: A Short Account of a Strange Jurisdiction* (W Green & Son, Edinburgh, 1950). See also "The Inter-Relation of the Legal Systems of Scotland and England" (1937) 53 LQR 61.

The defining event in Gibb's analysis of Scots law was unquestionably the dissolution of the Scottish parliament under the terms of the Treaty of Union of 1707. The Union, in his view, had inevitably contributed to the eclipse of Scots law and culture, for under the doctrine of the sovereignty of the (English) parliament it was never the case that the Articles of Union could preserve distinctive Scottish institutions. The Union was a straight-forward amalgamation of the two systems in which, in the absence of safeguards, it was inevitable that the weaker would be taken over by the stronger: "the inevitable tendency of the Union was to turn Scotland into a province of England".[1] There had, thus, been a betrayal of these institu-tions by those Scots who had negotiated the union, for they must have known that nothing could be preserved by law. Not only had this amounted to a surrendering of control over Scotland's own affairs and destiny, but it had had fundamental implications for all subsequent rela-tions between the two countries. The pacification of a hostile neighbour on her northern border, allowed England to build her empire—an enterprise which depended on Scottish resources and resourcefulness, even if this was never of direct benefit to Scotland. This led indirectly to the neglect of Scottish institutions, as the government of empire took priority. The empire thus cast a long shadow over such Scottish institutions as remained—and the law in particular.

There were three broad categories of threat to Scots law. The main threat was legislation of the UK parliament. In his earlier writings Gibb drew a distinction between legislation that dealt with matters of social class and that which dealt primarily with individuals—principally, though not exclusively, legislation affecting private law.[2] He did not challenge the necessity of the former category, though he frequently bemoaned the quality of the legislation that was produced (in his later work he turns against even this in a significant manner). Legislation relating to private law, however, was a matter of greater concern, since this interfered in precisely those areas of law where he believed that there was at least a moral obligation to respect the autonomy of Scots law. Here, he describes a lengthy (and familiar) pattern of intervention and abuse of Scots law, beginning with the passing of the Treason Act in 1708 and continuing through the introduction of a Court of Exchequer and civil jury trial.[3] This legislation, moreover, frequently did little more than extend English law to Scotland, with little respect or sensitivity to the different legal context.

The second major threat came from the development of the appellate jurisdiction of the House of Lords in relation to Scottish cases. The problem here was in part due to the fact that while Article XIX of the Treaty of Union did not provide for a a right of appeal to the House of Lords, neither did it exclude it. This jurisdiction was something that the House of Lords had taken on itself in the early eighteenth century, by drawing an analogy

---

1 *The Shadow on Parliament House*, p 13. *Cf.* the later nationalist view, most famously argued in *MacCormick v HM Advocate* 1953 SC 396, that the Union was fundamental law.
2 *The Shadow on Parliament House*, p 14.
3 Seeing, rather surprisingly, the jury as "the prime instrument of legal blackmail": *The Shadow on Parliament House*, p 20.

with the older right of appeal to the (now abolished) Scottish parliament. The result was the production of a system that was both expensive and massively inconvenient to the Scottish litigant—though this did not prevent a considerable number of litigants from trying their luck in London. More importantly, it meant that until 1876, when provision was made for a Scottish law lord to sit in Scottish appeals, Scots law was being administered and developed by judges with neither interest in, nor knowledge of, the system. He drew attention to many cases in which Scots law had been either wilfully or negligently transformed by this process. The situation was compounded for Gibb by the fact that the English common law was inelegant, complex and of a "vicious subtlety", when compared to the plainer virtues of Scots law.[1]

The final threat to Scots law came from within the system, and was the apathy or indifference of Scots lawyers to the destruction of their system. Academic lawyers, such as Erskine and Hume, had adopted anglicised rather than romanised treatments of the law, while practitioners acquiesced in the use of English authorities.[2] This, he argued, was at worst an abandonment of the Scottish legal heritage and at best amounted to wilful neglect. He castigated the legal profession for their willingness to accept that the convergence of the systems was inevitable and necessary, linking this to a wider analysis which criticised the attitude of all Scots because of their unthinking acceptance of the benefits of Union. That Scots law had survived, and even retained its vitality, under such adverse circumstances, was to be attributed to its inherent virtue and purity. The future, the lifting of the shadow, lay in the reform and modernisation of this system, for:

> "The possession of a system of law consonant, despite all that has happened, with the spirit of the people, is destined to be a steadying factor of incalculable worth when the kingdom of Scotland regains control of its own fortunes."[3]

Elements of this position will be familiar to contemporary readers as it has become part of a widespread conventional understanding of Scots law. It is worth noting, for instance, that in spite of his dismissal of Gibb's work, D M Walker uses a similar tripartite analysis of the threats to Scots law in his textbook on the Scottish legal system,[4] and it is equally commonplace for academics to lambast Scots lawyers for their apathy towards the principles or foundations of their legal system.[5] We should not let this blind us,

---

1 *The Shadow on Parliament House*, p 10.
2 See *Law From Over the Border*, p 2; *The Shadow on Parliament House*, p 21.
3 *The Shadow on Parliament House*, p 9. His agenda for reform, set out in the same pamphlet (pp 29 ff), is strikingly modern: the decentralisation of the administration of justice and the strengthening of local courts; abolition of the judicial functions of the sheriff principal; reduction of costs; codification of the law in line with other civilian systems ("the most vital and valuable legal change" p 36); a review commission for the law; bringing the law reports under state control; reforming the feudal system of land ownership; and a national legal service.
4 D M Walker, *Scottish Legal System*, 7th edn (W Green & Son, Edinburgh, 1997), p 160.
5 See e.g. R Black, "Practice and Precept in Scots Law" (1982) *Juridical Review* 31.

however, to what is distinctive about Gibb's position, and what it contributed to the development of legal nationalism.

A striking feature of Gibb's analysis is the ubiquity of the reference to empire. While his guileless celebration in *Scottish Empire* of the role of Scots in the subjugation of native peoples around the globe might be discomfiting to the modern reader, we should resist the temptation to regard it as extraneous to his analysis of Scots law. The recognition of the contribution of Scots to the building of the empire was not simply a matter of righting the historical record, but was linked to a demand for the contemporary recognition of Scots law. In the first place it was connected to his view of Scots law as a world system of law, part of the common heritage of English-speaking lawyers around the globe. Scotland was properly to be counted as a mother-nation of the British empire, and both her law and people were Aryan and independent and should remain so.[1] However, Gibb gave this familiar account a less familiar twist, as he used an argument about the decline of empire to argue for the future independence of Scotland and Scots law.[2] The ending of the imperial role was a matter of regret, but also offered new opportunity as he considered that the history of empire gave ample demonstration of the virtues of the national character and of the fitness of the Scots for rule. The recognition of this would be central to the destruction of the inferiority complex under which many Scots laboured and to the revival of political and cultural identity. In Scotland, then, "with her imperial task ended, she will seek to form and to justify a new conception of her function in the framework of European civilisation".[3] We thus see here the reinvention of the imperial role in the belief that the destiny of Scots law lay in being a bridge between the two great systems of law—common law and civil law—in a European context.

There is one further point that needs to be made in connection with the theme of empire. We have noted the connection he drew between the purity and virility of the national character and that of the legal system. Yet, his patriotism readily slipped into a virulent racism when racial and legal purity were seen to be threatened. The converse of the imperial role was the maintenance of the identity of the motherland. Gibb's belief in the purity of the Scots character was primarily (though not exclusively) expresssed in strong anti-Catholic and anti-Irish sentiment.[4] He regarded the "great Irish trek" to Scotland as "a national problem and a national evil of the first importance", for the Irish were not only responsible for most crime and poverty in Scotland, but also bred unchecked (and were even

---

1 This view of law as a bond of empire was common at the time he wrote. See A Rodger, "Thinking About Scots Law" (1996) 1 ELR 3 at pp 19–23.

2 "The hour is past when the law of Scotland can be called upon to perform an Imperial task. The British Empire is the poorer for that": *The Shadow on Parliament House: Has Scots Law a Future?* (Porpoise Press, Edinburgh, 1932), p 38.

3 *Scottish Empire* (Maclehose, London, 1937), p 315. This view is central to the Cooper/Smith vision of the Scottish legal tradition.

4 See *Scotland in Eclipse* (Toulmin, London 1930), Ch 4; *Scotland Resurgent* (A Mackay, Stirling, 1950), pp 179–184. Cf. the beliefs of Gibb's erstwhile political associate in the Scottish party: G M Thomson, *The Re-Discovery of Scotland* (Kegan Paul, London, 1928), pp 42–53.

encouraged to do so by their own "medicine men").[1] He thus concluded that "in the heart of a dwindling though virile and intelligent race there is growing up another people inferior in every way",[2] and urged that the Irish issue be used as a catalyst for the development of a sense of national identity and purpose.[3] The sense of ethnic and legal identity was thus narrow and extremist, depending on the defence of a narrow core and the exclusion of certain arbitrarily defined harmful influences.

Gibb's views on empire were also central to his understanding of nation and state. This connection is clearest in his book, *Scotland Resurgent*, published in 1950, where he most fully developed his argument for the post-imperial role of the nation-state. Writing at the conclusion of the Second World War and in the twilight of Empire, the tone is more muted and reflective as he considered not only the benefits of nationalism but also the evils that had been committed in its name.[4] He worked hard to defend a version of nationalism against the view that it (and national socialism in particular) was necessarily aggressive and expansionist. He did this by arguing that while nationalism had historically been the begetter of harmful empires—specifically the tyrannies of Rome, Moscow, Germany and England—the primary evil of the age in which he wrote was the "insane" levels of over-government.[5] He argued that the virtue of nationalism was that it offered a means of arresting the march of collectivism and totalitarian government.[6] This mutation in his view of nationalism gave rise to a whole new vocabulary with which to condemn the Union of 1707 as he compared the Union to the annexation of Austria in 1938 and characterised the advocates of union as collaborators. In Scotland, the consequence of the union had initially been a form of dictatorship as power was concentrated in the hands of the Lord Advocate; with the subsequent development of party politics this has led to collectivism and a different sort of dictatorship through the massive amount of social legislation that was being generated by the Westminster parliament.[7]

---

1 *Scotland in Eclipse*, p 53.
2 *Scotland in Eclipse*, p 56. He dismissed the argument that the infusion of Celtic influences would enhance the Scottish aesthetic sensibility: "The finest manure makes no impression on concrete" (p 61).
3 Gibb had at times expressed clear fascist and anti-semitic sympathies: "I have every respect for Hitler and Mussolini and intense admiration for them in almost every way ... I agree that communism is too largely Jewish in origin and development..." (quoted in Finlay, *Independent and Free: Scottish Politics and the Origins of the Scottish National Party 1918–1945* (John Donald, Edinburgh, 1994), pp 197–198). He was unrepentant in his later writing: see *Scotland Resurgent* (A Mackay, Stirling, 1950), p 179. In *Scottish Empire* (Maclehose, London, 1937), at page 309, he also claims that the Scots are less racist than the English.
4 *Scotland Resurgent*, Ch 1. See also *Scottish Empire*, Ch 1.
5 See e.g. *A Preface to Scots Law* (W Green & Son, Edinburgh) (3rd edn, 1961), pv. For an application of this argument in a specific legal context, see "Vicarious Liability for Crime" 1955 SLT (Notes) 21.
6 While on an international level a union of smaller nations could stand against the great powers: *Scotland Resurgent*, esp Chs 1 and 10.
7 A similar view can be found in the writings of Lord Cooper and T B Smith. This is discussed in L Farmer, *Criminal Law, Tradition and Legal Order* (Cambridge University Press, Cambridge, 1997) pp 38–39.

Against this backdrop it is perhaps only minimally surprising to discover that Gibb's view of politics was one that prioritised the role that could be played by certain elite institutions, such as the legal profession, above the need for democratic institutions. Indeed, he makes no reference to any real or imagined tradition of popular sovereignty in Scotland, advocating instead a politics where the power of the legal profession would, if anything, be enhanced. The old Scottish parliament was praised, but less for the constitutional values that it embodied, than the quality of the legislation it produced, and its value as an institution which was in close proximity to the people and affairs being governed.[1] He argued that in the event of independence lawyers could be a key force for social change, and indeed that Scotland would look to her lawyers for leadership.[2] He saw the Bar as a potential "focus of national thought and development", due to its tradition of service and "fine honour".[3] It followed from this that there was a strong emphasis on legal education, which should stress a greater breadth of subjects so that lawyers would be capable of giving the necessary moral and civic leadership.[4] This call of lawyers to arms was concluded bathetically, though perhaps rather presciently, with the claim that in a free Scotland at least "legal unemployment would ... disappear".[5]

It is appropriate at this point to return to the question of the relationship between legal and political nationalism, for we can now see that this distinction is of rather less analytical value than originally appeared to be the case. It is clear that for men like Gibb there was no distinction between the two forms of nationalism. However, this was not because they saw the law as a political force that might lead to liberation, but rather the opposite—that their notion of political nationalism was contained within their understanding of the role of law in Scottish civic and political life.[6] In a stateless nation, politics was carried out, and defined by, institutions such as the law which had historically defined for themselves a role of civil and political leadership. Nationalist politics was thus not driven by either a

---

1 Cf. E Attwooll, *The Tapestry of the Law: Scotland, Legal Culture and Legal Theory* (Kluwer, Dordrecht, 1997) Ch 3, where it is claimed that there is historically a constitutional culture in Scotland.

2 On the elitism of Gibb and the Scottish Party, see Finlay *Independent and Free: Scottish Politics and the Origins of the Scottish National Party 1918–1945* (John Donald, Edinburgh, 1994), Ch 3 esp. at pp 94–95. On the elitism of the Scottish legal tradition, see I D Willock, "The Scottish Legal Heritage Revisited", p 4, in J Grant (ed), *Independence and Devolution: The Legal Implications for Scotland* (W Green & Son, Edinburgh, 1976).

3 A D Gibb, *The Shadow on Parliament House: Has Scots Law a Future?* (Porpoise Press, Edinburgh, 1932), p 29. This is perhaps an oblique reference to the famous lecture by Lord Inglis on the historical study of law (1863).

4 "A Scottish law school of today gives little more encouragement to true legal scholarship than a Baptist church seminary": *The Shadow on Parliament House*, p 6. See also J M Mackay, "Stand Scots Lawyers Where They Could?" (1946) 58 *Juridical Review* 26. This analysis of legal education is not unlike the views expressed in G E Davie, *The Democratic Intellect* (Edinburgh University Press, Edinburgh, 1961).

5 *The Shadow on Parliament House*, p 30.

6 This may be close to what Christopher Harvie means when he talks about the legalism of Scottish political culture, "The Most Mighty of Goddesses: The Scots and the Law" in *Travelling Scot: Scotus Viator: Essays on the History, Politics and Future of the Scots* (Argyle Publishing, Glendaruel, 1999).

democratic ethos or even the desire for political liberation, but rather the more cramped and nostalgic aim of freeing these institutions and elites from the constraints imposed by the development of government from Westminster. To put this another way, Gibb and others like him had a narrow conception of the political, based on the historical role of the legal profession in the government of Scotland, and it was this that shaped, and indeed limited, their understanding of nationalism. It was not that they harboured secret feelings of unionism, but that they were unable to think of nationalism as meaning anything other than the renewal of those institutions which had formerly governed Scotland. The legal system was for him uniquely fitted to carry the additional burden of being an institution of national identity for, because of their singular position straddling civil and political society, lawyers were not only the interpreters of the law, but also of the state of the nation. The weakness of this view lay in its failure to see its own historical position, and recognise that in the post-war period both nation and state were being irrevocably transformed.

RE-ASSESSING THE SCOTTISH LEGAL TRADITION

This re-assessment of the work of Andrew Dewar Gibb throws new light on the Scottish legal tradition. It is not so much that this reveals new information about the content of the beliefs lawyers have held about Scots law, though we can see that there are both clear similarities and differences from the version of the Scottish legal tradition so energetically promoted by Lord Cooper and Professor T B Smith. It is important primarily because it draws attention to the historical forces that shaped the "Scottish legal renaissance" of the middle years of the twentieth century. There are two factors that are of special importance here—which, though they were operating on the nationalist movement as whole, had a particular influence in the legal sphere.

On the one hand, there is the conscious attempt to formulate a post-imperial role for Scots law, that would leave its identity intact, without merging it with the larger group of commonwealth or English-speaking systems. This took an extreme form in the claim that the convergence of common law and civilian systems meant that Scots law represented the global destiny of legal systems. More prosaically it has been suggested that Scots law demonstrates a means of "bridging" these different families, a potential "model" for future codes.[1] On the other hand, the tradition must be seen as a reaction to the growth of the role of government with the rise of the welfare state. While social legislation offered a particular challenge to the private law basis of Scots law, this was also a reaction to a change in

---

1 It is tempting to see this as an idea whose time has come, with current initiatives for the development of a European civil code: see eg Hector MacQueen's article in this volume. However, it is clear that the success or failure of this venture depends more on the supra-national developments, such as the European Union, than on any specific virtues of Scots law.

the form of government and politics that broke decisively with the past and threatened the political influence of the legal profession. The Scottish legal tradition thus appears as an attempt to defend the position of Scots lawyers against these threats, in part resisting intrusion through the professionalisation of law in Scotland, but also through a more direct emotional appeal for the defence of Scottish institutions. However, as we seek a more coherent explanation for its emergence, we should not ignore the more ignoble roots of the tradition in the right-wing, racist and elitist politics of the 1930s. These are shameful elements of our past that have been either suppressed or ignored, and while they need not discredit the entire tradition, they are an important reminder of the extremism that seems inherent in certain nationalist beliefs.

However, even as we revisit these origins, it is important to ask the question of whether it is either desirable or necessary that the legal system continue to take on the additional responsibility of being an institution of national identity. More recent statements about the Scottish legal tradition range from the calculated ambivalence of Professor Robert Black's inaugural lecture in 1981,[1] to the clear view of the current Lord President that the tradition is an unnecessary and wearisome burden to the contemporary Scots lawyer.[2] Certainly, the "legal nationalism" typical of Gibb and his successors may not survive the devolution settlement, for the transformation of Scottish political institutions underlines the separation between legal and political nationalism that has been recognised since the 1970s, while undermining the importance of the distinction. It may be less plausible now, as we learn to live with our new parliament, than at any other time in the past to claim that lawyers are uniquely placed to be the interpreters of national sentiment or political opinion. The development of a new Scottish political realm can free the legal system from some of the burdens of its past even as the legal system must take on the new and demanding responsibility of seeking to regulate governmental and political institutions.

However, none of these speculations should be seen as freeing lawyers from a responsibility to reflect critically on Scots law and its past. Indeed, this may be even more important given the recent growth of public law in Scotland, for, far from being a novelty, there is a rich, if neglected, history of constitutional thought in Scotland that has surely not exhausted its relevance.[3] Given that it is traditional to finish papers such as this with a call to action, I shall not disappoint. In place of the usual exhortation to work harder to discover and promulgate the true principles of Scots law, however, I want to suggest that there is a greater need for reflection and analysis of the role of law, lawyers and legal thought in social and political life. This must take the place of both the search for principle which,

---

1 See R Black, "Practice and Precept in Scots Law" (1982) *Juridical Review* 31.
2 See A Rodger, "Thinking About Scots Law" (1996) 1 ELR 3. Lord Rodger's comments were, appropriately, delivered at the first W A Wilson Memorial Lecture.
3 See the essays by Paul Maharg, Scott Veitch and Neil Walker in this volume.

consciously or unconsciously, seeks a unity which can be presented to and defended against the world, or the temptation unthinkingly to celebrate Scots law and lawyers. The future of Scots law lies in Scotland, in its ability to serve the needs, and to respect and protect the identities and interests of those who live there. To this end we should become more aware of the limitations, the failures and the blindspots in our perception of the law, both past and present, for it is on an awareness and recognition of these factors that the legitimacy of any legal system ultimately depends.

Index

Ackerman, Robert, 146
Act of Union 1707
  appeal to House of Lords, and, 157–158
  federal Union, as, 108
  incorporating Union, as, 99, 108, 111
  national identity, and, 136–137, 157
Administrative law
  increasing importance of, 8–9
Advocate General for Scotland
  generally, 29, 33
  legislative jurisdiction, powers, 30
Allan, David, 144–145
Allott, Philip, 149
Anderson, B, 149
Arshad, Rowena, 39
Ascherson, Neal, 139n
Asylum-seekers
  Scottish and Westminster Parliaments,
    tensions between, 130
Attorney General
  legislative jurisdiction, powers, 30
Attwooll, Elspeth, 29, 128n, 143, 161n

Bachofen, Jakob, 144
Barnett Formula, 32
Bartonshill Coal Co v Reid, 34
Belfast Agreement, 110, 114, 117
  British-Irish Council, 117
  British-Irish Intergovernmental
    Conference, 117
  North-South Ministerial Council, 117
Benhabib, Seyla, 129, 132
Black, Robert, 163
Blackie, John, 72
Blackstone, Sir William, 106–107
Blair, Tony, 34
Bloom, Harold, 96n
  misprision, theory of, 137, 148
Boswell, James, 141, 142
Boyd, Colin, 29
Brazier, R, 115
British Railways Board v Pickin, 12
Broadcasting Act 1990
  minority populations, 41, 42
Brown, Alice, 136–137
Brown, Allan, 50
Brown v Stott, 4
Buchanan, George, 143
Buchanan, J M, 104

Caird, John, 143–144
Cairns, John, 140
Carlyle, Thomas, 142

Cessante ratione legis cessat lex ipsa rule,
  81–82, 85
Clancy, Thomas Owen
  The Triumph Tree, 37–38
Clancy v Caird, 4
Clark, Lynda, 29, 33
Clark v Kelly, 4
Clarke, Peter, 50
Clive, Eric, 71
Colley, Linda, 88n, 138, 141
Commission on European Contract Law,
  61–62, 64, 67, 72
Commission for Racial Equality (CRE),
  40–41
Common law
  ancient writings, interpretation of, 80–81
  English, 59
  European private law and Scots law,
    59–73, 83, 87–88
Comparative law
  old and foreign law, 75–96
Constitution
  British, 138–139
    Parliamentary sovereignty, 12, 99–100,
      107
    unitary character of, 100–102
      flexibility, 102–109, 112
    diarchical, 103n
  European Union, 115
  federal, 103–104
    parliamentary sovereignty, and,
      108–109
  nature of, generally, 149–150
  pluralism, 103–107
  unitary, Scottish self-government and,
    97–119
Constitutionalism, 11
  Acts of Scottish Parliament, and, 12
  common law, 107
  constitutional denial, 115
  constitutions and national identity, 136
  devolution, and, 8, 11, 28, 126–127
  Human Rights Act, and, 8, 12
  interpretation and, 137–138
  metaconstitutionalism, 113–115
    cosmopolitan, 113
    counterfactual, 114
    human rights law, 116
    modification of internal state
      constitutional structure, 117
    non-state polities, 117–118
  status of Scots constitution, 11, 128, 135–136
  transitional jurisprudence, and, 123–128

Contemporanea expositio rule, 80, 82–83, 86
Contract law
  breach
    concept of, 65–66
    repudiation as, 66
    "self-help" remedies, 66–67
  Commission on European Contract Law,
      61–62
  English doctrines, assimilation into Scots
      law, 68–69
  exceptio non adimpleti contractus, 65
  misrepresentation, doctrine of, 68
  mixed Scots law, 63–68
  performance as creditor's primary right,
      64–65
  postal acceptance, 63
  Principles of European Contract Law
      (PECL), 62–65
  reduction of contract, grounds for, 68
  revocability, 63
  Scottish Law Commission, 69
  third party, for benefit of, 64
  undisclosed principal in
      agency/representation, 67
  unilateral or gratuitous promise, 63
Cooper, Thomas (Lord Cooper), 156, 162
Council of Europe
  European Charter for Regional or
      Minority Languages, 45, 56
  Framework Convention for the Protection
      of National Minorities, 39, 43–46
*County Properties Ltd v The Scottish
    Ministers*, 4
Court of Session
  collegiate court, as, 81
Cover, Robert, 132
Craig, Cairns, 141, 144
Craig, Paul, 104, 105
Cranworth, Lord, 34
Crawford, Robert, 141–143, 146, 147, 149
Cunningham, Roseanna, 29

Dahl, R, 104
Darwinism, 146
Declaration of Arbroath
  recent debates using, 143
Devolution
  1979 failure, 110, 139–140
  arguments for, 97–99
  constitutionalism, and, 11, 28, 126–127
  Gladstone's concept, 139
  incomplete nature, 126–127
  independence, and, 114
  Joint Ministerial Committee on
      Devolution, 117, 118
  Judicial Committee of Privy Council,
      18–19, 30, 128
  judicial review of devolution issues, 16,
      18–20
  lawyers, effect on, 27, 29–31
  national identity, and, 139–140

Devolution – *contd*
  politics and the devolution settlement,
      7–8, 31–35
  review or challenge of Scottish
      Parliament procedures, 30–31
  Scots Law Schools, 27
  transitional jurisprudence, 122–123, 132,
      134
  unitary constitution and Scottish self-
      government, 97–119
  Westminster Parliament's powers, 30,
      32–34
    reserved matters, 14, 32, 42
Dewar, Donald, 28, 29
Dicey, A V, 105, 106
Douglas-Hamilton, James, 29
"Dundas Despotism", 27–28, 34–35
  Dundas, Henry, 1st Viscount Melville, 27
  Dundas, Robert, 2nd Viscount Melville,
      27
Dunn, Douglas, 140

Education
  linguistic minorities, 43, 44, 46–47, 52–57
  religion, separation on grounds of, 43,
      52–55
  Scots legal education, 8–9, 27, 141
English regional government
  proposals for, 111–112
Erskine, John, 158
Ethnic group
  what constitutes, 47–50
Ethnology
  anthropological subjects and law,
      143–147
**European Charter for Regional or Minority
    Languages**, 45, 56
European Civil Code
  projected, 72–73
**European Convention on Human Rights
    (ECHR)**
  Brown v Stott, 4
  cases involving, 2–6
  compatibility of legislation with, 6
  impartiality and judicial debate, 5–6
  judicial review and the executive,
      19–21
  Lord Advocate, compatibility with
      ECHR, 3–4
  minority populations, 41
  Scottish Executive members and, 3
  Scottish incorporation, 14–15, 31, 77, 116,
      125–126, 132, 148
  Starrs v Ruxton, 3–4
European Union
  model constitution, and, 115
  sovereignty, and, 99, 117–118, 125–126,
      131–133
  supranational legal framework, 117–118
Ewing, Fergus, 29
Ewing, Winnie, 29

Federalism
European, 108
federal constitutions, generally, 103–104,
108–109
parliamentary sovereignty, and, 108–109
quasi-federal positions, 109
Treaty of Union, and, 108
Fenyo, Krisztina, 51
Field, Frank, 33
Financial Services and Markets Bill
judicialisation of politics, 22
Finn, Gerry, 43, 53–54, 57
First Minister
appointment, 32
role, 28
Foreign law
European private law and Scots law,
59–73
foreign decisions. *See* SCOTS LAW
Fraser, Lord, 47
Frazer, J G, 142, 145–146, 149

Gibb, Andrew Dewar, 147
legal and political nationalism, 154–162,
163
written works, 11, 156, 159, 160
Gladstone, William Ewart
Home Rule proposals, 139, 147
Midlothian campaign, 138–139
Globalisation
effect, generally, 148–149
Goldie, Annabel, 29
Grant, J, 152
Gray, Alasdair
1982, Janine, 140
Lanark, 147–148
Gwynedd County Council v Jones, 48–49

Haakonssen, Knud, 136
Habermas, Jürgen, 132–133
Hailes, Lord, 145
Hall, Stuart, 136
Hart, H L A, 131
Hart-Fuller debate, 121, 123
Harvie, Christopher, 153–154
Hervey, Tamara, 38
High Court of Justiciary
collegiate court, as, 81
Himsworth, C M G, 136, 137
History and historiography
Scots law, 75–96, 140–141, 143–145
Hobbes, Thomas, 122
Hoekstra v HM Advocate
judicial impartiality, 5
Hope, Lord, 23
House of Lords
appellate jurisdiction, 157–158
Human rights. *See also* EUROPEAN CONVENTION
ON HUMAN RIGHTS
common law constitutionalism, and, 107
metaconstitutionalism, 116

Human Rights Act 1998
court's power to declare legislation
incompatible with, 12
freedom of expression and opinion,
41–42
impact, generally, 1–3
minority populations, 41, 45
pre-legislative scrutiny, 20
Hume, David, 92, 145, 158

**International Institute for the Unification
of Law (Unidroit),** 62
International law
minority populations, 130
transitional jurisprudence, role in, 116,
124, 125
Ius Commune
Scots law, and 59–73, 83, 87–88

Jenkins, Roy, 39
John of Fordun, 50
**Joint Ministerial Committee on
Devolution,** 117, 118
Journal of Jurisprudence, 147
Judicial Committee of Privy Council
judicial review of devolution issues, 4–5,
18–19, 30, 128
Judicial power
growth, 6
Judicial review
abstract and concrete, 15–18
administrative action, of, unitary
constitution, 107
consequences
courts, judicial review and, 22–24
executive, judicial review and the,
19–21
generally, 19
Parliament, judicial review and, 21–22
courts, and, 16, 22–24
devolution issues, 16, 18–20
executive, and, 19–21
generally, 12
lawyers, and, 27
legislation, of, 12–14, 30–31
generally, 19–21
legitimacy of legislation, 24–25
rationales for, 13–15
Parliament, and, 21–22
political opposition, as weapon of,
17–18
Scotland Act 1998, 8, 16–19
UK model, 15–19
US model, 15–16
who may refer, 17–18
Judiciary
impartiality of, 5–6
transitional jurisprudence, role in, 124,
125, 128
Juridical Review, 147
Juridification, 19

Jurisprudence
  Hegelianism and, 143
  legal identity and jurisprudential
      thought, 135
  Scottish
      development, 147–150
      identity, 141–143
  transitional. *See* TRANSITIONAL JURISPRUDENCE

Kant, Immanuel, 122
Keith, Lord
  quoted, 13
Kelly, Michael, 50–51
Kelsen, Hans, 131
Kötz, H, 59–60, 61, 69
Kuper, Adam, 146

Lando, Ole, 61
Lawyers
  Dundas Despotism, 27–28
  role in Scottish political system
      Bills, drafting, 27
      historically, 153–154
      judicial review, 27
      legal nationalism, 153–154
  Scottish
      devolution, effect, 27, 29–31
      historical position, 28–29
Legal culture
  politicisation, 7–8, 19, 22–24, 35
Legal texts
  anthropological subjects, 143–147
  what constitute, 143
Lévy-Ullmann, H, 59, 61, 73
Linguistic minorities
  discrimination in favour of, 48–49
  education, 43, 44, 46–47, 52–57
  European Charter for Regional or
      Minority Languages, 45, 56
  Gaels, 46–47, 49–52, 56–57
  rights, generally, 44
Literary criticism
  law, and, 137–138, 148–149
  Scottish literature, place in British context,
      141–142
"Lobbygate Case", 31
Lockerbie trial, 1
Lord Advocate
  confusion of roles, 27, 28, 160
  ECHR, compatibility with, 3–4
  impartiality and judicial debate,
      5–6
  judicial appointments by, 3–4, 28
  legislative jurisdiction of Scottish
      Parliament, and, 30
  Starrs v Ruxton, 3–4
Lorimer, James, 143–144, 149
Lynch, Michael, 140

Maan, Bashir, 51–52
MacAskill, Kenny, 29

McCluskey, Lord
  impartiality and judicial debate, 5–6
MacCormick, John, 155
MacCormick, Neil, 29, 98*n*, 102*n*, 131, 153
McCrone, D, 136–137
MacDiarmid, Hugh, 156
Macfarlane v Tayside Health Board, 89
MacInnes, Dr John, 50
McLeish, Henry, 34
McLennan, John Ferguson, 145–146, 149
McLetchie, David, 29
MacMillan, James, 37
MacQueen, Hector, 140
McWhinney, Edward
  Supreme Courts and Judicial Law-Making,
      24
Main v Leask, 91
Maine, Sir Henry James Sumner, 145
Mandla v Dowell Lee, 47–50
Marquand, D, 105
**Mental Health (Public Safety and
  Appeals) (Scotland) Act 1999**
  ECHR, breach of, 20
Millar, Galbraith, 147
Millar, John, 145
Millar v Dickson, 4
Minority populations
  autochthonous, 46
  concept of, problems arising, 45–46
  cultural rights, concept of, 44–45
  discrimination, protection from, 40–41
  ethnic group, what constitutes, 47–50
  European Charter for Regional or
      Minority Languages, 45
  European Convention on Human Rights,
      41
  Framework Convention for the Protection
      of National Minorities, 39, 43–46
  Gaels, 46–47, 49–52, 56–57
  homosexuals, 130
  Human Rights Act 1998, 41, 45
  international law, invocation, 130
  linguistic, 43, 44, 46–47, 49–52, 56–57
  Minority Languages Charter, 56
  national minority, use of term, 45–46
  policies towards
      assimilation, 38, 44
      British, 38–39, 45–46
      Broadcasting Act 1990, 41, 42
      cultural pluralism, 38–39
      freedom of expression and opinion,
          and, 41–42
      preservation and promotion, 43, 44,
          52–57
      protection, 40–44
      Scottish, 39, 45
      separate education, 43, 44, 46–47, 52–57
      suppression, 40
      Race Relations Act 1976, 40–42, 45
      entitlement to protection under, 46
      racial groups, 46–48

Minority populations – *contd*
  definition, 42, 47
  racially-aggravated harassment, 42
  religious, 43, 52–55, 130
  Scottish, 37–38
  Scottish court decisions, 130
  Scottish Parliament decisions, 129–130
  United Nations International Covenant
    on Civil and Political Rights, 54–55
Misprision, theory of, 137–138, 148
Mixed system
  European Civil Code, 72–73
  Scots law as, 9–10, 59–62, 72–73, 162
  contract law, 63–68
Montgomery v HM Advocate, 5–6
Morgan, Edwin, 140
Morgan, Lewis Henry, 145
Morris, Lord, 12
Munro, C R, 136, 137

Nairn, Tom, 114*n*, 126–127, 138
National identity
  Act of Union, and, 136–137, 157
  arts and humanities, 140, 148
  constitution and, 136
  devolution, and, 139–140
  rhetorical concept, as, 142–143
  Scots law, and, 9, 152
  Scottish history, and, 140–141
  Scottish literature, and, 141–142
  Scottish Parliament, effect of, 137–138
  United Kingdom, 138
Nationalism. *See also* POST-NATIONALISM
  civic and ethnic, 98, 131
  economic, arguments for, 98–99
  legal
    elements of, 151–152
    Gibb, A D, 154–163
    political nationalism distinct from,
      151–153
    role of lawyers, 153–154
  nature of, generally, 149
  transitional jurisprudence, and, 130–133
Natural law
  anthropological writers, influence, 146
  national identity, and, 136
  transitional jurisprudence, and, 123–124
Northern Ireland
  early release scheme, 125
Northern Ireland Act 1920, 110
Northern Ireland Act 1998, 110–111, 114,
  115*n*
Northern Irish Assembly
  human rights law, 116
  unitary constitution, and, 109–110
Northern Joint Police Board v Power, 47–48

Old decisions. *See* SCOTS LAW

Pater, Walter, 143
Paterson, L, 136–137

Plessis, Jacques du, 60–61
Pluralism
  asymmetrical government, 111–112
  countervailing group power, 104
  diarchical constitutional arrangements,
    103*n*
  federal constitutions, 103–104, 108–109
  free-market-orientation, 104–105
  nature of, generally, 105–107
  parliamentary sovereignty, and, 108–109
  post-nationalism, 112–114
  public choice theory, 104
  socialism, 104
  union state, 111
  unitary legal conception's view of,
    111–112
Political culture
  increasing legislation, 7–8
  judicialisation, 19, 21–24, 34–35
  politics and the devolution settlement,
    31–34
Politicisation of law, 7–8, 19, 22–24, 35
Positivism
  anthropological writers, influence, 146
  transitional jurisprudence, and, 123–124
Post-nationalism, 112–114
Poulter, Sebastian, 38–39, 42
Principles of European Contract Law
  (PECL), 62–65
Private international law
  cases involving, 76, 77
Prosser, Lord
  quoted, 6
Public law
  Scots law, and, 8–9

Race Relations Act 1976
  entitlement to protection under, 46
  ethnic group, what constitutes, 47–50
  linguistic minorities, 48–49
  minority populations, 40–42, 45
Racial group
  definition, 42, 47
Racial hatred
  inciting, 41
  meaning, 41
Racially-aggravated harassment
  offence, generally, 42
Ramsay, Baroness, 33
Reed, Lord, 10, 24
Regulatory bodies
  increasing use, 8
Reid, John, 33
Robertson, William, 145
Rodger, Lord, 9*n*, 88, 152, 163

Saltire Society, 156
Sande, Johannes, 77
Santos, Boaventura de Sousa, 137, 148–149
Scheinin, Martin, 55
Schmitt, Carl, 19

Scotland Act 1978, 110
Scotland Act 1998
  competence of legislation under, 6, 12
    Judicial Committee of the Privy
        Council, powers, 30
  impact, generally, 1–3, 6–8, 110–111,
        126–127
  judicial review of legislation under,
        12–14, 19–21
    pre-legislative scrutiny, 20
    rationales for, 13–15
  Westminster Parliament's powers
        reserved, 14, 110
Scotland Office, 33
  budget, 33
Scotland's Parliament White Paper, 20
Scots law
  "bridging" role as model for future codes,
        59–68, 162
  cessante ratione legis cessat lex ipsa rule,
        81–82, 85
  codification, 70–71
  comparative study, 71, 75–96
  contemporanea expositio rule, 80, 82–83, 86
  English decisions, assimilation, 68–69, 77,
        95
  European Convention on Human Rights,
        2, 14–15, 31, 77, 116
  foreign decisions
    age of decision, 85–90
    cultural change influencing usage,
        92–93
    generally, 76
    old decisions, interaction with, 85–95
    rejuvenation of old decisions, 90–92
    use of term foreign, 77
  foreign influences, 9–10
  history and historiography, 75–96,
        140–141, 143–145
  legal nationalism, 151–154
  mixed system, as, 9–10, 59–68, 72–73, 162
  national identity and, 152
  old decisions
    ancient writings, interpretation, 80
    "cut off points", 81–83
    "early" case, use of term, 79–80, 84
    foreign decisions, interaction with,
        85–95
    generally, 76
    interpretation, problems arising, 81–82,
        85–87
    legal rules relating to use of, 80–82
    "modern" case, use of term, 79–80
    power to overrule, 81–82
    premature ageing, 82, 84–85, 91
    rejuvenation, 81, 83–85, 90–92
    use of term old, 78–80, 83
  post-imperial role, 162
  threats to
    appellate jurisdiction of House of
        Lords, 157–158

Scots law – *contd*
  Gibb's analysis, 157–159
  legislation of UK parliament, 157
Scott, Sir Walter, 142, 152
Scottish Consolidated Fund, 32
Scottish Constitutional Convention
  proposals of, 99, 139–140
Scottish Executive
  ECHR, compatibility with, 3–4
  establishment, 28
  judicial review and, 19–21
  ultra vires tests, 35
  Westminster Parliament's powers over,
        30
Scottish Law Commission
  contract law, 69
  generally, 69, 70
Scottish National Party (SNP), 29, 32, 154
  formation, 155
Scottish Parliament
  Bills
    drafting, 27
    ultra vires, 30
  establishment, 98
  judicial review and, 21–22
  metaconstitutionalism, 114
  ministers, appointment, 32
  minority groups, treatment of, 129–130
  national identity, and, 137–138
  opposition, 32
  Presiding Officer, role, 30
  private law, legislative powers, 69–71
  procedures, review or challenge of, 30–31
  reserved matters, 14, 32, 42
  ultra vires tests, 35
  unitary constitution, and, 109–110, 114
  Westminster Parliament
    powers of, over Scottish Parliament, 30,
        32–34
    sovereignty of, doctrine, 12, 99–100, 107
Secretary for Scotland
  establishment of post, 27–28, 33
  powers, 30
Smith, Robertson, 145–147
Smith, T B, 12–13, 34, 155, 162
Smits, Jan, 61
Smollett, Tobias, 142
Stair Society, 156
Starrs v Ruxton, 3–4
Steel, Sir David, 29, 30
Stevenson, John, 140
Stirling v Earl of Lauderdale, 93
Stuart, Gilbert, 145
Sturgeon, Nicola, 29

Teitel, Ruti, 123–125, 127, 128
Thatcher, Margaret, 125
  Thatcherism, 105–106
Thomson, G M, 155
Transitional jurisprudence
  constitutionalism, and, 123–128

Transitional jurisprudence – *contd*
  criminal prosecutions or amnesties, 124,
    125
  ethnos and *demos*, 123, 129–134
  generally, 121–122
  international law, role of, 124, 125
  judiciary, role of, 124, 125, 128
  legal aspects, 123–129
  nationalism, and, 130–133
  natural law, and, 123–124
  positivism, and, 123–124
  the UK, in, 121–134
    constitutionalism, 126–128
    criminal justice dimension, 125
    devolution, 122–123, 126–127, 132, 134
    European Convention on Human
      Rights, 125–126, 132
    European Union, and the, 123, 125–126,
      132
    generally, 122–123, 125–126
Treaty of Union 1707, 108. *See also* ACT OF
  UNION 1707
Turnbull, Gordon, 141
Twining, W, 149
Tyler, William, 145

Ultra vires
  Parliamentary sovereignty, doctrine of,
    107
  Scottish legislation, 30, 35
Unitary constitution
  British constitution as, 100–108
  flexibility, 102–109, 112
  ideologies embracing, 106–107

Unitary constitution – *contd*
  judicial review of administrative action,
    107
  pluralist systems, view of, 111–112
  Scottish self-government and, 97–119
**United Nations International Covenant on
  Civil and Political Rights**, 54–55
Unjustified enrichment
  draft codification of law, 71

**Vienna Convention on the International
  Sale of Goods (CISG)**, 62, 69

Walker, D M, 156*n*, 158
Wallace, Jim, 29
We Can't All Be White (Rowntree Trust), 42
West Lothian Question, 33
Westminster Parliament
  English Parliament, as, 33
  judicialisation of politics, 22
  ministers, appointment, 32
  Parliamentary sovereignty, doctrine of,
    12, 99–100, 107, 110
  power to legislate for Scotland, 14, 30,
    32–34, 110
    Act of Union, 99
    reserved matters, 14, 32, 42
  Scottish Question Time, 33
  "Strasbourg proofing" system, 20–21
Whaley v Lord Watson, 6, 31
"Writing Scotland's History" symposium,
  140

Zweigert, K, 59–61, 69